ABOUT THE AUTHOR

MIKE FREEMAN is a national columnist for CBSSports.com. Previously, he covered the National Football League, the National Basketball Association, Major League Baseball, and several college sports, and was an investigative and enterprise reporter for the *New York Times* and a columnist for the *Florida Times-Union*. He has also previously been a sports reporter, features writer, and investigative writer for the *Washington Post, Boston Globe,* and *Dallas Morning News*. Freeman is the author of three critically acclaimed books: *ESPN: The Uncensored History*; *Bloody Sundays: Inside the Dazzling, Rough-and-Tumble World of the NFL*; and *Jim Brown: The Fierce Life of an American Hero*. His most recent book is *The All-Time Biggest Sports Jerks: And Other Goofballs, Cads, Miscreants, Reprobates, and Weirdos (Plus a Few Good Guys)*.

BOWDEN

ALSO BY MIKE FREEMAN

THE ALL-TIME BIGGEST SPORTS JERKS:
And Other Goofballs, Cads, Miscreants,
Reprobates, and Weirdos (Plus a Few
Good Guys)

JIM BROWN:
The Fierce Life of an American Hero

BLOODY SUNDAYS:
Inside the Dazzling, Rough-and-Tumble World of
the NFL

ESPN:
The Uncensored History

BOWDEN

HOW BOBBY BOWDEN FORGED A FOOTBALL DYNASTY

MIKE FREEMAN

*it*books

AN IMPRINT OF HARPERCOLLINS PUBLISHERS

*it***books**

The photograph on page 8 courtesy of the *Florida Times-Union*.

A hardcover edition of this book was published in 2009 by It Books, an imprint of HarperCollins Publishers.

HarperCollins books may be purchased for educational, business, or sales promotional use. For information please write: Special Markets Department, HarperCollins Publishers, 10 East 53rd Street, New York, NY 10022.

FIRST IT BOOKS PAPERBACK PUBLISHED 2010.

Designed by Renato Stanisic

The Library of Congress has catalogued the hardcover edition as follows:

Freeman, Mike.
   Bowden : how Bobby Bowden forged a football dynasty / Mike Freeman. —
1st ed.
     p. cm.
   Includes bibliographical references.
   ISBN 978-0-06-147419-4
   1. Bowden, Bobby. 2. Football coaches—United States—Biography. 3. Florida State University—Football. 4. Florida State Seminoles (Football team) I. Title.
   GV939.B66F74 2009
   796.332092—dc22
   [B]

2009019885

ISBN 978-0-06-147420-0 (pbk.)

10 11 12 13 14 OV/RRD 10 9 8 7 6 5 4 3 2 1

TO KELLY . . . THE ETERNAL LOVE

CONTENTS

AUTHOR'S NOTE: Fathers and Sons 1

INTRODUCTION 9

CHAPTER ONE: Tragedy 29

CHAPTER TWO: Son Under Fire 36

CHAPTER THREE: The Fever 53

CHAPTER FOUR: April Fool's in Love 63

CHAPTER FIVE: The Coaching Life 69

CHAPTER SIX: Mountaineer 79

CHAPTER SEVEN: Papa 'Nole 99

CHAPTER EIGHT: Matriarch 110

CHAPTER NINE: Terry 126

CHAPTER TEN: "Take Five Minutes a Day to Hate FSU" 137

CHAPTER ELEVEN: Tommy 151

CHAPTER TWELVE: Bobby's Song 163

CHAPTER THIRTEEN: Law and Order 177

CHAPTER FOURTEEN: Wide Right 192

CHAPTER FIFTEEN: Champion 214

CHAPTER SIXTEEN: Steve 243

Afterword: Last Man Standing 251

Acknowledgments 265

Notes 267

Bibliography 275

Index 277

FATHERS AND SONS

It may seem odd to begin a book about a legendary football coach with a story about a legendary basketball player, but only a handful of people know what it is like to be a Bowden. One of them is a man named Walton.

Bill Walton, at the age of seventeen, played for the U.S. team in the 1970 FIBA (International Basketball Federation) World Championship. As a teenager he was on the cover of *Sports Illustrated*, and while at UCLA he was part of perhaps the greatest sports dynasty ever assembled. An impressive NBA career and the basketball Hall of Fame followed.

Like Bobby Bowden, what people didn't see was Walton the father who raised four boys with his first wife, Susie. The Walton children would end up like their dad: intelligent, thoughtful, and athletic. And, also as in Bowden's case, it's impossible for many people to understand the difficulty of raising children while living in the radioactive glare that is public life.

"I admire Bobby Bowden," Walton said. "From what I know about him, he's done such a good job of raising that family while being in the spotlight. That's not easy to do, and add to that some of his sons went into coaching. Then you factor in how he competed against some of his sons. I don't know if people truly understand how difficult a strain it must've been for that family. No one should feel sorry for Coach Bowden or me or anyone else in our situation, but there's no question it's a challenge. People think kids like Coach Bowden's or mine have it easy and have it made, but that's not necessarily the case."

There are families in which the fathers were sports heroes who then watched their sons grow into outstanding athletes like their dads, such as in the NFL's Manning family. Both of NFL quarterback Archie Manning's sons, Peyton and Eli, have Super Bowl rings. Tennis star Yannick Noah watched his son Joakim Noah win two national titles in basketball at the University of Florida. The Ripken baseball dynasty—rich with the patriarch and his kingly son named Cal—lives in the hearts of all Baltimoreans. Olympic gold medalist swimmer Mark Spitz has an athlete son, Matt, who has been attempting to qualify for the PGA Tour. There is the Earnhardt racing dynasty.

Other fathers and sons possess more complicated public and private lives. Imagine being the son of PGA golfer John Daly. Pete Rose is a baseball exile, banned from the Hall of Fame. His son, Pete Rose Jr., was indicted in 2005 for distributing to baseball teammates gamma-butyrolactone (GBL), a drug that is more commonly known as a date rape drug but also can be used as a performance enhancer for athletes. He was convicted over a year later and sentenced to one month in federal prison. Philadelphia Eagles coach Andy Reid watched his two sons suffer through severe drug addictions that landed both in prison. Jim Brown's sons struggled dealing with being the children of an NFL Hall of Famer. One of Brown's sons, Kevin, was a recovering drug addict who says Jim never embraced him as a child and only hugged Kevin after Kevin entered adulthood. MLB first basemen Cecil and Prince Fielder have had problems in their relationship as well.

Bowden has seen his own share of family drama in the profession. All three coaching sons were forced out of their various positions, leaving Bobby, ironically, as the last Bowden standing. (Recently Terry Bowden returned to coaching.)

College football is of course no stranger to father-and-son coaching relationships. University of Oklahoma coach Bob Stoops made his brother, Mike, the team's defensive coordinator in 1999.

Then Mike left for Arizona to become that team's head coach, and he hired brother Mark to coordinate the defense.

Other examples such as these exist, but no father has faced the daunting familial challenge of coaching against his son while another served as his offensive coordinator.

Bowden once told coaching sons Tommy and Terry, "Somewhere along the line, I hope you've learned from my experience that you've got to run smart as well as hard. You've got to stay on the good side of the university administrators and the boosters. And while you're doing all that, you've got to hold together a marriage and family."

Walton has preached a similar message to his sons. He has four in Chris, Nathan, Adam, and Luke. Chris played basketball for San Diego State, Nathan played basketball for Princeton and later earned an MBA from Stanford business school, Adam played at LSU, and then of course there's Luke. He only plays for the Los Angeles Lakers.

Walton stuck to three main principles when raising his sons: keep their lives as normal as possible; remind them how fortunate they are that the family was able to earn a living through sports; and stress that his love for them was unconditional and endless.

"One of the other things we did in raising them was to tell them no," said Walton. "That's with all kids for sure. Except with my kids when you told them no, they'd joke, 'We hate you! When we grow up we're going to Notre Dame!'"

Sometimes when the kids would play basketball at the house and their jump shot was astray, they'd approach Walton and ask him to summon some superhero assistance. "Dad, can you call Magic or Larry [as in Hall of Famers Magic Johnson and Larry Bird] and ask him to help me," they'd joke. Walton would respond, "Sometimes, kids, you have to work things out on your own."

As Luke in particular started to sprout into a gifted athlete, playing at the University of Arizona and then for the Lakers, Walton consistently reiterated how it was necessary to take the positives with the bad. "Failure and criticism," he would say, "are as much a part of it as winning and championships. You decided to do this, no one forced you." Walton's words sound remarkably similar to what Bowden told his football sons as they entered the family business.

Walton experienced one of the great satisfactions of his life when in June 2008 Luke's Lakers played the Boston Celtics in the NBA Finals. Bill and Luke came remarkably close to being only the third father-and-son team to win an NBA title. Ironically, Game 5 of the series came on Father's Day. Luke would eventually win an NBA title in 2009.

Luke's treks through the postseason brought back memories for Bill when Bill the father did everything in his power to attend his sons' games as the boys grew up. "There is no better feeling than when you go to your son's game and afterwards he says to you, 'Thanks for coming, Dad.'"

TO SAY THAT BOBBY Bowden is a highly decent man comfortable in his own cleats is a dramatic understatement. In two decades of covering almost every sport, I have never quite met anyone like Bowden. I am not a friend or a colleague but have quickly become an admirer. He is easily the most sincere coach I've ever encountered.

As I researched this book and heard the numerous stories about Bowden's good heart and sincerity, I had my doubts. I searched for hardened enemies. I admittedly looked for undiscovered dirt.

I could find neither. They don't exist. I can't even find a time he didn't help an old lady cross Osceola Street in downtown Tallahassee.

"We all have things in our closet we're ashamed of," said former Florida State running back Warrick Dunn. "But Bobby is the one guy who has a sparkling clean closet. Not even a little piece of dust."

That doesn't mean Bowden is without faults, and this book will explore the total Bowden, who is a far more complex individual than most people know. The same could be said regarding his familial dynamics.

This is the first independent biography on Bowden's entire career and life ever written. The idea for this book originated with a series I wrote for the *Florida Times-Union* newspaper in 2005 that the Associated Press Sports Editors organization cited as one of the top features of that year. I spoke extensively then with members of the Bowden family, including lengthy talks with Bobby and his wife, Ann. Many of those conversations and writings appear here. Later I spoke, again, with Bowden extensively and specifically for this book.

The voice of Ann is a constant throughout because she is the most important figure in Bowden's life and a key part of his success.

Bowden has coauthored a number of books, including several with his sons. Some information from those books—as well as numerous other sources—appears here and is credited. I also looked at each edition of the *Tallahassee Democrat* from 1975 to 2008. Information from the *Democrat* appears here as well as do some of the writings of one of that newspaper's writers, Andrew Carter, who pens one of the best football blogs in the country. The *Lakeland Ledger* wrote an outstanding twelve-part series on Bowden some years ago and that was a resource as well. Sources also include Rivals.com and Scout.com, particularly for the Paul Piurowski section, and the quotes from Garrett Ford were from MSNsportsnet.com. The book *FSU One Time! The Bowden Years* was also helpful. So were the player profiles in *What It Means to Be a Seminole*. I used some of those profiles to help me discuss several of the key players Bowden recruited in the Decade of the Seminoles, the 1990s. The book *Pure Gold* was also helpful, as was a January 2000 *Sports Illustrated* article. The Clevan Thomas anecdote was first reported by the *Tallahassee Democrat* and the book *Saint Bobby and the Barbarians* was useful.

What I hoped to do with this effort is present the total Bowden picture with dozens of interviews revealing other viewpoints. You also cannot discuss college football without addressing the topics of race, class, and exploitation, and the latter is a discussion Bowden did not include in his books but will be addressed here.

The main impetus for this book was similar to the reasons I

wrote a book about football legend Jim Brown. The passage of time, shortening attention spans, and the lack of familiarity many have with sports history leads a significant number to forget just how great a player Brown was as well as his importance to the NFL. The same applies to Bowden. The fact that Florida State has been average much of this decade has obscured Bowden's talent, brilliance, and influence. How he raised the Seminoles from practically the dead remains arguably the greatest achievement in college football history.

This is why the book focuses more on Bowden's early years than the better-known championship years.

Since this is one of the final—if not the final—independent biographies that will be written on Bowden, I wanted Bowden and his family to do most of the talking. They do.

To call Bowden St. Bobby—as he's been referred to by some—is an oversimplification, particularly since there are those who believe Bowden has allowed problematic players too much leeway in his program. A fair point, which will be debated. He may not be a saint in the literal sense but he is, in my opinion, the last of the college football legends who possesses, well, a conscience.

BOWDEN

INTRODUCTION

I've always told Bobby, "I'll support you and let you spend as much time away as you need. But if you're at the office, your feet kicked up on the desk, and chewing tobacco, then that's a problem."

—ANN BOWDEN

A man who coached against Bobby Bowden was asked a simple question: Just how good is the legendary Florida State coach?

"The best way to answer that is with a story not even Bobby knows about," says the former college coach, now in the NFL. "Our team cheated against Florida State, and we still couldn't beat him. We cheated badly, and that bastard still won.

"Bobby's team was coming in to play us," continued the coach, who asked not to be identified, referring to a time period within the past several decades, "and we were scared to death of Florida State. They were killing teams. They were winning by huge margins and running all kinds of trick plays. They were very intimidating.

"So we did some things I regret to this day. One thing we did was send someone to spy on his practices. We saw a lot of their plays and what they were planning to do. Mainly we saw some of their trick plays they were practicing. We got tons of information.

"Then we put microphones in the visitors' locker room of our stadium. We heard just about everything before the game and at halftime [that] Florida State was planning. At halftime we listened in to what Bobby told the team. We knew some of the plays they were going to run. Bobby and his assistants were talking about some defensive stuff too. We stole a bunch of stuff.

"I would guess we knew probably 30 or 40 percent of what they were going to do based on cheating like that. It might have been more. But you know what? We still lost. We wired Bobby's locker room and still lost.

"So how good a coach is Bowden? We had some pretty good players on our team when we faced him. Our coaches were cutthroat fuckers with no conscience, but we were good. We spied on his practices. We wired his locker like we were the damn CIA. We did all that, and he still beat us. I thought after that, 'This is the greatest coach I've ever seen.' Nothing has happened since then to change my mind. No one was better than Bobby, and no one ever will be. That's just my opinion as someone who has been in football for a long time and in college coached against some of the great coaches. People don't give Bobby enough credit for being very smart and a great tactical coach.

"You know I always thought Bobby knew what we did. He probably laughed at us. He probably said to himself, 'Nice dadgum try.'"

RADIO HOST RUSH LIMBAUGH answered his open call-in line one Friday in January 2008 and took a break from grinding Democrats into the New York City dirt with his wide heel.

> Limbaugh: Nick in Tallahassee, nice to have you, sir, on Open Line Friday.
> Caller: Yes, sir. How are you doing today?
> Limbaugh: Good, sir.
> Caller: I actually had some questions or just a thought— or wanted to know your thoughts on some stuff. Bobby Bowden being the most winningest coach in college football and everything, I was just wondering what your thoughts were on him and whether he needed to retire or

whether he should try to stick it out and hopefully turn this program around . . .

Limbaugh: I played golf with Bobby Bowden once down here in Florida prior to a boosters' dinner. This was in the spring, after spring practice. It's been about five or six years ago. It was over in Naples, Fort Myers, somewhere. He was just feisty as he could be. He was a blast to be around; he was actually a pretty good golfer. You know, he is the face of that team. I think if they hadn't designated—who was it the offensive coordinator or defensive coordinator to be the head coach when he retires?

Caller: Jimbo Fisher.

Limbaugh: Jimbo Fisher. What is he, defense or offensive coordinator?

Caller: He's offensive coordinator.

Limbaugh: Okay. If they hadn't done that, there would have been a problem recruiting and all.

Caller: Yeah.

Limbaugh: But now they can go recruit guys out of high school and say, "There's continuity here. Jimbo Fisher going to take over," and Jimbo Fisher, by the way, rejected opportunities to go somewhere else. He's established his loyalty. So, you know, Bobby Bowden is the face of that program and he's entrenched and they're going to kick him out of there, or he's going to have kick himself out, like Joe Paterno at Penn State.

Caller: Right.

Limbaugh: I have all the respect in the world for Bobby Bowden . . . I really enjoyed having gotten to meet him, his kids, his sons—I've never met them, but they seem to be really good guys, too, the ultimate plus for the program, from an outsider looking in like me with no intimate inside knowledge.

You know you have achieved greatness when you're one of the few people in the known universe adored by Rush Limbaugh.

. . . .

BOBBY BOWDEN NEVER DREAMED he would make it this far. How many small-town Alabama boys go on to nurture a decades-long dynasty? And the stories. There are so many. So, so many. He sits at his desk, which is neat, in an office surrounded by photos and scrapbooks from a rich and rewarding life. Bowden's demeanor almost always stays the same. There is often a smile on his face, and the stories roll off his tongue with ease. Like the time he almost died. Twice.

Forty years ago, when Bowden was an assistant at West Virginia University, he was offered the head coaching position at Marshall, a burgeoning school with a solid athletic program and football team. They wanted him, but Bowden wasn't so sure if he wanted them. He thought: something about this just doesn't feel right. He spoke to his wife, Ann, and couldn't fully explain why even to her. In the end, he didn't leave for Marshall.

A short time after that decision, at approximately 7:35 P.M. on November 14, 1970, on a cloudy and foggy night, the entire Marshall team perished when their ninety-five-seat twin-engine Douglas DC-9, registration number N97S, crashed into a hill just short of the Huntington, West Virginia, airport. All seventy-five souls onboard were lost, including thirty-seven players, twenty-one boosters, seven staff members, five coaches, and five crew members. "All these years later," Bowden says, "I still think about how close I came to being on that plane."

Bowden would brush with death again near the beginning of his improbable tenure at Florida State, which would see Bowden emerge as one of the winningest major college coaches and a symbol of perhaps the grandest period in college football history, the 1990s. The year was 1979, and Bowden was in the middle of Florida State's first 11–0 regular-season record. That season would be the first time any Seminole team went unbeaten playing a major college schedule.

After years of dismal football futility, Bowden had transformed Florida State from a wrecked program into a relevant one. The unbeaten season had attracted interest off the football field as well as on it. In Bowden's first season as head coach, school president Bernard Sliger asked Bowden to visit academically promising students as Bowden made his dozens of recruiting trips. The extra help was needed. It seems hard to believe now, but the university had a difficult time attracting students. That changed after the Seminoles went 11–0 and played in the Orange Bowl. Sliger informed Bowden that the football success had dramatically increased student interest. There were some twenty-five hundred positions available for incoming freshmen but more than five thousand applicants, with hopeful Seminoles coming from Michigan, California, and Colorado. "He said, 'Football was getting our message out' and I was almost amazed," Bowden remembered. "I never expected that kind of platform."

Hopeful students weren't the only ones with their interests piqued. The football community noticed as well. Several NFL teams considered hiring him as a head coach. College athletic directors and various universities were enthralled. One of them was Louisiana State University; the school pursued Bowden throughout that year. The persistent courtship was flattering to Bowden, who was also beginning to wonder if Florida State had gone as far as it could. "I told myself," Bowden recalls, "that if we lost to LSU, then my instincts were right and I'd take the job." He again conferred with Ann, and it seemed only a matter of time before Bowden left Florida State for the Tigers.

Then something odd happened: Florida State won the game against LSU, 24–19. It was one of the more significant wins in Bowden's career not solely because the Seminoles beat a more established power—something practically unimaginable just three or four years earlier—but also because the win convinced Bowden that the football program could one day be a force in the sport.

"I was wrong," Bowden told Ann. "We can win big here."

He told LSU he was staying at Florida State, and just a short time later Bowden signed a long-term contract with the Seminoles.

The Tigers looked elsewhere for a coach and hired Bo Rein from North Carolina State. At the time Rein was one of the hottest young coaching prospects in the sport. In January 1980, just a matter of months after Bowden rejected LSU, Rein was returning from a recruiting trip for LSU in a Cessna 441 when radar contact with the plane was lost. When controllers discovered Rein's plane, it had climbed to 40,000 feet, much higher than the safe ceiling for the Cessna. Eventually military aircraft spotted the plane near North Carolina more than a thousand miles off course. The Cessna crashed into the Atlantic Ocean, and the bodies of Rein and the pilot were never found. Rein was dead at thirty-four.

"I think about that boy's family all the time," says Bowden. "If anyone ever scoffs at my religious faith, I tell them those two stories. I don't know why, but I think this is the place God wanted me to be."

HIS WIFE IS A fighter, his daughters are defenders, and his sons were and are coaches. Sometimes those sons were also competitors. In 1994, Terry Bowden, one of Bobby's coaching sons, was attempting to snag a great recruiting prize: the top-ranked defensive player in the entire state of Florida, Martavius Houston, a speedy and durable defensive back born in Lauderdale Lakes, Florida.

Houston had narrowed his choice to two schools—Terry's Auburn University or Bobby's Florida State. This wasn't the first time it was Bowden versus Bowden, and it wouldn't be the last.

Terry decided to make one final strategic push to land Houston. Bowden is like his parents; there is a compelling mind and genuine smarts tucked underneath thick layers of accent and southern guffaws. Terry thought the best time to make his single NCAA-sanctioned home visit was during a ninety-minute window in the evening on a Thursday, one day before Houston played in a high school basketball game on Friday. The lateness in the week of the basketball game, Terry reasoned, would prevent other recruiters from swooping in at the last minute.

Terry's visit went well. Houston remembers Terry as being genuine and thorough. Terry was also a stunning salesman, just like his dad. "You're going to win two Heisman Trophies at Auburn,"

Terry told Houston. In some versions of the story, Terry actually told Houston he'd win three.

Terry walked out of Houston's home confident the young man would pick Auburn. There was almost a strut in his step as he prepared to skip off Houston's front porch, when a long black limousine pulled in front of the house. Out of the back of the limousine stepped Bobby.

Bobby had scheduled a recruiting visit immediately following Terry's. He approached the porch where Terry, Houston, and his mother were standing. Bobby greeted them all and then, in full view of the recruit and his mother, turned to Terry and said: "When you get home, your momma wants you to call her." Bobby patted Terry on the head.

Bobby's actions and words were simultaneously humorous and instructional. He was going to do everything to win this recruit, even if it meant playfully teasing his own son in front of Houston. The Bowden men are close, and they love one another deeply, despite the fact that Bobby hasn't always said so and even if the brothers don't always communicate that love directly to each other. Bobby is the kind of überfather every son wishes for; likewise the sons are fiercely protective of their dad. In West Virginia, when Bobby became the head coach, and struggled for wins, Mountaineer fans, not known for their civility, stuck FOR SALE signs in front of the Bowden home and phoned in death threats; one was intercepted by Bowden's daughter Ginger, who was a teenager at the time. Students draped FIRE BOWDEN signs scrawled on sheets from their dorm room windows. Once, upon seeing one, Terry and a friend angrily approached the room of the student and banged on the door. A scrawny, pimply-faced young man opened it. As angry as Terry was, he didn't have the heart to physically confront such a wimp.

Despite Terry's deep affection for his father, and his father's for him, love had its sideline boundaries. There was still no way the old man was letting his boy beat him to a solid recruit like Houston without a good fight.

Terry would need to be ready for that battle and he knew it, because few coaches—if any—were better recruiters than Bowden. When Bowden would recruit running back Nick Maddox in 1999, Bowden traveled to Kannapolis, North Carolina, and dined with Maddox and his mother, who had cooked up a mouthwatering meal of chicken, pinto beans, corn, and potato salad. Maddox liked Bowden and once referred to Bowden as "his cousin," smiling at the differences in their ethnicities.

Maddox went to Florida State, but happenstance played as much a part as good cooking and Bowden's charm. Maddox was worth the effort because he was one of the top high school players in the nation, scoring a then state record 114 touchdowns in high school. Scholarship offers arrived from across the country, but it came down to three schools: Georgia, North Carolina, and Florida State. Maddox had visions of being a Bulldog so he was all set to cancel his visit to Tallahassee, but Maddox's mother convinced him to go anyway, and they made the ten-hour drive. Maddox enjoyed the visit, but he decided to stick with his gut and attend Georgia.

On the drive back, their car overheated and stalled on the highway. Maddox called one of the Florida State assistants who told them to sit tight, help was on the way. Instead of a tow truck, under ten minutes later, someone else showed up. It was Charlie Ward Sr., the father of Charlie Ward Jr., who Maddox knew had won the Heisman Trophy six years earlier. Dad took the two to his home and waited for help. In the meantime, part conversation, part recruiting at the Ward home took place. "My mom talked to his wife, and I sat down and talked with Senior," Maddox said. "He showed me all of Charlie's trophies and stuff. But the most important part was what he told me that day. He didn't try to get me to go to Florida State. He just told me to be comfortable with my decision. I was so impressed with that, and I never forgot it."

Maddox changed his mind and went to Florida State. He'd be a key contributor to the team's 1999 championship.

Tommy Bowden also had his recruiting battles against his dad. When he was an assistant at Alabama, they were recruiting a player in Florida. Tommy called the player's home and his mother answered. "This is Coach Bowden," Tommy said. Tommy could hear the prospect in the background saying, "Which [Bowden] is it? Is it the real one or the other one?"

As for the Houston recruiting battle, Terry would win it despite going against the Babe Ruth of recruiting coaches. He topped Dad. Houston went to Auburn instead of Florida State.

But he didn't win a Heisman. Or two. Or three.

Instead, Terry eventually kicked Houston off the Auburn team for repeatedly violating team rules. Terry told the media at the time: "This saddens me for him, and I hope somewhere down the road he can be a little more responsible. He did make mistakes that violated team rules . . . and we had no choice but to dismiss him."

Maybe the old man had beaten his son after all, since it was Terry who had incurred the Houston headache, not Bobby.

"IF THERE WAS ONE thing in this world I could eradicate," says Bowden, "it would be racial prejudice."

Bowden was raised in the segregated South and witnessed the unconscionable hostility and colored-only sections of Birmingham, Alabama. He was aware of Jim Crow, but it didn't directly affect him. So he went on with his young life, untouched by segregation, until one day a moment on a golf course opened his eyes.

During Bowden's senior year at Howard College in Alabama (now Samford University), he ignited a lifelong passion for golf. He took a class there and spent hours hitting balls on the football field.

Eventually Bowden was able to talk his way onto a local golf course. Even at that young age Bowden possessed the ability to smooth talk. Just after daybreak he was there with a friend and a group of black caddies who were walking the course looking for errant golf balls to later resell. It was a typical Bowden moment. He had chatted his way onto what was considered a fairly exclusive course and was able to play for free.

The ethnicity of the caddies mattered little to Bowden. He struck up a conversation with them and offered a young teen his club, giving him a chance to hit. The caddie took it. In his naïveté,

Bowden failed to realize that simple gesture demonstratively violated the social norms of the time.

Someone spotted the black caddy on the segregated golf course and reported the group. The group of boys looked up to see a large, creaky truck speeding down the middle of the fairway toward them. Bowden tensed, thinking he was about to get tossed off the course.

The truck lurched to a stop and a white man holding a small-caliber pistol jumped out. He didn't even look at Bowden; he marched right to the black caddy who'd taken the shot and held the gun to the caddy's head. "You know you're not supposed to be here," he screamed at the caddy. The man pushed the young caddy into the back of the truck and drove off.

"I never knew what happened to him," Bowden says now. "I think they just scared him and let him go. But I can't say for sure."

"Do you mind if I use the term 'black' or do you prefer African American?" Bowden politely asks a visitor to his office.

"Black is fine and it's nice of you to ask," the visitor responded.

"That [golfing] incident really opened my eyes," Bowden says. "It changed my viewpoint about race. I know I should've felt that way before, but it took something like that to make the point. There was a lot of ignorance and I wasn't going to be a part of it. I was never going to tolerate racism again."

Bowden has stayed true to his word for his career and life. Unlike his hero, Bear Bryant, Bowden was never forced to integrate. He did so willingly. As a head coach, Bowden would fight off alumni seeking to limit the number of blacks on his teams. In the 1990s, Bowden started an African American at quarterback when some other major college programs wouldn't. Every African American player interviewed who ever played for Bowden maintains he was one of the most color-blind white coaches they ever knew.

Bowden witnessed segregation, but the prejudice didn't stay with him. "I grew up in the south back in the 1930s and 1940s," Bowden wrote in his 1994 book *More Than Just a Game*. "Black folks lived in one part of town; white folks lived in another. That's just the way it was. I thought that was the way it was supposed to be. I never thought to wonder, 'Why?' I knew there were white rest rooms and 'colored' rest rooms, white water fountains and 'colored' water fountains, but it never occurred to me to question that stuff. I didn't know the injustice of it and how serious it was. How could I? All I was interested in was playing sports and having a good time."

Interestingly, Bowden's legacy in terms of race and college football is exactly the opposite of his mentor and the man he greatly admired in Bryant. Bryant's reputation is mixed. Mississippi State coach Sylvester Croom has told the story that Bryant approached Croom's father, Sylvester Croom Sr., and pleaded for the young Croom to play at Alabama in a deeply segregated South. "Don't give him nothing because he's black," the older Croom told Bryant. "Don't take nothing away from him because he's black."

Yet in 2006, *Sports Illustrated* wrote of Bryant: "It is certainly illuminative of his nature that the Bear took no lead whatsoever in the matter of integration. His defenders will claim that [Governor George] Wallace kept his hands tied, that the Bear wasn't even allowed to schedule teams with black players, much less dress any of them in Crimson, and there may be a measure of truth in that. But given the Bear's surpassing popularity, he had it within his power to assume a burden of leadership. Yet he held back on race and let other—less entrenched—Southern coaches stick their necks out first. Only after Southern Cal and Sam (Bam) Cunningham ran all over the skinny white boys in a 1970 game, only when it was evident that the Tide couldn't win any longer lily-white, only then did the Bear learn his civics. It is consistent that the one knock against him as a coach is that he never had the faith or daring to be an innovator."

There is no such mixed record with Bowden. The first African American player Bowden ever coached was Garrett Ford at West Virginia. Bowden was the team's offensive coordinator in 1966 when he first met Ford. Initially, Ford viewed Bowden with great suspicion. Ford was from Washington, D.C., and had paid close attention to the civil rights battles in his own city, and farther below the Mason-Dixon line. Ford knew Bowden was from Birmingham, the hotbed for segregation and mob attacks on civil rights marchers, and the site where police turned fire hoses on children singing "We Shall Overcome" in a city park.

When Bowden and Ford first met, Bowden said to Ford, "How ya' doin', boy?" Ford was initially taken aback, not knowing that Bowden—then and sometimes now—calls almost anyone, regardless of their race, "boy" if they are younger than he is. "This is the mid-1960s, Bull Connor had his dogs in Birmingham and you've got the Freedom Marchers," Ford remembered. "Coach Bowden had never coached a black kid until he came to [West Virginia]. The first thing he said to us was, 'How ya' doin', boy?' He had that Southern accent and back then the Black Power was getting popular.

"Well, he'd say 'boy' and he meant nothing by it. My attitude was like, 'You're a white man from the South and you don't know me.' That was the way I was coming at him."

Bowden sensed the tension and perhaps his poor choice of words. So he took what for the time period was an unusual step. Bowden invited Ford over to dinner at his home with Ann and the family. "I had never been in a white person's house for dinner and here was this man from Alabama and he wanted me to come over to his house to eat with his family," Ford said. "I didn't want to go but I had to because he was my coach. I went to the house and I'm bouncing [sons] Terry and Tommy on my knees. They were just little kids. They turned out to be the nicest people you'd ever want to meet."

As for Ford, like many people who played for Bowden, he remains Bowden's friend to this day.

It's no surprise Bowden made the gesture. Son Terry remembers growing up in the Bowden household and never hearing the word *nigger* or any other racial slur used by his parents or siblings.

When Bowden became West Virginia's head coach, he named Ford to his staff, making Ford the first African American coach in any Mountaineer sport in school history. That was February 1970 and his annual salary was $9,600.

Bowden did help make history with the Mountaineers, but he could only go so far with Ford. The culture in West Virginia was racially charged, and giving Ford too much power would outrage alumni. Ford didn't have a great deal of authority; he couldn't send his players into the game, though the white assistants could. Bowden also could do little to protect Ford from the humiliation and racial grenades tossed his way at football-related functions. On occasion boosters would drink too much and the slurs and racial insults would fly with Ford well within earshot.

Bowden did fight other battles. Some of the older West Virginia alumni insisted to Bowden that only a small number of blacks be allowed to play on the team. In other words, they wanted quotas. Bowden refused. "White people used to come up to me and say, 'How many black guys you got on the team?'" Bowden remembered. "I'd say, 'I don't know. I don't count.' They're all some momma's son to me.

"It's funny how that works." Bowden laughed. "Once we started winning with more black players that quota talk went away real quick."

BOWDEN IS MORE THAN just a storyteller. He is more than a tactician and recruiting's version of The Closer. He is more than a surrogate father to the athletes he coaches. In some ways, for much of his Florida State career, he has been a blend of all these things. Above all, he's the best Division I coach college football has ever seen.

Calling Bowden the best college football coach in history is certain to generate vehement disagreement. Indeed, as Bowden's career has reached its end, his critics have grown in numbers and harshness. SportingNews.com ranked its top coaches in the Atlantic Coast Conference (ACC) in 2007 and Bowden finished behind Wake Forest's Jim Grobe, Virginia Tech's Frank Beamer, and N.C. State's Tom O'Brien. It didn't help Bowden's case when the NCAA ruled against Florida State in March 2009 for an academic cheating scandal, which led to Bowden forfeiting some of his victories.

My opinion, however, is based on six defensible factors:

1. Winning—purely the numbers. In his first fifteen years at
   Florida State, Bowden won 132 games, which is only 18 fewer
   than the school's entire football existence before his tenure.
   Between 1990 and 1999 the Seminoles led the nation in bowl
   wins (7), bowl appearances (9), All-American players (19),
   ten-win seasons (10), weeks at the No. 1 ranking (58), first-
   round NFL draft picks (13), and top-five finishes (10). The
   Seminoles have not had a losing season since Bowden's first
   year in 1976. In the two decades before that year, Florida
   State had ten losing seasons and only one bowl victory, the
   1965 Gator Bowl. By the time Bowden retires, which will be
   soon, it's likely only Paterno will have more wins than he does.
   That's an incredible feat. Winning is the definitive factor in
   sports. It's true that Bowden has accumulated some of those
   wins through attrition. Some critics in the media maintain he's
   gotten them only by hanging on for so long. But he's gotten
   them, and he's won over several different eras and generations.
2. Building—constructing a college football program from the
   ground up is one of the hardest things to do in all of sports.
   A large part of building a program is being a master recruiter.
   Bowden could walk into a recruit's living room and not only
   sign the player but also snag the dedication of the player's
   momma.
3. Innovation—did coaches create offensive or defensive systems?
   Did they expound on ones already created? To a large degree,
   Bowden did both. He instituted a fast-break offense under
   mobile quarterback Charlie Ward that was later duplicated by
   numerous programs. The offense was run with the type of
   speed and aggression not seen in college football before. As for
   expounding on systems, Bowden embraced the passing game
   in college football in the 1970s after long shunning it. But
   once Bowden did digest the passing game, he passed the ball
   extensively, doing so when the running game was seen as the
   only way to win games.

4. Longevity—one of the more underrated factors in coaching, particularly in a world where the media and fans quickly forget a coach's past accomplishments. "Longevity is another word for old," Bowden joked to the author. Yes, it is; however, growing old in their jobs is something most college football coaches don't get to experience because they're usually fired. Part of this depends on your perspective. Has Bowden stayed in the game more as an observer or something different? Current and former players on the team maintain that although he isn't calling plays, he remains a key component in formulating game plans and tactics.

5. Ability to deal with the modern athlete—today's players are far more independent and stubborn and less likely to take coaching. Even on the college level, they need coaxing and convincing. Few coaches in college history have been better at getting players to listen. Listen, that is, on the field. Where Bowden has had trouble reaching some of his players is in how they behave off the field. So in this category it's mixed.

6. Ability to handle the media—Alonzo Stagg never had to deal with a jackal writing a college football blog. In the past, when newspapers dominated, no one could work a room like Bowden. Now, in the age of the website and blogger, for a man who thinks the Internet is a fancy way to trap salmon, Bowden has remained remarkably adaptive. Friends and Florida State officials make him aware of blogger criticism, but it doesn't get under his skin the way a good cyberspace ripping does other top coaches.

When you factor all of those criteria, the top four Division I coaches, in my opinion, are Bowden, Paterno, Bear Bryant, and Stagg. How can Bowden rank ahead of Stagg, one of the great in-novators in college football history? Stagg pioneered the lateral pass, presnap motion, the tackling dummy, the huddle, the re-verse, and uniform numbers. Stagg was to college football what Paul Brown was to the pros. He was brilliant. But the bulk of his wins and accomplishments came in the era of football's infancy.

There was little competition, no ESPN commentators analyzing every move he made, no blogs rating his recruiting classes.

Bowden topping Bryant is a far tougher case to make. Bryant won six national championships over an eighteen-year period beginning in 1961. His legacy is almost unmatched, as he was not only a vibrant winner but also a great builder of programs (and not just at Alabama). Here's the problem with Bryant: I'm not so certain he would have been able to coach today's athletes. In fact, he would have struggled greatly. If Bryant attempted in the twenty-first century what he did at that Texas campsite in 1954, there would be no Junction Boys; they would've mutinied. There would've been lawsuits and members of the press decrying the brutal treatments of the players. Since then the NCAA has drastically limited practice times and the amount of physical punishment a team can inflict on a player.

"Times have changed," Bowden said. "I've coached in the '50s, '60s, '70s, '80s, and '90s; now in the 2000s. Coaching in 2000 ain't anywhere close to what it was in the 1960s; ain't even close. . . . If a coach don't change, he's fixing to get fired. I don't think Coach Bryant could coach now the way he did back in the '60s. I don't think kids would go along with it."

Alphonso Carreker played on Florida State's defensive line from 1980 to 1983. He put this thought perfectly in the book *What It Means to Be a Seminole:* "When you watch these guys nowadays, I don't think they could have played with us. Not because they don't have the talent, but because I don't think they could have dealt with the discipline during my era. It's almost like the kids today, with the way they're raised and the things that are given to them, they don't have respect for their elders. We were heads above all that because things weren't tolerated like they are now. That's what made you gain the respect of your coaches, because nothing was tolerated. The game is just played totally different now."

In addition, Alabama's football program was already firmly in place when Bryant became head coach in 1958. The Crimson Tide had won just four games in the three years before his arrival, but Alabama had won a national championship in 1934. Florida State from 1947 until Bowden took over in 1976 had no national titles, and barely half of those seasons were winning ones. In that pre-Bowden period, the Seminoles' only titles were three Dixie Conference championships.

Bowden and Paterno bridge the gap between old-school coaches like Bryant and Ohio State's Woody Hayes and the newer generation of talented coaches like Pete Carroll, Jim Tressel, and Urban Meyer. Bowden and Paterno both fare well in the above criteria, though Bowden prevails in innovation. Paterno had a magical resurgence in 2008, but overall Bowden performed better in those previously mentioned six factors than Paterno. Even in an era when bowl games are more plentiful than Derek Jeter girlfriends, Bowden's record of twenty-one bowl wins is nevertheless remarkable (he trails only Paterno). He led Florida State to its twenty-fifth straight bowl game in 2006, and in 2008 the Seminoles' 42–13 smothering of Wisconsin was the largest bowl victory in FSU history. Bowden is the only coach in history to secure a top-five position in the Associated Press rankings fourteen straight times. Although Bowden was not the innovator that Stagg was, it was Bowden who helped to usher in the pro passing game to major college football after initially thinking it wouldn't work. After Bowden won his first national title in 1993 with an up-tempo offense quarterbacked by Charlie Ward—Bowden once called it the "Kentucky Derby offense," but it was more commonly known as the fast-break offense—dozens of schools copied what Bowden did. This revolution erupted after Bowden took control of a program that was considered one of the nation's worst. Remember: after the 1975 season, the Florida State president almost terminated the football program for lack of success and interest. Then later, because of Bowden, from September 1992 to September 2001 the Seminoles played fifty-four home games at Doak Campbell Stadium (now Bobby Bowden Field at Doak Campbell Stadium) and didn't lose one.

What Bowden has also been able to do (as well as Paterno) is survive fan fickleness. This is an extremely underrated aspect of Bowden's legacy. Some look at Bowden's long career as a man holding on for the sake of earning the all-time wins record. It's more than that. Bowden is one of the more persistent personalities in the history of all sports, and to many that counts for a great deal. "One of the things that's changed over the years is that there is so much scrutiny and so much attention on coaches and programs now," Colorado coach Dan Hawkins told the media before playing Bowden in 2008. "Part of that is what makes college football awesome. But eventually people get tired of your offense, they get tired of your recruiting. That's just the nature of society." Bowden has weathered all of this. He hasn't been unblemished, but his surviving for such a lengthy amount of time says a great deal about him.

Bowden remains locked in a battle with Paterno for all-time career victories. Although both say they don't care about who earns the mark, if you believe that, you are currently waiting for Santa to slide down the chimney any moment now. "I won't lose any sleep one way or the other," Bowden said. "Would I love for it to be me? Yes. But will I lose a lot of sleep if it isn't? No. I will not lose a minute of sleep. I'll just be happy to be here. They always call me 'Avis' anyway."

Ivan Maisel, a much respected college football writer, named Knute Rockne, Bryant, Paterno, and Bowden as the four college coaches who eternally transcend the game. "Florida State seemed like an unlikely setting for a dynasty," Maisel wrote in June 2008. "When Bobby Bowden arrived in 1976, the team he inherited had won four games in three years. The bumper stickers, Bowden joked, said, 'Beat Anybody.' Bowden proceeded to beat everybody. The heights to which he took the Seminoles—14 consecutive top-five finishes and two national championships—are dizzying when you consider the depths in which Bowden began. Bowden assembled the best coaching staff in the country. He recruited a talent-rich state. And he put to work his considerable personal talents: a nimble offensive mind, personal magnetism and simple fearlessness. He would call any play. He would play anywhere. In 1981, the Seminoles played consecutive road games at Nebraska, Ohio State, Notre Dame, Pittsburgh and LSU and won three of them.

In 32 seasons in Tallahassee, Bowden has produced 31 consensus All-Americans, 18 10-win seasons and millions of laughs. In 42 seasons as a head coach, he has won 373 games—more than anyone in the history of major college football." And consider that when Bowden was hired at Florida State he was considered somewhat of a risk. His initial base salary of $37,500 was reasonable for coaches at the time but barely so.

Ernie Accorsi, the longtime former NFL executive and general manager for the New York Giants who is also a football historian, believes both Bowden and Paterno are the greatest of their generation but not of all time. The two men as of 2009 were in an awkward standoff: whoever blinks and retires is the loser; the other wears the laurels of the most wins, though after the NCAA's ruling against Florida State the title is all but Paterno's.

"I think they're the perfect odd couple," said Accorsi, who is close friends with Paterno. "They really like and respect each other. I know Joe really loves Bobby. But they're so different and what is interesting is I think this 'most wins of all time' thing is going to go right down to the wire. My favorite moment between them is after the last game they coached against each other, the bowl game in Florida a few years ago that would not end, afterward Bowden said, 'This is way past Joe and my bed times.'

"Of course, although I confess to not being totally objective, I think Joe has had the tougher job. There are just a lot more great high school football players in Florida than Pennsylvania, which has helped him [Bowden]. But they're both great. To me, they are the two greatest coaches of their generation. It's tough to say all time. Bear Bryant was incredible. [Notre Dame coach Frank] Leahy didn't lose a game for four years between 1946 and '50.

"[The late New York Giants general manager] George Young used to love to quote Knute Rockne's line about Amos Alonzo Stagg, which was spoken in the late 1920s: 'Everything that has ever been used in college football and will ever be used has already been invented by Stagg.' Stagg was hired as head coach at the University of Chicago just as the university was created and shortly had them dominating the Big Ten.

"But Bowden and Paterno have another major characteristic in [common]. They have not only turned their football programs into immortal programs but elevated the status of their universities to a prestigious level beyond football. When I was a student at Wake Forest we played Florida State but never thought of it as a big deal. They were kind of in the Tulane category. Now kids all over the country want to grow up and play for Florida State. I remember asking [Giants executive] Frank Mara's son, Sean, a pretty good quarterback prospect at Iona Prep a few years ago: 'What is your dream school?' He said, 'Florida State.' This is an Irish Catholic kid who grew up in suburban New York. That says it all."

MOSTLY, BOWDEN IS ABOUT family. A strong, devoted wife and bright and dedicated children have served as a protective splint as Bowden traversed from the 1990s, the last decade of the super-power program, when many appreciated Bowden, into the new, more complicated world of text-messaged recruiting ("I don't know what e-mail looks like," he once said. "The Internet? Don't know what it is. Maybe if I retired I'd have time to learn.") and a football landscape where parity has watered down Florida State's once-dominant empire.

"When you look at a coach like Bobby," says longtime broad-caster Pat Summerall, "you basically see one of the few coaches who has lived through several different generations of college foot-ball. Not only has he lived through it, he's prospered. Some people like to criticize Bobby now. But think about what he's done. His longevity and what he's accomplished is almost impossible to do. We'll never see it again."

CHAPTER ONE

TRAGEDY

Ann was sixteen when I married her. I was nineteen. I'm not embarrassed to tell the story. You see, both Ann and I were taught you must be married before sex. We had been dating since she was thirteen or fourteen. You know how intimate you get. Well, we were so in love with each other, we couldn't control it. We needed to go get married.

—Bobby Bowden

You cannot probe the life of Bowden without discussing the life of Ann and their umbilical connection. Theirs are two lives intertwined after decades of marriage. It is more than a fair statement to say Bowden wouldn't have had his success without her. By taking the responsibility for the day-to-day operations of the Bowden home, Ann allowed Bobby to dedicate most of his life to Florida State football. Such a sacrifice hasn't been easy for Ann, and there have been plenty of moments of bitterness and even regret over the loss of her own professional life.

They've weathered practically everything together, including perhaps the most brutal period the Bowden family has ever experienced. It's a period that begins with challenges to Bowden's once unquestioned authority, unyielding attacks on his offensive coordinator son, accusations that Bowden was again catering to bad-boy athletes, and an unfathomable tragedy that demonstrated just how close—and strong—the Bowden family is.

IT WAS 10:05 ON a warm Friday morning in September 2004 when Bowden sat at a desk in his room at the Miami Airport Hilton to rally his family yet again. He began this time by writing the following words: "My Dear Children."

The season opener against the Miami Hurricanes was just hours away. There were plenty of last-minute details to fix and conversations to have with his staff, but a football game was the last thing on Bowden's mind at that moment. Several days earlier, Bowden's grandchild—the son of his daughter Ginger—and former son-in-law were killed after their car skidded off a dark, rain-soaked highway.

Bowden is from a different generation, a time when men did not easily share their emotions. That's why what he did that day in Miami was so poignant. Fighting back tears, he penned a one-page, handwritten letter to his six children, a note that for years had not been seen outside the Bowden family.

"When the tragedy occurred last week I saw again the bond of love our family has for each other," Bowden wrote. "I witnessed the inner strength of Ginger in a time of mortal crisis and the love of her mother, brothers, sisters, spouses, nephews, nieces, children as well as in-laws and friends. Oh, how I love all of you!" Bowden then made a plea: "Keep in mind, at this time, our family will be together forever if we all trust in Jesus and surrender our lives to him. I don't mean change our jobs or schools, etc. But just make your life available to Christ as your grandparents did and Ann and I have tried to do.

"When I die and go to heaven (I know I will) if all of you and your family are not there with me when your time comes," he wrote, "I will consider myself to have failed in life. All the statues, trophies, championships, etc. will be in vain. Somewhere along the line, I failed you if you are not there."

Bowden remembers: "That was one of the toughest things I've

ever had to do. It might be the toughest. I was just trying to make sure the family knew my thoughts and Ann's thoughts, that we were thinking about everyone."

It had been a turbulent few days for Bobby. He went to the funeral and then flew with his son Jeff and several Florida State officials to the game in Miami. "Bobby does not want to be away from his players very long," Seminole assistant Mickey Andrews told the media. "Football is not the most important thing in his life. But he feels responsible to all these players. He doesn't want to let them down."

Bowden's letter was in some ways atypical for him. Yet in other ways the letter typifies the Bowden family, the roots of which were established by the marriage of Bobby Bowden and Julia Ann Estock six decades ago, an intersection of two highly decent people that produced a great American love story and first coaching family of college football.

The Bowden children are a collection of coaches, mothers, fathers, educators, entrepreneurs, and legal minds. Terry is a former Auburn coach turned college football media analyst turned head coach again, this time at the University of North Alabama. Tommy coached at Clemson until he was fired in the fall of 2008. Jeff is a former Florida State assistant who once coached under his father until intense pressure from boosters and others forced him to resign. Steve is a financial planner who would endure his own personal pain and be accused by prosecutors of taking part in a sinister scheme that would eventually touch the entire Bowden family. Ginger is a prosecutor, and Robyn Hines teaches elementary school.

Although often portrayed in one-dimensional snippets—the tough mom, the driven sons, the aw-shucks grandfatherly Bobby—the Bowdens are much more multifaceted, much more complicated, much more human.

There was an example of that complication after the firing of Tommy by Clemson. The father and sons had done well in their careers, winning 579 games in a combined seventy seasons as of late 2008. They had accumulated three unbeaten seasons, numerous conference titles and bowl games, and lots of laughs as well as a few cries and a handful of wide rights. Tommy's firing was a painful chapter in the family's life mainly because of the behavior by some Clemson fans who plastered blogs with highly personal and offensive posts about Tommy. The family was incensed, and Bobby reached out to his son in a brief but emotional discussion, telling him it wasn't the end of the line.

Terry took a different approach. In his column for Yahoo! Sports, Terry defended his brother but also took him to task in what was a public and blunt assessment of his brother's tenure at Clemson. "So, did Tommy Bowden deserve what happened to him . . . ?" wrote Terry. "Unfortunately, yes. He deserved it because he, of all people, knew what to expect when he got into this business. We grew up in it. He knew what to expect when he went to Clemson. He knew that no matter where you go, there is an expectation of success that must be met. After nine years at Clemson, he knew exactly what those expectations were and he knew they had not been met. Clemson expects to win the conference championship once in a while—and they should. After 10 years of falling short, they deserve the right to try to find a coach they believe can get them there." Some family members weren't ecstatic about Terry's remarks, but Bobby took it in his usual stride. "Terry speaks his mind," said Bobby. Then he said laughing: "Sometimes he speaks his mind too much."

Indeed, though the family is close, there is variance across the spectrum. Their political beliefs, for example, cross the gamut. Between November 1999 and July 2006, Bobby contributed thousands to the campaigns of Republicans George W. Bush, Mel Martinez, Bill McCollum, and (the infamous) Katherine Harris. Bobby also contributed to the Republican National Committee and the Republican Party of Florida. All of those donations totaled $17,750. Steve, however, between 2007 and 2008, contributed to Democrats John Edwards, Kay Hagan, and Barack Obama. Ann gave to Black America's PAC, an organization dedicated, in part, to expanding economic opportunities in historically disadvantaged American communities, as well as $500 to the Bush campaign.

Their political variance aside, one thing about the family is certain: the Bowdens have built their coaching dynasty with sweat, intelligence, honesty, and goodwill. But the empire also has seen despair and dysfunction. To endure the rough times, Bobby does what he always has done: lean on his family for support.

The terrible car accident was one of these moments. At 5:47 P.M. on September 5, 2004, John Allen Madden, Ginger's former husband, and their son, sixteen-year-old Bowden Madden, were riding in their 1993 BMW, driving westbound on Interstate 10 in northern Florida. The highway was slick with standing water from the final breaths of Hurricane Frances, which had reached Category 4 strength with sustained winds of 145 mph. Madden's vehicle was in the outside lane, a police report states, and a 2002 Dodge van driven by Larry Maines was in the inside lane. Madden, for unknown reasons, according to an accident report, veered left into the Dodge carrying Maines and his wife, Margaret. The left side of Madden's car struck the right front of the van. "I heard a thump and, before I know it, I was sliding across the highway," Larry Maines said in an interview. Both vehicles careened across the median into the eastbound lane, according to the report. A medium-size utility truck traveling 45 mph missed Maines's car by eighteen inches and crashed into Madden's. The entire accident took less than twenty seconds.

Emergency services arrived at the scene at 5:59 P.M. One minute later, both John and Bowden Madden were dead, the police report states. Later that night, at approximately ten o'clock, the longtime head of security for Seminole coaches, Billy Smith, a former member of the Florida Highway Patrol, rang the doorbell of the Bowden home. Ginger answered. "Ginger, we need to sit down," Smith told her. "I've got some bad, bad news." He barely got the words out before Ginger exploded in grief. Ann was asleep on the couch and woke up. Bobby was upstairs sleeping and raced downstairs when he heard the screaming.

Later more officers arrived, several of whom had actually been at the terrible crash. Bobby did something the experienced officers hadn't really seen before. He asked them to diagram exactly how the accident had occurred. So the police officers did. Bobby needed to know exactly what happened, and he best processed that information the way he would a football play.

Amid Ginger's devastation, she drew comfort from a family that was by her side in a matter of hours.

"That was awful," Bobby says. "One of the worst experiences I've ever had. To see it happen. To see my daughter as patrolmen come up to my house and tell her. That's something I'll never get over and she'll never get over. But she has to go on with life because that's the way life is. It was a big lesson right there. We are all going to go one of these days. Everybody thinks someone else is going to go. 'I ain't gonna die. Y'all are.' There are reminders of that like this, unfortunately."

In dealing with the tragedy, the family relied on faith and almost as important, they relied on football. "We flew to the funeral in Panama City with them," said T. K. Wetherell, the school president who once played for Bowden. "I think the only way they got through it was with the family, and that family is really, really tight. They spent a lot of time, when I was there, all talking football. The sons, Tommy, Jeff, and Terry, would talk about this game or that game. They were about to have a service, and Bobby and Jeff were sitting there and saying, 'Tommy, you couldn't run a blitz on third-and-whatever' or 'I can't believe you ran that play.'

"It's just how they dealt with it; it wasn't callous," he added. "The loss of family shook them more than anything, but that's the way they dealt with it—through football and their faith. They immersed themselves in football and used football to get through that time."

Months after the accident, Ann told her doctor she was having trouble speaking about it without breaking into tears.

"I always thought I had the perfect family. But you know, Doctor, now it's broken, and I can't fix it," she said.

The doctor nodded and held her hand, but there was only so much comfort a family practitioner could deliver. She again turned to prayer. "Lord, just please put us back together . . . and help me fix myself," she'd pray.

Ann was consumed with why it happened—not the technical causes of the accident, but why it was allowed to happen, particularly since one of the victims was so young. "Mom, it doesn't matter why it happened," Ginger told her. "It just happened." Ginger, a highly accomplished county prosecutor in Florida, sought her own answers, as she had a consuming desire to understand the cause of the tragedy.

She examined the accident almost methodically, in what was a remarkably detached, lawyerlike manner. She spoke to each of the witnesses and in the end came up with a smart, and in all probability accurate, theory of what happened. An intense wind event from the hurricane remnants, she reasoned, caused John to lose control of the vehicle.

Ginger has the tenacity and openness of her father, the high intelligence and sophistication of her brother Steve, and the emotional freedom of Ann. She also possesses the Bowden sense of humor. When she applied to law school, Ginger started her essay: "I was born on a dark night. My mother was unconscious. My father was out recruiting. And I've been trying to get their attention ever since."

"Ginger is a very strong person," says Ann. "She got up at 5 A.M. to study. Took the kids to school. Went to her law classes. Then the library in the afternoon. Then she'd pick up the kids and spend the early evening with them. Passed the Florida Bar the first time she took it. She loves being a mother."

Ginger remembers how, soon after the accident, she made a pact to herself that she would not curse God or any person. She would come to understand that, unfortunately, these types of things happen to many families. Just because she was a Bowden, a member of a powerful football trust, she thought, the Bowden name didn't offer a shield from devastation, the same way the Kennedy name did not protect any of them from various horrific events.

"I was not going to say, 'Why me?'" Ginger said.

CHAPTER TWO

SON UNDER FIRE

Nothing compares to losing a young child. It would be foolish to put football on the same plane. Yet the Bowdens were tested again just a short time later, this instance coming in a more familiar arena—on the football field. It is here where Bobby for practically his entire Florida State career had gone unchallenged by fans and the media because his nearly unparalleled success served as armor from criticism (well, mostly it did). That all began to change when Bobby appointed Jeff as the team's offensive coordinator in 2001.

To many, Jeff became a symbol of the decline of the Seminoles. To numerous others, he was more than a symbol; he was a punching bag, a conduit for launching unprecedented attacks on Bobby, and the originating source of almost riotous outrage from hardline Seminole fans and the blogosphere.

It's no shock when prominent alumni scream about a coordinator's strategy or fire off notes to the university president demanding various resignations. What was stunning was how people inside of and close to the program began to express their displeasure over Jeff's command of Florida State's offense. Indeed, Bobby's stubborn loyalty to his son strained even the closest of relationships with some of Bobby's longtime coaching friends.

Jeff, of course, wasn't always a human dartboard. Of all the Bowden coaching men, he was, in effect, the fourth most known behind Bobby, Terry, and Tommy. "Jeff is an outdoorsman," said

Ann. "Likes to fish. Good golfer. He's got his personality, and he's a little bit rough around the edges. Sensitive person. He [handled] his job very well because he [had] a lot of criticism."

This also wasn't the first time Jeff was at the center of some controversy involving him and his father. Jeff played wide receiver for the 1981 and 1982 Seminole teams under his head coach father, when the 1982 Gator Bowl saw Florida State beat Bowden's old team, West Virginia, 31–12. Late in the game, with the Seminoles comfortably ahead and inside Mountaineer territory, Bowden ordered a pass to one of the receivers. The media and some fans thought Bowden was trying to run up the score on his former school. It wasn't that. The receiver who had gotten the pass attempt was Jeff. He caught it. It was the only catch of Jeff's college career.

When the pressure on Jeff to resign grew to a crushing force, family members never saw him succumb to it. He stayed the same Jeff he'd always been. As sister Robyn Hines explained, Jeff bought into Bobby's persistent motif: if you decided to go into the family business, you have no right to complain when the wolves start tugging at your coattails. And complain Jeff never did. Not once. He blew off steam in the off-season with long fishing trips and mostly stayed away from reading about himself on the Internet.

Ann remembers calling Jeff in the winter of 2005 as the heat on him increased. "I didn't raise any quitters," she told Jeff. "I'm not a quitter and your dad has never quit, so you're not going to give up now either."

What often was lost in Jeff's public beating was that he was actually qualified for the job. Jeff spent four productive seasons as offensive coordinator for brother Terry's teams at Salem College in West Virginia and at Samford University in Birmingham. There, Jeff's offense put up impressive numbers. After that, Jeff spent three years as receivers coach at Southern Mississippi University before coming back to Florida State and coaching receivers again. In that role, Jeff oversaw some of the school's most talented wideouts.

He was more than qualified, yet his qualifications almost didn't matter—as the thoughts and reservations of former Florida State president Talbot D'Alemberte would eventually demonstrate. D'Alemberte, who retired from Florida State in 2003, expressed in several media interviews after his departure that Jeff was in a no-win situation. If the offense did well, Bobby would get the credit. If it didn't, there would be cries of nepotism and Jeff would become a convenient target.

The rapidity and ferocity of the attacks on Jeff shocked even the Bowdens, a family hardened by the hot vitriol that accompanies coaching life. Robyn has seen the coaching profession from all sides. She is the oldest daughter of a famous coach, the sister of three coaching brothers, and the wife of Jack Hines, a former assistant coach at Clemson under Tommy. Robyn has closely watched how the college football world works, on the field and off. She enjoys the competition and camaraderie of the team sport but despises what she believes has been an increase in fan hostility toward coaches, a meaner media, and a nasty talk-radio and Internet culture. When she once heard a radio talk-show host blast Bobby for being a disloyal cad because he departed West Virginia for FSU decades ago (the accusation wasn't true), Robyn was so infuriated she was tempted to call the station. Bowden didn't abandon West Virginia, he left for a better Florida State job after West Virginia fans had turned on him. Instead, she called Ann to commiserate. "I hate it, too, but this is just part of the life," Ann told her.

"The animosity of fans and some people in the media has gotten so much worse over the past ten or twenty years," Hines says. "I don't know how my father and brothers and husband put up with it. I'm to the point where I'm tired of the hassle and watching my family get hassled, and I want them all to get out of coaching."

"Fans are much more vocal now than they have ever been," Hines continues. "It's because they think they have more inside information because of things like the Internet and instant replay. Every fan has a little bit of knowledge, but a little bit of knowledge is a dangerous thing."

Her son once considered going into the family business. "Then he decided against it," Robyn says, "and I can't tell you how happy I am."

Robyn has always been the planner in the family. When she was just sixteen years old, she made a list of the qualities she wanted in a husband. She's also always been a protector of her siblings. "[Robyn's] a lot like me," said Ann. "She's very open. Very friendly. Everyone loves Robyn. She's very sweet. Attractive. Not overly aggressive but a strong defender of the family, like the other children."

As the oldest, she was assigned by her parents to look after the kids while Bobby was away at practice or when Ann had to run errands. Although Robyn is quick to point out how much she loves football, her desire to protect her brothers and sisters is stronger.

She bristles at charges of Bowden nepotism when it comes to Jeff. "Why is it an unspoken rule in our society," Robyn asked, "that if you work for your family or your parents, you automatically can't be any good?" Bobby felt strongly the body blows to Jeff were really a thinly veiled passive-aggressive attack on him (which would later be neither veiled nor passive but definitely aggressive). Terry agreed, but he handled the destruction of his brother with his usual sense of humor. At one point, during the height of the criticism, while hosting his radio show, Terry had listeners call in and vote Jeff on or off the field. "You're not going to break my father," he told his audience, "so if you need to vent, do it here."

The cornerstone of the attacks on Jeff came on two fronts. First, critics maintained Jeff got his job solely because his last name was Bowden. Second, they claimed he was grossly overmatched as offensive coordinator.

Jeff took over the offense in 2001, following the redoubtable Mark Richt, who left for the head coaching position at the University of Georgia. Richt is one of Bowden's successful protégés. Some of Bowden's former assistants would spend decades coaching in the NFL, whereas others like Richt stayed in college coaching. Although it's unfair to state that Bowden's nonfamilial assistants have had more success than former assistants with genetic linkings to Bowden—Terry after all did have an impressive run at Auburn until the situation imploded, as did Tommy at Clemson to some degree—coaches like Richt and George Henshaw did produce a solid Bowden legacy. It wasn't as bountiful or well known as Bear

Bryant's, but it's been noticeable. "I don't want to compare my sons to other coaches; that's not fair," said Bobby. "My kids have done pretty doggone good if you ask me. Jeff did better than some people want to give him credit for, and Terry and Tommy produced some good results where they were. Mark was very good and very loyal. He was almost like one of my kids."

If you want to trace to one moment when things not only got ugly for Jeff but when the doubts about Bobby began to rumble vociferously—and the memory loss of what Bowden had done for Florida State started to bloom fully—2001 is when the ugliness began in earnest.

The smart and quick Richt departing around that time didn't help. Richt would leave the Seminoles and lead the Georgia Bulldogs to an impressive 71–19 career record prior to the 2008 season. Still, Richt at one point in his life seemed like an unlikely candidate for a longtime Bowden right-hand man. He was a career backup for the University of Miami and tried odd jobs like valet parking cars and bartending. When he was fired as a bartender for watching too much football, he was forced to clean the bar at closing. Richt then went on to prepare for a career as a life insurance salesman. He never got to finish that career either. One day he showed up to work and witnessed his boss being handcuffed and put into a police car. End of life insurance career. Richt would eventually get into coaching, and Bowden would call him a genius; indeed, few offensive coordinators in the history of the sport could take apart a defense like Richt.

The Seminoles are in many ways the prototypical victims of their own success. The unprecedented trek of fourteen consecutive seasons in which they never lost more than two games began in 1987, a year in which they finished in the top five of the Associated Press rankings. Along the way, Florida State won two national championships and would have captured several more if not for a few wide right (and left) field goal tries along the way. Quite simply, that lengthy period of dominance, one could easily argue, is the most impressive long-term coaching achievement in modern football history. Bowden's ACC record at one point was 96–8.

Then came that pesky year: 2001. After that, everything quickly changed. At one point, from 2001 to 2007, there were six consecutive seasons Florida State finished with at least three losses. In that time it was not unusual for FSU to inhabit the bottom of the ACC; and, in fact, from 2004 and entering the 2008–09 season Florida State had a very average 18–14 conference record, tying them for second with Clemson and Virginia. Remember, this is a league Florida State dominated in its early years after being admitted, winning a dozen titles in its initial fourteen seasons.

The Seminoles' overall record (conference and nonconference) in the previous thirty-four games entering 2008 was only 17–17. The rallying cry for Florida State was no longer "win a championship"; it had become "just get bowl eligible."

When the losing started, the criticism and potshots from fans in particular resembled an out-of-control sprinkler system. "We're an also-ran," Monk Bonasorte, one of Bowden's earliest stars at Florida State, told the Associated Press in 2007. "We're in the middle of the pack in the ACC, or actually below the middle of the pack. We're not talked about on ESPN anymore. The only thing that's talked about is how Florida State is in last place. That's hard for a program that has the national prominence we have."

After one particular season, when the Seminoles averaged twenty-three-year lows in yards per game and points averaged, FSU administrators, powerful trustees, and others attempted to persuade Bobby to fire his son. There was at least one former Florida State coach who approached Bowden with concerns about Jeff as well. Bobby angrily refused to take action. After all, Bobby had stood by former coordinator Richt when Seminole fans early in Richt's career called for his firing, bombarded Richt's office and home with nasty letters and phone calls, and started the Evict Richt Club. Bobby says he actually lost friends over his insistence on keeping Richt (and temporarily did so over Jeff, though some of those relationships were later repaired). So if Bobby was going to be loyal to Richt, he was certainly going to stand by his son.

It wasn't easy to do even for a dedicated father. It was even harder to hear and see your son metaphorically burned at the stake. After

Florida State barely beat North Carolina State in 2004, ESPN analyst and former Seminole player Lee Corso called the offense the worst he has seen at that school in fifty years. Signs popped up at games that read SEND JEFF TO UF. A website, hirejeffbowden .com, sarcastically asked another school to take him off the school's hands. "Jeff Bowden is a young coach that is currently toiling in his legendary father's shadow at Florida State University," the site stated. "Unfortunately for Jeff, at FSU he will never be more than 'that other Bowden.' For this reason and others on these pages, we ask that you support our effort to help Jeff land a head coaching position somewhere where he can gain his own identity."

In 2006, millionaire booster Larry D. Beltz, a personal injury attorney used to playing hardball, wrote a scathing e-mail questioning Jeff's competence to school president Wetherell, who played football for Florida State and was loyal to Bowden. "The fans are not upset with losing, although we all enjoy winning," Beltz wrote. "They are upset with how FSU football has lost all its excitement since Mark Richt left and Jeff Bowden took over. He is not competent to coach the quality of players that FSU has. He has continued to demonstrate this year after year for the last six years. If his name wasn't Bowden, he would have been gone long ago, and if that's not true, then you would have to consider Bobby's abilities at this point. Are FSU fans doomed until Bobby retires or, God forbid, dies before we're rid of Jeff?" Beltz also threatened to hold back significant amounts of financial donations until Jeff was dismissed. Another prominent booster, Peter Mettler, also wrote Wetherell, and while he expressed respect for Bobby's career, he added it was time for him to step down as well. "As our president, I urge you to be the leader I know you are, and do what has to be done," he wrote.

"I think a lot of former players or prominent alumni were getting pressure from other boosters to try and get not just Jeff to step down but Bobby as well," says former Seminole player LeRoy Butler. "I was definitely getting pressure. People were approaching me and saying, 'It's time for Bobby to go.' And I would say, 'He should go out when he wants to.' Many, if not all, of the great things associated with Florida State are because of Bobby; it can all be traced back to Bobby and not just football either. The school owes him. But I think there was such a frenzy people were forgetting that."

"I'm not saying he's the same coach he was ten years ago," said former player Warrick Dunn. "Maybe that's true. But a lot of Coach Bowden's former players feel like people have forgotten what he's done for Florida State. Many fans, I feel, betrayed him. I think a lot of players felt, 'The man should step down whenever the hell he wants to. He's more than earned that right.'"

One Florida State fan started retirecoachbowden.com. On the site was a photo of Bobby with a caption underneath that read: "Dazed and Confused."

"We mourn the demise of Florida State University Seminole football at the hands of its most trusted builder," the site stated. It tracked and detailed each of Florida State's 23 losses since the start of the 2001 season, calling that time period the "Bobby and Jeff Pony Show." The website no longer exists, making it something else Bowden has outlasted.

Former Florida State quarterback Peter Tom Willis, the team's color announcer, called the offense "a high school offense." He was later so critical of Jeff during one broadcast Bobby pushed for his ouster from the network and got it. Willis was gone.

"In my opinion, you saw a few cowards come out of the woodwork," Bobby says now.

THE CRITICISM MARKED A dramatic shift in the treatment of the Bowden Empire. For the first time, it was open season not solely on Jeff but on Bobby too.

"In my coaching career there were two coaches I felt who were for most of their careers untouchable in terms of the media and fans," said Bowden's friend and former assistant coach George Henshaw. "One was Don Shula and the other was Bobby Bowden. That changed for Bobby around 2000 or 2001. The things that were being said about him I thought I'd never see. Some of the critics were very, very vicious. I think Bobby took the criticism very personally. I think it hurt him."

The criticism, over a variety of issues, got so bad that media allies who had long been friends began to suggest draconian measures for Bowden and his program. Ron Morris, the columnist at the *State* newspaper in Columbia, South Carolina, was once the sports editor of the *Tallahassee Democrat*. When the academic cheating scandal engulfed much of the Florida State athletic department in 2007 and 2008, Morris ripped Bowden perhaps like no journalist had ever before. In one column excerpt he wrote: "The NCAA needs to give Florida State the 'death penalty' and shut down the program, thus preventing Bowden from gaining necessary wins to overcome [Joe] Paterno." Morris also wrote: "What has become apparent over the past decade or so is that Bowden remains the coach for personal, selfish and egotistical reasons. He has not coached a down of football in about 15 years and is as much a figurehead as anyone in college athletics. Yet he sticks around solely so he can become the all-time leader in victories."

Bowden is gentle and fair and sturdy. He's also human. He alternated between feeling angry, betrayed, and greatly saddened at the criticism, though he was reluctant to publicly admit it. At times, Bowden couldn't hide his disappointment over the treatment of his son. Former Florida State running back Lorenzo Booker says that in Jeff's final season in 2006 he saw a different Bobby. "Coach Bowden was always a constant, his personality was a constant," says Booker. "He was always energetic and upbeat. But that year got to him. Usually when he spoke to us as a team, his speeches were very enthusiastic. But when all the criticism about Jeff happened, his speeches weren't as enthusiastic. I was at Florida State for half a decade. I got to know Coach Bowden well and that year I had never seen him so down."

For much of his Florida State career, Bobby's offense was innovative and unpredictable. If there was one criticism of Jeff that was accurate, it was that the offense had become less so under him. There were fewer multiple formations, and the staple of a Bowden game plan—the trick play—had all but disappeared. Several defensive coaches who opposed Jeff's schemes claimed it was easy to discern what play was coming. Some former opposing players who went against Bowden told the author that his team would call out what play was coming during key moments in games; and not just "run" or "pass" but what direction the play was going. Often such claims are exaggerated and self-serving, but several opposing coaches and players who faced Florida State during Jeff's tenure swore their claims were accurate. (These coaches were different from the ones who used electronic eavesdropping to steal portions of Bowden's offense.)

Jeff had become such a polarizing force even some of the Florida State players began to question his competence. Whether their questions were legitimate or whether they were doing what some athletes do, which is seek excuses for their own ineptitude, is an interesting debate. The end result was, according to several players, the loss of respect for Jeff as a coach. Booker said in an interview that while he liked Jeff personally, some thought there was a feeling that Jeff wasn't holding himself accountable for the problems with the offense. "Jeff always blamed us," said Booker, who now plays for the Philadelphia Eagles. "Everything was always our fault. Some of it was, but some of it had to be his." Booker added: "My last year there was bad. I just wanted to get the hell out of there." Those are simply not comments you're used to hearing Florida State players making.

Booker says he was so miserable that he counted down the days on the calendar until his last Florida State game, the Emerald Bowl in San Francisco in December 2006. He marked through the days with an X.

"It was the last day in Tallahassee, before we flew to California," Booker said. "And [the calendar] said, 'One more game—it's finally over.' It was like six in the morning, and I'm thinking, 'I'm not even going to be back here.' And I just crossed it off. I haven't been back there since.

"Jeff Bowden would consistently come into meetings and tell us it was all our fault, all our fault. He told one coach, 'I just call plays off the top of my head.' Who does that? This isn't *Madden*. You've got to actually put a game plan together. There was just no accountability, and a person who doesn't have accountability can't teach another person to have it. I had coaches come up to me and apologize to me when I left Florida State. They said, 'You guys deserved better.'"

Then, referring to the $537,000 buyout Jeff received, Booker said, "I love all the coaches I played for. They worked hard, and some people lost their jobs because of that, and none of them walked away with half a million dollars. I never said that I was perfect. I'll pull up tape right now and let you know that there's a bunch of plays I messed up. But I'll tell you this: when I didn't do what I was supposed to do, I was punished for it. If I fumble, you're going to take me out of a game. But when you continuously make bad calls, then let someone else call the plays. Don't just tell us we're not doing our job and it's nothing you did. I think JB's a great person. I'm not talking about the person. But everybody individually has to see what they could have done better, and if you don't have everybody doing that, then the team will never be what it could be."

(Booker told the *Florida Times-Union* in 2006 that Jeff "always [has] been a great guy to talk to. There have been times when I've gone in there and felt like I could get the ball more, and he was more than happy to talk to me.")

Former Florida State quarterback Chris Rix, who makes it clear he respects Bowden, nevertheless agrees with the central theme of Booker's assessment. Rix believes the coaching staff has deflected blame to the players from itself. When the author asked Rix what was the single biggest reason why the Seminoles haven't won a championship in recent years, Rix, now a college football analyst for Fox, responded in an e-mail: "I believe there are various reasons why we haven't won a title or as many games as people expect us to win, but if I had to point out the biggest single reason in my opinion, I would have to say . . . accountability. At times on the player's behalf, but mainly on the coaches' behalf. Accountability in coaching, accountability in their decisions, and accountability in their decisions as coaches."

Again, Booker's critical comments about Jeff are extraordinary (and to a smaller degree so are the comments from Rix), because no player had ever publicly made those kinds of statements about Bobby's program. The comments are also indicative of just how divided and splintered—to some degree—the Seminole program had become. The situation was more complicated than some Florida fans and media members wanted to believe. Jeff wasn't the offensive coordinator boogeyman, but he was also no Richt. Then again, few people were.

Perhaps a more wholly accurate take is that Jeff suffered from bad timing. In the 1990s, Bowden and a handful of elite programs had their picks of the upper echelon of high school talent. That changed beginning in the twenty-first century. The state of Florida became a more competitive recruiting battleground because coaches like Urban Meyer at the University of Florida and later Randy Shannon at Miami were fighting effectively in the same living rooms as Bowden. Bowden actually made the admission that Shannon was reclaiming vital and fertile South Florida recruiting turf where Bowden had historically done well. From the years 2004 to 2006 Bowden signed seven players from the Miami area, but in the two years after, according to the *Miami Herald*, he had signed only one. Bowden says Shannon's recruiting skills are so effective that Shannon reminded Bowden of Miami coaching legend Howard Schnellenberger, who is considered one of the best recruiters in college football history.

Recruiting is also a remarkably inexact science. In his early years with the Seminoles, Bowden was able to build a program practically from scratch by successfully mining Florida's talent. He did this probably as quickly as any coach in college football history. There was both skill and great luck involved in doing this, and as fortunate as Bowden was in those years he was as unlucky in recent seasons. In 2002, the recruiting bible Rivals.com declared that Florida State produced a monster recruiting class and ranked four Seminole recruits in its top twenty—running backs Booker and Leon Washington and wide receivers Chris Davis and DiShon Platt. Platt never made it to Florida State because of academic issues, and although Booker, Washington, and Davis would make it to the pros (Washington is a special teams star for the New York Jets), none truly became huge stars while with the Seminoles, and Florida State failed to finish in the Associated Press top ten with them onboard.

There's also the matter of the wallet. Florida State just couldn't keep up with some wealthier private schools that were dramatically increasing their recruiting budgets. The *Chronicle for Higher Education* ranked the top twenty spenders in sports recruiting and the Seminoles weren't among them, beaten out by schools such as Tennessee, Notre Dame, the University of Florida, Auburn, and Ohio State.

The increased competition was bound to lead to more losses for the superpowers. The first decade of the BCS era, which began in the late 1990s, was dominated by names like USC's Pete Carroll, Ohio State's Jim Tressel, Oklahoma's Bob Stoops, and Texas's Mack Brown. Critics point to Bowden's performance in these BCS bowl games and use his record as proof of how modern football passed him by. That wasn't exactly accurate; college football's shrinking talent pie was the bigger factor, meaning smaller programs were capable of stealing more talent from the big boys. A Boise State could not only compete with Oklahoma on the field but in some of the recruiting wars off it. Kids turned down Notre Dame for lesser programs, something unfathomable just a decade or so ago.

Florida State participated in each of the first three BCS title contests, falling to No. 1 Tennessee in 1999, beating second-ranked Virginia Tech in the 2000 Sugar Bowl, and losing to No. 1 Oklahoma in the 2001 Orange Bowl. Since then the Seminoles haven't been nearly as big a factor in the national championship hunt. Again, the problem with blaming Bowden is that many of the traditionally great college football powers have suffered similar cyclical fates as Florida State.

Where Bowden did misstep was policing the attitude of his team over the last few seasons. At some point, in recent years, Florida State players got cocky and believed their reputation alone would help them win games. "I think we had an identity crisis at some point," quarterback Drew Weatherford said in July 2008. "I can't put my finger on when that was, but we got to the point where we were relying on being Florida State way more than we were relying on us getting the job done. We were walking onto the field and thinking because we had a spear on our helmet, because we were Florida State, because we had won two national championships, been in the top five fourteen years in a row, that was enough. . . . That's not what it's all about. Good teams have a lot of chemistry and a lot of intangible things that make great teams, championship teams."

"I know when I first got here in 2005, you look at the legacy that was built there, and sometimes you do get complacent," said defensive end Everette Brown in 2008. "You think . . . so when we go out there on the field, everybody is going to lay down and everything will fall into place. We've got the big stadium with all the trophies. Well, I'm a part of that. Well, you didn't earn any of that. You didn't play in that national championship game. You didn't play in the ACC championship. What are you going to do to build onto the legacy before you . . . ?"

All of these nuances were lost on some fans. The main reason Jeff's offense was seen as predictable was because there were more second- and third-and-long plays. The reason there were more second- and third-and-long plays is because the talent pool had rapidly shallowed for Florida State. It was a dastardly cycle. The talent on the field wasn't as good as some fans believed because there was much more parity in the sport due to reasons already stated. Rather than deal with that uncomfortable fact, it was easier for fans to light Jeff's pants on fire.

TheBigLead.com website might have captured this phenomenon best when it wrote: "Florida State and Nebraska have been hit the hardest since dominance in the 90's, and both have sunk into mediocrity. Florida State, Miami and Nebraska used to win 80 percent of their games; now that number is in the low 60's while perennially bad teams like Kansas and Rutgers have caught up. There was a time when the notion of Navy beating Notre Dame was as foreign to college football fans as restraint was to Catholic priests. These truly are trying times to be a fan of the old guard."

There was proof the offensive woes weren't solely the fault of Jeff. It emerged after Jeff stepped down on November 26, 2006, one day following the season finale against Florida. The following season new formations were added, the offensive coaching staff was over-hauled, and the ball was better distributed into the hands of play-makers; yet by November 2007, the media buzzed with stories of how things failed to get dramatically better in Jeff's absence. As the Atlantic Coast Conference season came to an end, the Seminoles had scored 30 points only once in eleven games, twice less than the year before under Jeff. The offense, now being run by Bobby's hand-picked successor, Jimbo Fisher, who turned the portly JaMarcus Russell from LSU into a top NFL draft pick at quarterback, had in-creased in yards per game but the scoring average was down slightly. Fisher, anointed by Bowden as the head coach–in-waiting, signed a contract in December 2007 that would give him $2.5 million if he's not hired to replace Bowden in three years. Likewise, Fisher would have to pay the same amount if he wanted to leave before then.

So Fisher will be Bowden's successor, not Jeff. The people who wanted Jeff gone finally got their wish in November 2006. Bobby at-tempted to talk Jeff out of leaving, but Jeff, the honorable son, whom Bobby calls Jeffrey, knew what his presence was doing to Bobby's image. Indeed, Jeff had wanted to resign one year before, but Bobby talked him out of it. Bobby, Ann, and Jeff had several simple, low-key conversations at Bobby and Ann's home leading up to the decision. There were no fireworks or highly teary moments, just thought-ful conversations sometimes at poolside. Three days after Florida State was shut out in a brutal 30–0 loss to Wake Forest in November 2006—the first shutout at Florida State's Doak Campbell Stadium in Bowden's then thirty-one years as coach—Jeff announced in a press conference he was stepping down. Jeff mentioned how his father had always taught him to never quit but to also do what's right. "And that's the reason I am here," Jeff said, "because I believe in my heart that for Bobby Bowden this is the decision that I need to make."

By 2008, Bowden had undergone experiences in just a few years he had not seen in his many decades of being in the public eye. The year should've been one of great enjoyment. Bowden was at 500 games coached, an accomplishment only reached by Stagg and Paterno. Bowden had coached so many games, he had faced opponents from thirty-one different states and coached in a dozen different bowl games. The milestone didn't matter because in a short time span that year and into 2009, Bowden had witnessed more ugliness than maybe in his entire coaching life, enough to enervate any person, young or old. He had lost a grandson in a terrible car accident. His son Jeff stepped down as offensive coordinator. His players were in trouble again. (In October 2008, he dismissed senior fullback Joe Surratt for what were called administrative reasons.) And, despite an eighty-eight-year-old Supreme Court justice and a 2008 candidate for president of the United States in his seventies, Bobby was being assailed as an ineffective old coot.

The discontent of some fans had been building. In 2007, after a brutal loss to rival Miami, Bowden was leaving his home around 7:30 A.M. when he noticed a FOR SALE sign on his front lawn. He pulled it from the ground and casually laid the sign on its side, knowing of course that he didn't put it there, some unhappy fan did. Bowden publicly joked that "I'll save it for when I get ready to move. It'll save me a few bucks." But privately Bobby and Ann were angered by the callousness of the intrusion. The sign also brought back painful memories of the hardened troglodyte fans at West Virginia who left FOR SALE signs on the front lawn of his home toward the end of his tenure as head coach of the Mountaineers from 1970 to 1975.

Bowden wasn't immune from wisecracks from some in the coaching fraternity. Florida's Meyer will one day end up in the college Hall of Fame, but he is also Captain Smug. During his radio show in September 2008, Meyer, when speaking about the Gator and Miami rivalry, stated: "I'm forty-four years old. I'm not trying to be seventy-eight and playing those guys every year."

Pat Dye, the former Auburn coach, speaking in October 2008 at a luncheon to a group of college football fans, said that "all football coaches, and I include myself—they all got egos. It's all about who's going to win that one game more than the other one. I guarantee you, Coach Paterno, if they've got to put him on a damn gurney and take him out there . . ."

When the 2008 season began, the overall pressure on Bowden only worsened after Florida State was embarrassed by up-and-coming Wake Forest, led by Coach Jim Grobe, whose career was remarkably similar to a young Bowden's. Wake Forest was Florida State's first true test of the season and the team scored just three points, had five interceptions, and fumbled twice; and the quarter-backs outgained the running backs on the ground. "This was no boo-boo," wrote ESPN.com's Heather Dinich, "this was a black eye, broken nose and busted lip on picture day." CBSSports.com senior writer Dennis Dodd wrote that "at Florida State—where ACT used to mean Always Catching Touchdowns—the 'Noles would settle for a score, any score . . . College football awoke to a bizarro world Sunday that saw Vanderbilt ranked for the first time since 1984. Florida State was just rank."

It wasn't always like this. The greatest coach of his generation wasn't immersed in constant controversy and subject to taunts about his age. He was simply a coach, a father, a husband, and a man of unshakable faith, a faith sharply honed by a traumatic childhood experience.

CHAPTER THREE

THE FEVER

The document is frayed and blackened but still clearly legible, despite being delicately handwritten almost eighty years ago. The top of it reads in part: "Fifteenth Census of the United States: Population Schedule." The date is April 1930. The census was for the city of Birmingham in Jefferson County in Precinct 10. Toward the bottom of the report is a notable Birmingham family. They lived in a home valued at $40,000. The man identified by the census as the head of the family is Rob, whose occupation is listed as "bookkeeper" and whose industry is stated as "bank." His wife is Sunset. The daughter, two years old, is identified as Marion. The son, just four months old, is listed as Robert C. As Robert C. grew, almost everyone would simply come to call him Bobby.

Bobby was barely five years old when his father hoisted him up on his shoulders and ascended to the roof of their three-bedroom home in Birmingham to watch a nearby high school football team practice. Bob Bowden had just a handful of loves: his faith, his family, and football. In that regard, Bobby's dad was not so different from the many others in their neighborhood.

Woodlawn was annexed by Birmingham in the early 1900s and retained its small-town southern charm (or as much charm as a strictly segregated town could possess). By the year 1910, Woodlawn had built its first bank and a handful of elementary and segregated high schools. Two decades later, just as a young Bob was starting his family, Woodlawn neighbors could visit the town's first public library, as well as seven white churches and one black church.

The Woodlawn High School football team was a short distance away from Bobby's home, and he watched those practices for hours. Sometimes Bob would leave the rooftop and Bobby, not quite fully understanding what he was seeing, remained for hours until Bob came back to fetch him. Indeed, he was too young to fully understand what he was witnessing, but it was exciting to him nonetheless. He watched field goal kickers put the football through the uprights, tracing it through the sky until it landed in a nearby chicken coop. Bobby's infatuation with football continued when the family moved to a different section of Birmingham near Howard College in 1934. The home was a modest three-bedroom (like the previous home, but this one had larger rooms) and was just a few hundred yards from Berry Field. Again Bobby was consumed by football. Bob continued to encourage the infatuation by one day bringing home a Howard Bulldogs helmet and uniform.

Bowden's relationship with his father centered on football and religion; they connected closely on both. They sometimes played catch with a football given to Bobby by his uncle on Christmas. Bobby's admiration of his father was a form of idolization. Years later, in many ways, Bobby would become exactly like his dad: compassionate, resourceful, intelligent, stubborn, and deeply religious; but there were also few verbal expressions of love. Those types of things were understood but unspoken.

Bobby was well behaved, but he was still a kid and prone to bouts of ignoring the wishes of his parents. When he was ten years old, Bobby received a small BB gun for Christmas. Bobby was thrilled and his father could sense his son's excitement; knowing that children are children, however, he issued a stern warning. "You better not shoot anybody," he told Bobby. Then he added that if he did, a beating would follow. Bobby didn't listen. He saw a young boy standing on a street corner at a distance he believed the gun was incapable of reaching. Bobby took a shot, unaware that he'd struck the person. When Bobby got home, there was a man on the front porch. It was the boy's father and the unintended target had indeed been struck. Bobby got the forewarned beating, and the BB gun was taken away for a year.

But that kind of misbehaving wasn't necessarily chronic and became less so as Bobby increasingly got into sports. Bobby's football education continued through grammar school, and by the time he was thirteen years old he'd developed a fairly quick stride and some good strength in his upper body. He was smaller than other kids, and Bob wasn't so certain how much football was in his son's future. That was particularly true in January 1943. Bobby had finished playing basketball at the YMCA for nearly three hours and began the walk home when he felt a stinging in both of his knees. A short while later as Bobby approached the house, he unlaced his shoes to see severely swollen feet. Bobby spoke to his mother, Sunset, who was horrified by what she saw. Bobby was taken to the doctor.

It took a brief examination for the doctor to determine that Bobby had rheumatic fever, an inflammatory disease that though largely rare now was less so when Bobby was a teenager. Then, it killed people. In the year 1950 alone, rheumatic fever–generated heart complications killed about fifteen thousand people in the United States. The fever started as strep throat and spread throughout Bobby's body and was mostly unnoticed until that walk home from basketball practice.

Bobby's doctor insisted on sustained rest and minimal movement because it was feared the disease would spread to the heart. Bobby went home immediately and stretched out in his bed. No sports. Not even a walk to the bathroom was allowed; he had to use a bedpan. He drank goat milk because folk medicine said it healed hearts. Days became weeks, and weeks became months. For much of 1943 Bobby was either bedridden or mostly confined to the home.

The radio became Bobby's constant companion. He listened to Edward R. Murrow for war updates from Europe, and there was of course the play-by-play of Alabama games. It was also during this time Bobby's voracious appetite for reading books was born.

In some ways his religious faith blossomed then too. Initially church was a chore, something Bob and Sunset insisted upon. Bobby used to see one of his heroes in church, Jim Tarrant, an all-Alabama high school player who went on to Howard College. Bowden thought: if a guy that cool was in church every Sunday, there must be something to it.

Bobby now talks about his belief in God in ways that seem hokey and insincere to many in a highly and understandably cynical world. But that belief is born from many decades of stubborn and earnest faith and also from those days when doctors told him he might die. When Bowden was in bed, his joints stinging and his muscles aching, Bowden and Sunset prayed constantly. She brought dinner to his room one night and after setting up the plate asked Bobby a question. "Do you believe in God?" she said.

The question caught Bowden by surprise though it shouldn't have. The Bowdens had a strictly patriarchal household, but Sunset was without question a leader in her own way. She was president of the Federation of Alabama Women's Clubs and taught a Sunday school class. She was direct and opinionated. They had prayed as a family many times and were regulars at church. In the Bowden home, there was no leisurely time on Sunday spent playing golf or reading the newspaper. The family went to church, always, without fail, so Bobby's answer to Sunset was easy.

"Yes, I believe in God, Momma," he responded.

"Then ask him," she said, "for a miracle."

Bobby was born on November 8, 1929, in Birmingham to Bob Pierce Bowden and Sunset Cleckler. He was a sturdy baby, just under seven pounds, and he arrived about a year and a half after his sister, Marion. Bobby and Marion were never close and mostly lived separate lives. Over the years Bobby has rarely mentioned her.

Bobby Bowden's father, Bob, grew up poor in Clayton, Alabama, a tiny city that was the birthplace of the fiery George Wallace, the four-term governor of Alabama and four-time candidate for U.S. president, and Congressman Bertram Tracy Clayton. Bob was one of thirteen children born—but only about half lived—and

Bob's father had died when Bob was six. The 1910 Census showed the family consisted of seven children, four sons and three daughters with ages ranging from two to seventeen. The 1920 Census showed five children with one occupation for a son listed as "returned soldier." One of the other sons' job title was "freight clerk" at a "railroad co." (The 1920 Census shows that Sunset was one of four children, one son and three daughters. The children were sixteen, thirteen, eleven, and eight.)

Bob lived an impoverished, painful upbringing. The family eventually moved to Birmingham where Bob, at seven years old, started selling newspapers on street corners and at a local drugstore to earn money. He was also a regular at Ruhama Baptist Church. The church was organized in March 1819 and is the first known Baptist church in the Birmingham area. It's also one of some fifty churches organized even before Alabama officially became a state.

Bob's extraordinarily poor childhood is something that stayed with him for much of his life and was the energizing source for his strong work ethic once he had a family of his own. Those lessons were not lost on the son either. Bobby would duplicate his father's blue-collar values and inherit the concerns regarding from where the next paycheck would come. The younger Bowden also emulated his father's desire to never (or at least rarely) use foul language. Instead of using God's name in vain Bob would shout "dadgum" around the house. Bowden later adopted this word—and his father's no-curse mantra—as his own. (So, too, would Bobby's son Tommy.)

Bob worked seventeen years as a bank teller for the First National Bank of Birmingham before eventually going into real estate. Initially, when Bobby was older, father wanted son to follow in his footsteps, but neither banking nor real estate was ever attractive to a young Bowden. "He wanted me to go in there with him . . . I wasn't interested," Bowden says. "He didn't press it. He said 'Do what you feel like you want to do, or need to do.'"

For Bob, working in banking during the Great Depression was dangerous considering the massive numbers of failed businesses, but Bob was savvy enough to keep his position at the bank while many across the country lost their jobs. Bob was fortunate, but young Bobby's grandfather, Robert Cleckler, who was in construction and built courthouses in two southern states, emerged from the Depression bankrupt. One day Robert walked into his bank and discovered that every penny he had earned was gone. Robert moved into the Bowden home and lived in Bobby's room with Bobby for years.

When Bobby became ill, the family's faith in prayer was tested. Bobby dealt with constant pain either from the disease or from the large syringes filled with salicylates that doctors sank almost daily deep into Bobby's vein. (Salicylate was a new drug extracted from willow bark, devised to combat rheumatic fever, which was later refined to become aspirin.) Bobby closed his eyes and took the pain each time, barely able to look at his sore and discolored limbs.

Doctors told Bobby he would never play sports again. At night, he cried himself to sleep, sometimes in his mother's arms, when the pain in his legs grew unbearable. So he prayed and the more he did, to him, the more the pain abated. To the doctors, the medicine and rest were healing him; to Bobby, God was. Soon he had enough energy to spend more time out of bed and work on a scrapbook overflowing with articles about the Auburn and Alabama teams. The small walks from the bed turned into trips around the house and short excursions to the front of the home. A constant stream of well-wishers from Ruhama Baptist Church kept his morale up.

By the mid-1940s, Bowden was close to fully recovering from his illness and slightly active again. His neighborhood was a stereotypically sleepy southern town. There was a handful of homes on the streets. The two across from Bowden's were not so different from his. They were painted white and ringed with picket fences; large trees shaded the backyards. Kids played constantly in the neighborhood, and Bowden's home was the nexus of much of the activity. He'd put on the football uniform Bob had given him—the one with the canvas pants and cardboard shoulder pads—and run routes with friends to a nearby telephone pole. A group of kids would play touch football at Berry Field, often with children older than them. One of the players was a twenty-three-year-old father of two. Larger competitors would physically pound the smaller Bowden on occasion, but he became known around the neighborhood as a highly competitive and unbreakable kid, if not a feisty one. It wasn't unusual for Bowden to physically challenge bigger neighborhood kids to a fight and get badly beaten. "I finally learned my lesson and grew out of that," Bowden says, "but it took a while." Bowden was tougher than he looked before and after the fever hit him (and he remains tougher than he looks to this day). He'd walk through large, hilly areas near his house or explore abandoned iron ore mines. Some days he'd run to the top of a daunting fire tower that stood dozens of feet high.

Initially upon entering Woodlawn High School, remarkably, physicians were still telling Bowden the aftereffects of rheumatic fever could kill him. Bobby was crushed. He pleaded with doctors and his parents to let him play football, but they understandably refused to relent. Instead of football, Bowden took up music. His parents had encouraged Bowden to play the piano since he was eight, and he also played the trumpet. (When Bobby took piano lessons and hit a wrong key his teacher rapped his knuckles with a ruler.) At Woodlawn he switched to the trombone and made the marching band. By his second year in high school, Bowden was so proficient at musical instruments he joined a twenty-piece brass jazz band called the Lee Jordan Band. Despite being still only fifteen years old, he actually played at a dinner club in the eastern section of Birmingham; the band also played New Year's Eve parties.

Despite his musical prowess, Bowden never forgot about football. Occasionally Bobby and Sunset would make the short drive back to the family's physician and the message was still the same. "If you play football," he told Bobby, "you'll be dead by the time you're forty." Doctors feared the disease had weakened Bobby's heart so much that participating in strenuous physical activity could cause the organ to fail immediately or sometime in the near future. Understandably this terrified Bowden's family.

Bowden figured he'd never play football again until Sunset decided to take him to a cardiologist. The doctor listened to his heart and then ran extensive tests. It took hours but when he returned to the room where Bobby was waiting, a smile came to the physician's face. Bowden's heart was enlarged and there was some scar tissue, but the specialist felt Bowden was more than healthy enough to play football.

Bowden was visibly emotional as was Sunset because they both knew Bobby's football career was finally about to begin. Sunset had asked Bobby to pray for a miracle and Bobby had. "Dear God," Bowden prayed, "I know that I may not be worthy of a miracle but if you could heal me or at least make me better, maybe even play again, then I'll use my life through athletics to serve you."

Bowden has long believed the year he spent ill from rheumatic fever, and his subsequent recovery, was one of the more instructive of his life. His high school football career isn't far behind when it comes to life lessons. Bowden tried out for the Woodlawn High School team just a short time after that meeting with the doctor. Bowden was still a shrimp even by the standards of that era when athletes weren't intimately familiar with the pinch of a steroid-filled syringe. Nevertheless, Bowden played with a sort of rage. He relished collisions despite being just barely five feet seven, and larger players didn't intimidate him. Bowden impressed Kenny Morgan, the team's coach and athletic director for the Birmingham city school system, and Morgan wasn't easy to please. He emphasized contact and brutality, again, both the norm for 1940s football. Then, even in high school, players were on offense and defense. In practice there were few breaks, and getting a drink of water could lead to getting kicked off the team.

Morgan quickly became fond of Bowden (and Morgan would become one of Bowden's lifelong heroes) and started playing him at tailback, asking Bowden to do the bulk of the blocking. He did, with no complaints. Despite his lack of physical prowess, Bowden was still an excellent blocker because of his ability to get extremely close to the ground. His short height was an aid, but he also used practically perfect technique, lowering his shoulders, squaring them, and placing his pads clean under his opponent's. Soon,

Morgan was using Bowden as a sort of human instructional video on how to make the precision block.

Ironically, it wasn't the physicality of blocking that led to Bowden's first significant injury in high school football. It was the simple act of catching a pass. Just ten days before the team's opening game on a hazy day, Bowden was running a short pass pattern when the football hit his right thumb, jamming it and breaking the bone clean. Bowden looked down at his hand, where his thumb rested neatly atop his wrist. Morgan trotted over, took Bowden's hand, and attempted to reset the thumb by pulling and twisting it. After propping up the thumb with a thick tape job, Morgan thought it had been repaired, but in actuality he'd likely turned a small fracture into a more serious and compound one because Bowden's thumb continued to badly ache. The thumb was indeed broken and later correctly reset by a specialist, but it was too late for Bowden to play that season. He sat out and by January 1947 was trying again. Bowden's second attempt was successful. Again, in a short period, Bowden became an integral part of the Wood-lawn program. When Morgan spoke to others about Bowden, it was always in complimentary terms.

Morgan became so close to Bowden the coach knew exactly how to motivate him. Several days before one of Woodlawn's bigger games, Morgan called Bowden into his office. Morgan informed Bobby he needed to share a rumor he'd heard. The opposing coach had told his team that Bowden wasn't hustling or playing hard and that basically the opposing team's players had been instructed to try and knock Bowden out of the game. Bowden left the office angry, and by game time on Friday night his anger had grown into fury. During warm-ups Bowden glared at the opposing coach and then went on to play one of the best games of his high school career. What Bowden didn't know at the time was that Morgan had made up the entire scenario as a way to goad Bowden into playing his best game.

Bobby wasn't a talker on the football field. It's not that he was shy (no Bowden is); he simply believed in action over words. He played numerous positions at Woodlawn: as a runner and passer, and sometimes even as a kicker. He also played defensive back. Word of Bowden's prowess spread not just throughout Woodlawn's two-thousand-student population, but also among the remainder of the power five programs in Birmingham that were Woodlawn, West End, Phillips, Ramsey, and Ensley. Although Bowden wasn't a star in the classroom, earning a solid C average, he'd almost become a legend in Birmingham football.

This was reflected in an October 1948 story that ran in the school's high school paper, the *Tattler*. The article also showed that even in the fresh and constantly shifting embers that compose the mind of a high schooler, Bowden, at the time a senior at Wood-lawn, knew what he wanted to do with the rest of his life.

"Some boys play football just to be playing something, but our prep personality this week is really interested in the game," the story said. "He is Bobby Bowden, co-captain of the Colonels. Bobby first became interested in football when he was about 8 and has worked and trained hard in high school. The game with Ramsay showed the results of sticking to training because Bobby can really play. He wants to become a coach after finishing college. Bobby's hobby is a football scrapbook. He has a dog named Sang and likes chocolate pie. His weight is 157 pounds and his height is 5-feet, 8 inches."

CHAPTER FOUR

APRIL FOOL'S IN LOVE

A nn Bowden stood smiling under a nearly room-sized white banner that read MRS. GEORGIA OF 1958. To her left stood two of the vanquished: Mrs. North Georgia and Mrs. Columbus. Ann was in the middle of the room, wearing a white gown that reached just above her ankles with the top of the gown reaching well above her cleavage. A tournament official lowered a crown onto a well-coifed mane of dark hair, though no crown was actually needed to determine who was the prettiest, most poised woman in the room.

Ann moved to Birmingham from Oak Ridge, Tennessee, just as Bobby was emerging as a high school football star in the late 1940s. Her home was only several streets away from Bobby's, and she'd sit on her front porch reading a book or just watching people pass by. Eventually the neighborhood boys started to notice Ann, and a few began hanging out on the stoop with her. As Ann physically matured, the visits to her porch by Bobby became more frequent.

They began to date a short time later. After Bowden headed to Alabama in the spring of 1949 to play football, they continued to date. Their love developed quickly, and it was so rapid it surprised even them. "If you can call it love at that young of an age, we were very much in love," Ann says now. "There's nothing like young love."

And nothing like the ancient emotion of jealousy. Ann was not above making certain Bobby knew how much she was pursued, just in case while he was away at Alabama there was a memory lapse. In February 1949 a roommate of Bobby's, Paul Crumbley, found Bobby one day and delivered some troubling news. "Aren't you going steady with Ann?" he asked Bobby.

The question puzzled Bobby because Crumbley knew the answer. That meant something was dead wrong. "Why do you ask?" Bobby responded.

"I probably should have kept my mouth shut," said a genuinely embarrassed Crumbley, "but I saw Shorty White and Ann riding the bus together." Bowden immediately contacted Ann. "She didn't say it wasn't true," Bowden remembers now. White played football at a rival Birmingham high school, and the two knew each other. Bowden wasn't happy and grew even more irritated when Ann confessed they had taken a downtown streetcar to go see a movie. To Ann, her innocent date was a sort of payback for Bowden, who had taken a beach trip with the fellas without telling her and flirted with several cute young women. The maneuver by Ann was a message to Bowden: I refuse to take any twaddle from you.

"Bobby was at the beach with some girls," Ann said. "He's a guy. He was doing what guys do when they're at the beach. He was messing around with some girls. You know guys always want to control women but guys want their freedom. They want to have their cake and eat it too. Bobby didn't want me dating Shorty. You know Bobby didn't want me dating anyone. Period."

If Bowden already didn't know, he knew then—his wife was a strong and independent woman. In many ways, she was more sturdy than Bowden.

When Bowden would return home to see Ann, their dates turned romantic and physical. Neither wanted to have intimate relations while unmarried, so they seriously discussed the subject of marriage with their respective families. The families didn't approve. At the time Bobby was nineteen and Ann was only sixteen, and the parents on both sides of the family wanted Bobby and Ann to first attend college. None of that mattered, because the attraction between Bobby and Ann was too strong. They were getting married one way or another.

The couple heard about others who crossed the state line into Georgia and were married there. "Eloping was something we thought about for a long time before we actually did it," said Ann. "We loved each other and thought it was the right thing to do."

On the first weekend of April, both sets of parents—the Bowdens and the Estocks—were out of town. Bobby's parents took the train to Atlanta on a business trip, leaving behind his father's 1949 Ford. Bobby and Ann saw the moment as an opportunity to finally follow through on their plans. Bobby jumped into his father's car and drove to Ann's house; then they both headed to Rising Fawn, Georgia, a small town located at the intersecting triangle where Alabama, Georgia, and Tennessee connect. But before departing town, Bowden stopped at a friend's house. He knocked on the bedroom window and asked to borrow as much money as he could spare. Bowden took $20 in various bills and coins and left. "Keep this a secret," Bowden said.

Then they left. Bowden couldn't believe what he was doing. In some ways it was the antithesis of his personality. Even for a young man he wasn't a terribly impulsive person, but his love for Ann had completely overwhelmed him. He pressed the accelerator on the car, pushing it faster and faster. So fast, in fact, a police officer stopped Bowden for speeding. He got a $5 ticket.

When they arrived in Rising Fawn, the car slowed to a crawl as they crossed a long dirt road to where the justice of the peace lived. They timidly knocked on the door, and a woman holding a chicken leg in her hands answered it. Bowden peeked inside and saw seven people sitting around a table eating dinner. The minister came to the door and asked about the ring. Bowden didn't have one. In his rush to marry Ann, he'd completely forgotten about the ring. Bowden proffered his high school ring, which apparently was acceptable. Bowden handed over $5, and the ceremony took only a few minutes. It was done. They were married. The date was April 1, 1949.

They had planned to keep their marriage a secret until they could find the proper moment to inform their families, but Ann had told members of her high school cheerleading team and the secret was out (Ann has always believed the secret was spilled by the friend who loaned Bobby the $20). They told their shocked parents soon after that.

Bobby was married and destined for a life in football. That was already clear. Although Bobby would also make great personal sacrifices for his family in the future by spending periods of time away from them, Ann's sacrifices were just as pronounced. Ann was one of many women in the 1950s who gave up a career and the idea of attending college to stay home with the kids. However, the life of a football wife requires more selflessness because of the amount of time coaches spend on the road recruiting or working in the office. Ann would raise a wonderful family, but there would also be moments of reflection about what her life would've been like had she gone to college or had a traditional career of her own.

"There have never been any regrets," Ann says now. "We've raised wonderful kids. I won't say regrets. I've wondered what my life would be like had I developed a career outside of the home. But look at our family. Our kids are terrific. How can I regret that?"

Bobby attended Alabama—his dream school—but athletes with superior size and skill, as well as Bobby's homesickness, forced him from the Crimson Tide and into Howard College. He simply wasn't physically ready for the size and speed difference the Alabama athletes presented. While Bobby went to school Ann worked in Bobby's father's real estate office. Ann was close with her in-laws, and Bobby continued to take his father's advice; namely, not to join the military. Bobby considered joining the Marine Corps Reserves because many of his friends were. Bob advised against it. "Don't sign anything," he told Bobby. "Think about it first." Bobby listened to his father and changed his mind. Just a short time later the Korean War erupted, and some of Bobby's friends headed off to Asia.

By the time Bowden graduated in 1953, he knew his playing career was over. He wasn't going to be a professional player, but he still wanted to be involved in football. The football coach at Howard told Bowden that if he earned his master's degree, there'd be a job for him at Howard. Bowden awoke at four in the morning every Monday and commuted the nearly two hundred miles from Birmingham to Peabody College (which would later become a part of Vanderbilt University), taking classes until Thursday and returning late that night. Sometimes Bowden drove, most of the time he carpooled, and occasionally he hitchhiked. Well, at least for a bit he hitchhiked. On one return trip a seemingly nice man stopped along a darkened highway and offered Bowden a ride. Bowden accepted, but when he started to hop in, the stranger asked if Bowden had a driver's license and if he would mind driving. Bowden said he didn't and off they went. A few minutes later the man reached into his glove compartment and pulled out a small-caliber gun. Bowden was understandably terrified. "I'll give you money or I'll pay for gas," Bowden pleaded, "whatever you want."

The man just glared at Bowden and didn't speak. He turned toward the passenger window, rolled it down, and began shooting into the darkness. Maybe the man was making a statement; mess with me and this is what you'll get. Or maybe the stranger was simply a gun-toting psychopath; whatever the case, Bowden clenched the wheel and his teeth and nervously drove. They made it to within a mile of Bobby's father's house where Ann and the growing Bowden family, which had mushroomed quickly to two kids, were now living. Their bedroom was tiny and full as son Steve slept in a crib at the foot of the bed and Robyn slept in a small bed on the side.

Bowden gladly and quickly got out of the car. It was almost 5 A.M. and Bowden was exhausted. Believing nothing like that could ever happen again, Bowden tried to hitch a ride for the final leg of his trip. A man pulled along Bowden; in a markedly effeminate voice, he asked him to get in. Bowden declined and never hitchhiked again.

The hard work in school (and hitching) paid off as Bowden earned that master's degree in physical education from Peabody College. Bowden was hired as an assistant coach for $3,600 a year at Howard. It was an interesting time for Bowden. To say that Howard had a tiny budget was an understatement. Money was tight. Bowden first had to fight for his full salary. The athletic department had promised Bowden $3,600 but initially wanted to pay him $300 less. Bowden only received the promised money after making a fuss.

The staff at Howard had only three coaches, led by sixty-two-year-old Bill "Cannonball" White. White had coached at Howard before in 1940 and 1941. He was experienced, and, more important, he was secure. White didn't mind handing over a significant chunk of the coaching duties to Bowden and allowed him to coach the offensive backs and receivers. The problem, again, was money. There were no scholarships, and the only way players could earn money to pay for school was doing janitorial services or shoveling coal into the oversized school furnace.

A coaching change forced Bowden to leave after just two seasons. He feared his coaching career was moving too slowly and maybe even had grinded to a halt, so he made alternate plans. Bowden applied to Columbia University with the intention of earning a doctorate in education, and the school accepted him. The thought of Birmingham Bobby in the concrete wilds of New York was amusing to Bowden, but he was ready to go.

Upon returning home one day, Bowden saw a letter in his mailbox. In it was a note from the president of South Georgia College, Dr. William Smith, who had heard of Bowden from friends and other coaches. "If you want to be head coach at South Georgia," the letter read, "phone me collect." Bowden called immediately, and the discussion between the two men lasted less than an hour. Bobby took the job without even going to the campus. One thing Smith said swayed Bowden. "Son, do you want to coach," Smith asked him, "or do you want to be a schoolteacher?"

CHAPTER FIVE

THE COACHING LIFE

When Bowden was fifteen years old, each day he'd rip through every Birmingham newspaper he could get his hands on, mainly the *Birmingham News*. Bobby searched for any news story or picture he could find about the Alabama football team (and normally didn't have to look long). He'd digest what he was reading like an archaeologist who had just made a brilliant discovery. Alabama football was Bowden's passion, and every article he read put him there next to his football heroes. After reading the story, he'd meticulously cut the words or picture out of the paper and carefully glue them on an 8-by-11-inch paper and insert it in a three-ring notebook. The only thing that stopped Bowden from amassing a scrapbook the size of a stack of encyclopedias was the business of high school life. Nevertheless, by the time he had stopped, the notebook was about three inches thick. (To this day, sixty years later, Bowden still possesses the book, neatly hidden away on a bookshelf just behind his office desk.)

South Georgia was a two-year college and a universe away from Alabama or even Howard College. It was infinitesimally smaller, with a tiny budget, and located in Douglas, a town of fewer than ten thousand people not far from the Okefenokee Swamp. The school offered fewer than two dozen partial scholarships: six for $120, six for $90, and six for $60. The annual tuition was about $200. Bowden realized the first thing he needed to do was raise significant amounts of capital to enhance the athletic budget.

Bowden literally went door-to-door in the downtown areas asking merchants for donations. People gave in small amounts, $5 and $10 chunks, sometimes larger, but they gave. By the summer, he had raised more than $3,000.

Bowden's work didn't stop with the coaching or fund-raising. By 1955, the year Bowden took the job, his marriage to Ann remained steady and their already significant family of three was growing to four. Bowden's salary meanwhile remained small. He was earning just $4,600 a year at South Georgia, and money was extremely tight. Bowden worked extra jobs, including duties as a lifeguard at the school's swimming pool during some of the summer months and a night job at a tobacco warehouse. His schedule was brutal, and Bowden grabbed sleep whenever he could.

At the tobacco storage facility Bowden removed large bales of tobacco from trucks and stacked them inside the warehouse. Unload, stack. Unload, stack. He did this from eight in the evening until eight the next morning and when things slowed, Bowden climbed the twenty-foot stacks, sprawled on top of them, then napped for an hour. Below him, portly rats scrambled about searching for food.

Ann had her own responsibilities. She and Bobby both worked as resident assistants in the college dorm, and during the Christmas months, Ann worked at Sears and Bobby delivered mail. Ann would actually see her husband hauling a hefty wagon full of letters and packages down one of the main streets for delivery to local businesses. She'd chuckle when seeing the wagon get stuck in one of the grooves of the hardened cobblestone streets.

Their new home was a modest and slightly renovated group of buildings that was once an army base used to house World War II troops. It was cheap living—just $25 a month—but there was a catch. The floors were concrete and Ann needed to spread newspapers on them in the winter to soak up the moisture.

Ann sometimes visited with the children to watch the football team's practices, where one of their young toddlers, Terry (with Ann close behind), occasionally wandered near the action. Some of the South Georgia players handed him soda pop and candy. Ann got irritated at the gesture and pinned a note to Terry's diaper that read: "Do not feed!" Sometime later Terry returned with the note reattached and reversed that read: "Well fed."

On the football field Bowden provided organization and discipline that South Georgia College hadn't truly seen before. The standards of the time allowed Bowden to run physically strenuous camps and practices on a weed-riddled field where the grass was ankle-high. Many of Bowden's players were Korean War veterans attending school on the G.I. bill, and some were even older than Bowden. Some had seen unspeakable war horrors. The players had nicknames like Ape, Bull, Stumpy, Possum, and Tiny; and despite the fact some had more life experience, they still respected Bowden and his authority. Although respecting authority was part of those times, they also witnessed and respected Bowden's work ethic. After all, in addition to his other duties, Bowden drove the team bus to away games, even if he wasn't the world's best driver. The bus was a dark blue, diesel-powered monstrosity called the Old Blue Goose. On one away trip, Bowden nearly hopped a curb and caused the bus to roll over. Soon after that the school got Bowden a driver.

As with any team there was the occasional brawl and lots of practical jokes. Bull once stuck a dead fish inside the mattress of an unsuspecting Stumpy and sewed the mattress up tight. Stumpy only knew about the dead fish once the smell was unmistakable. Some players threw firecrackers into the hallway of the girls' dormitory at night. The team had a sense of humor, that's for sure, but the players also kept their respect for the law and Bowden's rules.

The football was harsh. Punishing Oklahoma drills were the norm; so were broken bones and severe dehydration, because water breaks were not allowed, which was the custom at most programs. Sometimes, when the temperature became extreme, Bowden allowed the team manager to approach each player with a wet towel and wipe the dirt and sweat from his brow. Occasionally a player would grab the towel and suck the water from it. The players were physically smaller, far shorter than probably most high school teams today. Yet Bowden made sure no one would out-tough his boys—and no team did.

"Today's players are a lot bigger and faster, but they are not nearly as tough as players were when I first started coaching," Bowden said. "Today, when you tell a player to do something, you'll have to explain to him why. When I first started coaching, you could tell a player to run headfirst into a brick wall, and before you got the last word out of your mouth, he was already running toward the wall with his head down. . . ."

The conditions for college football at that time would have been deemed practically illegal today. In one contest, two players collided headfirst, and one of them, a player for Bowden, was out cold. A portion of the skin on the player's forehead was torn back, and some of his skull could be seen. Bowden ordered that the player go to a hospital, and in a sign of the times there was no ambulance parked at the stadium. The nearest hospital was forty miles away.

The 1955 season started on October 1. Bowden began the season 2–0, and the third game was against Jones County Junior College in Ellisville, Mississippi. Bowden remembers leaving around four or five in the morning and getting to Jones around nine or ten that night. Bowden's players unfolded cots and slept in the school gymnasium. The long ride and uncomfortable surroundings took their toll, and South Georgia trailed by 33 points at halftime. The team was destroyed by Jones County in the worst loss of Bowden's early coaching career.

Bowden's team later recovered, and despite some humiliating losses in his first season, Bowden had much to be proud of. So did the players. The season before Bowden arrived the school didn't win a single game. In Bowden's first year, he won five and a conference title. Bowden knew nothing about scouting, and in some ways his coaching was raw and unspectacular. It was totally instinctive. He was also busy serving as the school's head coach for the baseball and basketball teams in 1956. Those stints weren't nearly as successful. The only win Bowden had as basketball coach was against a ragtag team of sailors from Glynco Naval Air Station. Bowden actually quit as basketball coach after his best player abruptly left the team.

Bowden's multiple roles within the athletic department led to long absences from home. There was understandably some resentment—particularly when Bowden would return from a long practice and the conversation would be about nothing but football. Ann would steer the subject in a different direction only to have Bobby drive it back to sports. "Bobby, sometimes I think you love football more than you do me," Ann said once.

"Well, I love you more than I do basketball," Bobby responded.

Bowden may not have been ready to coach the Boston Celtics, but his football coaching skills were nevertheless proving to be formidable. In just a four-year period, Bowden won three state junior college championships and barely missed winning a fourth. Bowden's South Georgia teams won with tenacity and physicality, but Bowden also won with trickery and on-field deception. At least once in every game South Georgia engineered a play the opponent hadn't seen before. Once against Gordon Military there was a fake kick. Bowden remembers constantly practicing one play where the back faked a handoff, then threw it to one of the ends. Another of Bowden's more audacious trick plays (which would now be illegal) came when he sent only ten men onto the field. Only seconds before the ball was snapped the eleventh man crept onto the field, unnoticed, and received the pass.

The origin of Bowden's trick plays go, in some ways, back to his childhood. When Bowden and his young friends played football together, Bowden hated some of the deceptive plays his friend would pull on him, like a halfback pass. Bobby didn't call them tricks. He had a different name for them then: barnyard plays. It wasn't because at his first home he was within spitting distance of a chicken coop; rather, Bowden felt anyone who ran them was like the substance on the floor of a barn: chicken shit.

Bowden's feeling about the barnyard plays would change drastically once he got into high school—and beyond. As a small-boned high school football player he developed an underdog mentality and pulled every little ploy and advantage to compete with much stronger players. That mentality would stick with Bowden for decades, particularly when he took over what was an awful Florida State program. Then, Bowden needed a good ruse because of the dearth of talent. If he had tried to constantly play stronger teams

straight up, the Seminoles would have been battered. On-field deception in high school gave Bowden a chance to survive, and the
same strategy as a head coach gave Bowden a chance to win.

At South Georgia, Bowden learned the fundamentals of coaching: how to deal with players, how to motivate them, how to
criticize them, and how to organize his time. Bowden was able to
maintain discipline while maintaining the respect of the players,
which is no easy trick. Discipline was followed by praise and the
reverse was true. In one game, a Bowden player retaliated against
an opponent after the play was called dead. At practice after the
game Bowden made his player run a circle around two football
fields five times.

"Basically I was just learning how to coach," Bowden said. "I
wasn't really sure what the heck I was doing at first." And then?
"I discovered that being a football coach was like a lot of other
things," he said. "The harder you worked, the better you got."
In 1955 and again two years later, Bowden was named the state's
Junior College Coach of the Year.

Bowden's actual time at South Georgia was short, but his impact
on the players was dramatic and for many lasted a lifetime. Bowden
would return for a reunion with his surviving South Georgia players each year for the next several decades.

There is probably only one time in Bowden's long life when he was
outright misleading. It happened in the summer of 1959 as he departed South Georgia to coach football at his alma mater, Howard
College.

The Bowdens returned to Birmingham, and Bobby's work ethic
was as unchanged as the city itself. His father Bob, always looking for a solid business opportunity, purchased a portion of a car
repair shop. Bobby worked for his father when college was out. By
August, Bobby's mind focused on his first full year of coaching at
Howard. Bowden sat at his desk and wrote a letter to his players.
"Do you know football season is nearly upon us?" Bowden penned.
"It's hard to believe that in approximately three weeks we will be
wearing the togs again. I hope you are as excited about the coming

season as I am. I don't ever remember being as optimistic over prospects at Howard College as I have been this summer. I have a pleasant surprise for you about our first week of practice. We will spend the first seven days at a camp, where you will be able to swim, fish, and recreate yourselves between practice sessions." The only thing missing from Bowden's letter was the promise of virgins and a dessert buffet. The letter wasn't completely truthful.

Bowden rented a dusty and spartan camp in Cook Springs about forty miles from Birmingham, and his plan was simple. He was going to turn the training camp into a battle of the fittest and physically test his players. It didn't take long after his camp began for the punishment to take its toll. Bowden and his staff would turn out the lights as exhausted players climbed into bed. The only way you knew when people ran from Bowden's camp was when a car engine cranked in the middle of the night and the sound of screeching tires woke sound sleepers. Or the next morning when players were simply gone.

"When we started camp," Bowden says, "we had a nice-sized group of guys. When we were done, it was basically a lot smaller. A lot of guys quit, but the guys who stayed were strong. We had a bunch of tough guys."

That didn't mean they were impervious to harm. On a particularly steamy day, one player, Bill Kinghorn, almost died. Initially, he just fell to the ground. Bowden and his staff slapped Kinghorn and doused him with water, but after over a minute Kinghorn remained unconscious. Just as Bowden thought Kinghorn was going to die, Kinghorn awoke. In what was a sign of football in those times, Kinghorn simply shook his head several times and then went back to practicing. There was no sitting out the remainder of practice or a detailed exam by a medical staff. That's because there wasn't a medical staff.

The lounging by the pool and leisurely fishing Bowden promised in his letter to the players never came. There was only physical contact and pain. Although there was a pool, it was dark and algae-filled thanks to the lack of cleaning.

The camp lasted seven long days, and it came as a result of

Bowden's coaching naïveté. He thought that since a player had to be on both offense and defense, he had to be rugged and the only way to test a player's toughness was to run a camp like that one. "Looking back all this time later," Bowden says now, "that camp was a mistake. It was just too dang tough, you know? But I was doing at that camp what everybody else in college was doin'." Indeed, Bowden got the idea from Gene Stallings, who would later coach at Alabama. Stallings was an assistant under Bear Bryant who ran the infamous camp in Junction, Texas. Bryant's camp lasted ten days and is considered perhaps the most brutal training camp in college football history. In that camp, Bryant hauled three busloads of players out to it, but so many quit that he needed only one bus for the return trip. Bryant once said of practice: "I make my practices real hard because if a player is a quitter, I want him to quit in practice, not in a game."

Camp was bad, but spring practice wasn't exactly easy. Since Bowden had only a handful of assistant coaches, he utilized one to handle some of the offensive players and the other some of the defensive while Bowden coached the quarterbacks, wide receivers, and secondary. "Now you have these giant coaching staffs, you know?" Bowden says. "Then there were only two or three assistants at smaller colleges." The difference was that then there were no NCAA rules limiting the amount of time a player could practice. In the spring Bowden spent the entire month of February coaching the offense. That was several hours every day of the month. In March they'd switch to defense.

Although Bowden's camp (and to some degree his spring practices) were harsh, the purpose was served. Bowden was able to weed out the weaker players and build a highly unified Howard College team. The success cannot be solely attributed to Camp Bowden, however. Bowden also had the advantage of having a mature team that allowed Bowden to do more with less, including throw more schemes and harsher practices at his boys. As with South Georgia College the turnaround was stunning and had the typical Bowden trademark: a furiously rapid start and a type of precision and professionalism not seen before his arrival. Bowden guided Howard to a 5–0 start, and his defense held each team scoreless. Bowden won with physicality and discipline and of course a little deception. After going 8–1 in the regular season in that inaugural year, Bowden's team won its postseason game—in the momentous Textile Bowl—by five touchdowns. Bowden called for a naked bootleg, and it scored the first touchdown of the game.

Bowden went 31–6 in four years at Howard. In that first year, 1959, the Bulldogs went 9–1 and posted six shutouts. Bobby did this by demonstrating a brutal side as well as an always undervalued intellectual aspect to his personality. He soaked up all the bits of coaching techniques and strategies he could. Bowden wanted to learn more about the passing game, so he phoned a fellow Birmingham man named Bart Starr who lived in the area during the NFL off-season. By that point in the spring of 1960, Starr had not yet been transformed into the epic and dynastic catalyst he would become with the Green Bay Packers, but he was still regarded as a talented thrower. Besides, Bowden thought, he was an NFL quarterback who was learning under Vince Lombardi, and that meant he knew far more about the passing game than Bowden did.

Starr was pleasant and helpful. It didn't take long for him and Bowden to spend hours diagramming plays on a blackboard. "It was a lot of fun working with him," Starr told the author several years ago. "Our families became friends. I remember Bobby being very smart. I don't know if people think that about him. We talked football, and I told him some of the things the pros were doing." Starr opened Bowden's eyes to an entirely new thought process. "I never thought a high-tech passing game would ever work in college," Bowden said. "I actually thought we threw the ball a lot. Then I started working with Bart." Bowden had two passing game epiphanies. One would come later in his early days as an assistant at Florida State. The other arrived with Starr's help. Bowden and Starr met several times to discuss how the Packers ran their passing offense. Once, Bowden allowed Starr to coach the offense in a spring practice game. Bowden still believed primarily in the running game, but the passing game had tunneled its way deep into his mind.

Bowden also reached out to his idol Bear Bryant, who treated Bowden well. He scrutinized every aspect of Bryant's program. What Bowden noticed most was Bryant's attention to detail; Bryant monitored and commented on almost everything that occurred during practices. Bowden rarely spoke to Bryant—the coach intimidated Bowden the way he did almost everyone he came into contact with—so Bowden used assistant and friend Gene Stallings as a sort of translator and messenger.

Bowden put all of his lessons into his arsenal. Possessing these new stores of information was like handing an army general a sophisticated new weapon. At that point, college football was anchored and enamored with the running game; lower-level college football programs like Howard's knew almost nothing about passing the football. The organizational tidbits Bowden assimilated at Alabama under Bryant also helped Bowden separate himself. As Bowden's Howard College career progressed, he brashly destroyed teams that were unprepared for a more aggressive passing attack. Maybe brash isn't the word; shameless might be better. After his sessions with Starr and the Packers, and as Howard expanded its facilities by building a six-thousand-seat stadium into a large hillside, Bowden utterly embarrassed teams, beating one by an astonishing 12 touchdowns and scoring 80 points against another.

Bowden thoroughly appreciated what Starr did for him, but it was Bryant's lessons that stayed with Bowden for years, all the way to Florida State. Like Bryant, Bowden would take notes at practice and then share his thoughts with the staff. Like Bryant, Bowden would observe practices from a perch high above the ground.

As Bowden would later state, he desperately wanted to be around Bryant. To Bowden there was no better program than Alabama's, so he made a move to join Bryant's coaching staff. Bowden picked up a pen and wrote in part: "Coach Bryant, if a position ever opens on your staff, I'd sure love to have the opportunity to work for you." Bryant politely declined. Initially, not being able to join Bryant was disappointing, but Bowden would be too busy for the disappointment to last.

CHAPTER SIX

MOUNTAINEER

Bowden never made it a secret that he was a climber. He was always interested in coaching at a large school, and though he was proud of his work at Howard, there was little question he wanted something bigger. He got the big-college chance he'd been looking for when a school named Florida State called in the winter of 1963.

The head coach of the Seminoles, Bill Peterson, believed Bowden could add some brainpower to the offense, so Peterson contacted him. They agreed to meet at a later point, and Bowden went on with a previously arranged speaking engagement in Alabama. When Bowden arrived at his hotel, he barely had time to take off his coat before the phone started ringing. It was a reporter from Birmingham who'd already heard about Bowden's phone chat with Peterson. Even then, in the pre-Internet era, news traveled quickly. Bowden was stupefied but honest with the newspaper journalist. "It's only for an interview," he said. The writer said he'd keep the story quiet, but the following day a newspaper headline declared Bowden was leaving. The word of Bowden's imminent departure was now public, and just a short time later, Bobby was gone to Florida State.

Bowden's first stop at Florida State was a successful one. In 1964, the Seminoles went 9–1–1 and defeated Oklahoma in the Gator Bowl. The partnership between Bowden and Florida State worked primarily because Peterson loved the passing game. Bowden had doubted a consistent pass attack in college could work. He wasn't alone. At that time only a handful of programs—Baylor, Tulsa, and the Seminoles—incorporated a pro passing attack. Bowden's doubts were quickly erased after only a short period at Florida State.

Peterson's passing attack was already well established. So was his reputation. In some ways, Peterson cleared the way for Bowden by creating a degree of respectability at Florida State. He used the pass as a weapon in a way college football had rarely witnessed before. He also used grammar in interesting ways. Peterson became as well known for his misspoken words as his on-field deeds. He once told the team, "I'm the coach around here and don't you remember it." In one halftime speech, he told the players: "We can beat this team if we just capitalize on our mistakes." But the player and coaching talent he assembled was no joke. There was eventual Pro Football Hall of Fame wide receiver Fred Biletnikoff, and on Peterson's staff were names like Bowden, Joe Gibbs, and Bill Parcells.

What Bowden brought was precision and teaching. He made sure his receivers were in the proper stance, and if they weren't, he quietly instructed a defensive back to knock the sense out of any receiver who had his head down at the beginning of a play. In practice, Bowden put a white line on the field and receivers had to run down the line straight as an arrow—no drift—before making a cut.

BOWDEN CLIMBED THE COACHING ladder, but that didn't free him from the daily rigors of family life. In December 1965, Bowden and Ann packed the car with the kids for a trip from Tallahassee to Birmingham to see their families. Less than a hundred miles from Birmingham, the family stopped at a diner for a morning meal. They ate, Bobby paid the bill, Ann packed the kids into the car, and they resumed their trip. They'd driven more than forty miles when a state trooper suddenly appeared in Bobby's rearview mirror. Bobby looked at his speedometer. For once, he wasn't speeding. The police officer walked up to the car. Bobby rolled his window down and after asking why the officer stopped him, the officer said, "Are you missing anyone?" They were. It was their three-year-old daughter, Ginger. She'd wandered away from the table to mingle with others in the restaurant. She was temporarily out of sight and thus temporarily out of mind. They returned to the restaurant to reclaim their daughter with Ann crying the entire way there.

Bowden worked under Peterson at Florida State for only three years, but he racked up an impressive enough record to be recruited by West Virginia as offensive coordinator. He took that job because at the time West Virginia was a bigger and more prosperous program. Bowden moved the family to the wooded hills of Morgantown, and it didn't take long after getting there for the family to make an impression and Ann's protective side to again emerge. Heavy woods surrounded the home, and the kids would sometimes go running in them with the dogs. Steve found a rarely used old cabin and made it his own playpen. Despite the building being practically abandoned, the wife of the owner wasn't happy with the Bowden kids and expressed as much to Ann in a phone call. "What a sorry bunch of boys," she told Ann.

Ann is the toughest of the Bowdens, and insulting her kids was akin to punching her in the gut. She informed the woman that she wanted to speak to her in person. Sensing Ann's palpable anger, the woman declined. It was too late. Ann jumped into the car and drove along a stereotypical West Virginia dirt road, up a steep hill, and pulled in front of the woman's house. The lady was waiting for Ann, standing in the front yard with a daunting hunting rifle, holding it in front of her as if she was prepared to use it.

Ann saw the rifle and didn't care. Someone had insulted her family. The woman could have been manning a piece of heavy artillery and Ann still would've approached. She walked up close to the woman. "Put the rifle down or I'm calling the police," Ann said. The woman wouldn't oblige, so Ann shoved the rifle and the woman aside, marched into the woman's home, and used the woman's own telephone to call the police. The woman was dumbfounded and just stood there holding her weapon. The police arrived, calmed the two women down, and Ann went home. She'd made her point and never heard from the woman again.

By the summer of 1966, the Bowden family had settled comfortably into their new home near the West Virginia University campus. Ann had certainly done so. She discovered a grocery store that offered speedy delivery. She'd occasionally phone the store and ask if the green beans were fresh. The store clerk on the phone answered yes. Ann would then ask the clerk to prove it by snapping the beans in half as close to the phone's receiver as possible so Ann's probing ears could hear. Ann was only satisfied if there was a sufficient pop heard over the line.

Bobby had become just as discerning about his football as Ann was about the family's produce. When Bowden arrived in West Virginia, he was an entirely different coach—and human being—than the Bowden who was uncertain about the nuances of coaching during his Howard and South Georgia College days. He was far more confident and aggressive. His play calling was forward thinking for that era. His star was rapidly rising. He had the large family and wonderful wife he'd always wanted. Now came the shot to coach at West Virginia, a large and well-known program. Florida State was still seen as a smaller school with little promise while the Mountaineers were more established and respected. Everything was going so well, which is why it was so shocking that Bowden's life would suddenly become so miserable.

It didn't start that way at West Virginia. Bowden was the offensive coordinator in 1966 before being named head coach four years later. "The staff was all basically young," remembered Dick Inman, who coached with Bowden at West Virginia. "Bobby and I were the highest-paid assistants in the history of West Virginia, and we made $12,000 each. We were all in our thirties, and Bobby really stood out because he had some great ideas. He was on the edge, far ahead of a lot of college coaches, as far as the importance of speed."

Bowden brought a more concentrated and effective strength and conditioning program to West Virginia. Before Bowden's arrival, just two Mountaineer players could run faster than a five-second 40-yard dash, a speed considered infernally slow, even in 1960s college football. Soon the number of players who could run faster than a five-second 40 quadrupled and would continue to grow. Bowden also looked for more ways to attack defenses. Bowden attended clinics given by Sid Gillman, the innovative and mercurial NFL Chargers coach, who was taking the air attack to never-before-seen plateaus. Bowden observed the different camps of pro teams like the Redskins, Eagles, and Colts. What Bowden noticed when dissecting the tactics of the NFL coaches was that offenses constantly attacked, and Bobby convinced the Mountaineer staff to do the same. "Bobby wanted to score, score, score," said Inman.

It also meant that Bowden sometimes took his attacking mode too far. During one game, West Virginia, with Bowden as the offensive coordinator, was playing a smaller Southern Conference school. The Mountaineers led by a comfortable four touchdowns. West Virginia's head coach, Jim Carlen, ordered Bowden to stop passing the football. Bowden was irritated—he wanted to call a halfback pass. Bowden grew more agitated by the moment and decided to call the play anyway, clearly defying Carlen. As the backup quarterback ran onto the field, Bowden called the halfback pass. Bowden only stopped the play from being called after uproarious objection from other assistants on the staff.

The coaches at West Virginia had met few men with Bowden's energy. He brought his now trademark penchant for successful recruiting to the Mountaineers. Bowden talked his way into living rooms and the hearts of mothers throughout the state, and he was a key to the program's mini talent explosion. Some of Bowden's recruiting trips through the state's coal towns and rolling hills were standard fare, while others were more exotic. On one he asked a recruit to finish up a five-hour drive. The recruit agreed, and as Bowden slept heavily the young man drove Bowden's car into the back of a moving truck. Bowden awoke to shattered glass ripping through the cabin. Turned out the recruit who said he had a license actually didn't.

Bowden was innovative, but he also didn't mind doing what every coach does: borrow an idea or two. West Virginia ran the Houston option, which is a more basic version of the wishbone, but Bowden had an idea. When West Virginia received a Peach Bowl bid in 1969 to play South Carolina, Bowden wanted to spring a surprise on the Gamecocks. He phoned Texas coach Darrell Royal who put Bowden in touch with the team's offensive coordinator. Bowden picked the coach's brain for the secrets to the wishbone. West Virginia had four weeks to prepare for the bowl, and Bowden used the time to insert that hard-to-defend offense. The Houston option was somewhat similar but not completely. Bowden put an upback on the field and—presto—they were running the wishbone. South Carolina was totally unprepared for it, and West Virginia's fullback ran for 206 yards. Bowden never ran the wishbone again, however, feeling that system didn't fit the type of players he was recruiting. Bowden wanted a speedy, up-tempo passing offense, the polar opposite of the wishbone.

When Bowden finally was named the West Virginia coach, his first job heading a big program, the first person he wanted to tell was his father, Bob, who had retired in 1970 and subsequently suffered an aneurysm. The son went to visit his father in a Birmingham hospital, where Bob was lying in bed comatose. "I went to see him," Bowden told me. "He was just lying there, shrunk up. I didn't think he could hear me, but I told him anyway." Bobby leaned in close to his father. "Dad," he said, "I got the head job at West Virginia."

"I'd like to think he heard me," Bowden says.

Bowden was the best choice to become head coach after Carlen abruptly left for Texas Tech following the 1969 season, and he inherited a decent team. A season earlier, the Mountaineers captured a 10-win season and much of the team returned under Bowden, a fact Carlen, who coached the Mountaineers from 1966 to 1969 (amassing a record of 25–13–3), was not shy about discussing publicly. "I left Bobby a real good team," Carlen told a Houston reporter in mid-July before the start of the 1970 season. Although Carlen "didn't want to put any undue pressure on Bobby," he went on to say that he thought West Virginia had "at least a half-dozen players good enough for All-America consideration."

Of course, no pressure. There was, however, some question about Carlen's mathematical skills. West Virginia did have a solid and proud program, but the school failed to produce any All-Americans throughout the 1960s, though it had achieved a pre-season ranking for only the third time in school history. Bowden's emphasis on speed was starting to produce results, but overall, the Mountaineer players were still smallish and slow. When West Virginia would later play Duke University, the Mountaineers gave up 236 yards rushing and lost in what was considered a stunner.

Bowden also immediately established that though he was willing to listen to his coaching staff, he was clearly the boss. While watching practice Bowden would absorb every detail he could, some things that bothered him, some things that made him happy. He'd put all those thoughts on a tape recorder, and then at the start of staff meetings, he'd sit the tape on a table in the middle of the room and instruct his coaches to listen to it.

Bowden made clear the kind of program he desired to run off the field in an interview with the university's official game program in his first year as Mountaineer head coach. "I do not want our boys to smoke, drink or cut classes," Bowden said in October 1970, "and I will still insist on church attendance."

Coaches on the staff weren't exempt from Bowden's rules either. He asked his staff to live their lives the way he did; womanizing wasn't tolerated. After hiring a young, single freshman football coach, Bowden heard that the coach had purchased a case of beer and shared it with some of the West Virginia cheerleaders. When Bowden asked the assistant if it was true, the man said it was. Bowden fired him immediately.

George Henshaw, Bowden's longtime coaching friend, remembers during a staff meeting early in Bowden's tenure, the group of nine coaches was discussing an important roster issue. Bowden listened to everyone's opinion in the room, nodding and shaking his head in appreciation as everyone talked. When the last opinion was delivered, Bowden spoke. "I want you all to understand that I respect the opinion of each and every one of you," Bowden told his nine coaches. "You each have a vote. That's nine votes."

"But just so we understand each other," Bowden added, "I have ten."

Bowden retained some of Carlen's coaches and added his own when other valuable Carlen assistants departed for Texas Tech with their boss. The final mix turned out to be a potent one. At one point Henshaw was one of four graduate assistant coaches on Bowden's staff. Three of them—Henshaw, Joe Pendry, and Jack Henry—would each go on to coach in the NFL for more than fifteen years. There was almost a fourth. Bowden heard of a young rookie graduate assistant at Kent State who was helping his family deal with the death of his father. The graduate assistant was from West Virginia and Bowden wanted to make it easier on the young man so he phoned the assistant and offered him a job closer to home. "I don't really have a position for you," Bowden explained, "but I'll create one for you if you need to be close to your momma." The graduate assistant's name was Nick Saban, who eventually decided to stay at Kent State. Decades later, Saban became the highest-paid head coach in the country.

Bowden also liked the fact that some of his assistants were former players. Bowden long believed coaches with playing backgrounds gave their teams a slight advantage over teams with coaches who didn't have such backgrounds. Henshaw started every varsity Mountaineer game from 1967 to 1969, and Pendry played two seasons at West Virginia before a career-ending injury forced him into student coaching. Henry was no slouch. In his first season as an offensive assistant with the Detroit Lions, in 1997, he inherited a runner named Barry Sanders who ran for 2,053 yards, and the team finished second in the NFL in rushing.

The relationship Bowden had with his assistants was unique in college football, to say the least. Like his players, many of his assistants would admire Bowden to the point of adulation, and though there would be heated disagreements and even temporarily severed relationships with some of his assistants, nothing was ever permanent. Bowden's assistants trusted him to the point where sometimes they didn't even have contracts, just verbal promises of salary and number of years. "His word was stronger than any contract on paper," Henshaw says.

Henshaw witnessed this several times, including when Bowden

left West Virginia for Florida State. Bowden wanted Henshaw to join him on the Seminole staff, but Henshaw's family was comfortable in West Virginia and his wife dreaded the move. In the end, Bowden made a promise that was too tempting to ignore. "If you come to Florida State with me," Bowden told Henshaw, "the next coordinator's job is yours."

Henshaw followed Bowden, and it wasn't long before Bowden's word was tested. George Haffner left the Seminoles for Texas A&M after Florida State failed to make a bowl game. (Eventually Haffner's move paid off as he ended up at the University of Georgia as the team's offensive coordinator, winning a national championship, three conference titles, and almost a dozen bowl games.) Until that point, Henshaw had never been an offensive coordinator, but the day Haffner left, Bowden asked Henshaw, "You ready to be offensive coordinator?" Henshaw accepted, and Bowden's word was good yet again.

Even most of the disagreements between Bowden and his staff didn't possess the steel edge that coaching arguments did on other staffs. On one occasion, with the Seminoles facing a first and goal, Henshaw wanted to call a pass play while Bowden wanted to run the football. Henshaw remembers Bowden saying, "If it doesn't work, you're fired." It became almost a running joke, though Bowden, when the game was in play, wasn't always kidding. But he'd constantly remind Henshaw: "Whatever happens during a game doesn't count. If I fire you during a game, it doesn't count."

Players had the same trust in Bowden the staff did. In 1972, West Virginia won a heated recruiting battle over running back Artie Owens, who as a senior at Stroudsburg High School in Pennsylvania set state records for touchdowns and rushing yards. He was a quick, brilliant runner, and Bowden, as the Mountaineer head coach, won the fight to get Owens by making an unusual promise. Bowden told Owens he'd play extensively his freshman year at West Virginia, including the first game. Most college coaches—then and now—loathe playing freshmen, but Bowden needed to make that promise in order to get Owens to sign. Owens was convinced Bowden would keep his word so he signed with the Mountaineers.

Henshaw was coaching the freshman team when Owens joined West Virginia. As Henshaw prepped for the annual scrimmage, when the Mountaineer freshmen played the top Mountaineer veterans—normally a bloodied blowout in which the freshmen were pummeled—Henshaw was called into Bowden's office. "George," Bowden said, "I told Artie Owens he was going to play in our opener. Now if he looks terrible in this scrimmage I can't justify him playing. I'll look like a liar to him. So you've got to make him look good in this scrimmage." Henshaw left Bowden's office wondering how he was going to get a freshman runner to look impressive against a solid varsity defense. It was mission impossible.

Somehow, Henshaw was able to pull off the requested miracle. The freshmen beat the varsity 17–14, and Owens scored two impressive touchdowns. Henshaw had unwittingly embarrassed the other coaches by winning, and they were furious with him for doing so. One day later, while reviewing the scrimmage, Bowden angrily chastised the staff in what was a heated meeting. "He was absolutely furious," Henshaw remembered.

Though not at Henshaw, he wasn't. Henshaw managed to do exactly what Bowden hoped. He made Owens look solid so Bowden could keep his word and Owens could play. Three days after verbally destroying the staff, Bowden walked by Henshaw in the hallway and without breaking stride Bowden whispered, "Good job, George."

(It turns out that Owens would embarrass a number of defenses, not just West Virginia's. He rushed for a career 2,648 yards and is third on the school's all-purpose yardage list with 3,971.)

Bowden kept another such promise to an even bigger star, defensive lineman Ron Simmons, who would become one of the top players in Florida State history. Simmons was nicknamed "Float" not because of his quickness despite a massive and powerful frame (though that made perfect sense) but because of his favorite song, "Float On," by the rhythm and blues group The Floaters. Bowden had to overcome the fact that Simmons was from Georgia and every school in the state recruited him hard. When it was discovered that the Seminoles were in the lead to snag Simmons's services, schools began telling Simmons he was going to an all-girls' school with no tradition (Florida State was once a women's college).

Simmons would consider Bowden a second father; one of the reasons he did was because Bowden kept his word with Simmons as he did with others. In this instance, Bowden not only promised the high schooler Simmons that he would play for Florida State as a freshman, he promised Simmons he would start for the Seminoles. Such a guarantee was not just unusual in big-time college football, it was practically unheard of.

Not long after making that promise to Simmons, the coaching staff met and Bowden had a message for Henshaw. "Let me make one thing perfectly clear," Bowden told Henshaw. "You can play any ten players you want on defense. I get to pick one: Ron Simmons." Simmons started against LSU in the first game of the year and was practically unblockable. Bowden convinced a reluctant Simmons to play nose tackle. At that position the new Seminole would go on to become freshman of the year. His 4.56 40-yard dash speed would allow Simmons to dominate games like no Seminole player ever had. In his first game he blocked a punt, in a game against Auburn he had 19 tackles, and overall he is considered one of the more ferocious players in modern college football history.

Bowden's bluntness and honesty were refreshing and didn't apply solely to his team. That bluntness also sometimes cost him. Ron McCartney, a solid high school prospect at defensive end, was deciding between the Mountaineers and the University of Tennessee. McCartney met with Bowden and asked him a simple question: Could Bowden guarantee he'd coach McCartney throughout his entire college career? In other words, Bowden was being asked, will you be staying at West Virginia for a while? Many coaches would have lied and said yes. Bowden told the truth. "Son," he told McCartney, "I can't guarantee I'll coach you tomorrow." McCartney a short time later piled into his car, drove to Tennessee, and committed to the Volunteers.

And Bowden kept other, more personal promises, like the ones to his sons. As they grew and entered the football world, Bowden constantly reminded them there would be no special breaks or favors because they were Bowden kids. It's a lesson Bowden taught all of his children as his coaching acumen and fame grew. The family's integrity was put to the test when Terry and Tommy joined the West Virginia team as walk-ons while their father was head coach. Terry played running back; a lanky Tommy played wide receiver. Several practices had a particularly Bowden family flavor. Once, with Tommy at wide receiver and Bobby calling plays, Bobby called for Terry to run the ball directly up the middle. Terry did as told, and was smashed hard, returning to the huddle with a bloodied nose and his helmet askew. In the huddle, Tommy laughed at his brother and Coach Bowden, without hesitation, called the same play again. Bowden wanted to let Terry—and the team—completely understand: there would be no easing up on any player, even if that player's last name was Bowden.

During Bowden's tenure as head coach at West Virginia, indeed everyone (not just his sons) knew who was boss, but his authority sometimes came tempered with a smile or laugh. After being shut out by Penn State, Bowden and the team watched film of the game. He was livid. Bowden called his team's play disgusting, and as he screamed, his face turned deep red. He was partly genuinely angry and partly venting for effect. At the end of his tirade, he turned and stormed off. He meant to leave the room, but accidentally walked into a small, dark closet. The door locked behind him. He was sealed in. Players eventually recovered from his lambasting and started to laugh hysterically. Just then Bowden knocked on the door, and one of the coaches opened it. Even Bowden, furious just seconds earlier, couldn't help but giggle.

There was no laughing after a 1973 loss to Penn State, 62–14. It was the worst loss of Bowden's career. He was able to hide the naked disappointment of losing so badly from his staff and team but not from himself. Following the game, after the players and coaches had departed the locker room, Bowden sat on a small corner of a bench in a more isolated portion of the room. He'd showered, but the only thing draped around him was a towel. Bowden just sat there, his head down, silent. That's when Charleston, West Virginia, sportswriter Bill Smith, a friend of Bowden's, approached and tried to cheer up the coach. "It's not the end of the world," Smith told Bowden, "your team will bounce back."

"Naw, I'm just not getting the job done," Bowden responded. "I feel like hanging it up." Bowden added: "I ain't gonna die, but I'm so sick I could throw up."

He didn't quit (or throw up), and by 1974 Bowden was in his fifth season as head coach of the Mountaineers and was well ensconced, the horrific Penn State loss behind him. But the setting was beginning to wear on Bowden. The after-midnight four-hour drives postgame from Morgantown to Charleston to tape his television highlight show (there were no studios in Morgantown) were draining enough. Bobby and Ann hosted a party at their home following games, then slumped to their car, drove the several hundred miles, usually slept in a motel for about forty-five minutes, taped the show, then immediately drove back.

What strained Bowden more were the Mountaineer fans. Even now, all these years later, there's tension in Bowden's voice when speaking about his West Virginia days, and almost pure hate in the voices of other Bowden family members when asked about Mountaineer fans. In one conversation, Bowden makes it clear there is no bitterness about his time there. Then, in another, he speaks about the cruelty to which his family was subjected. Bowden will state how fans are the same everywhere—some loyal, others ungrateful and mean-spirited—but then discuss how Mountaineer fans were the most vicious he'd ever seen. "My family has never really been through anything like we experienced at West Virginia," he says now. "Never."

Part of the problem between Bowden and the West Virginia fans was cultural. To some northerners, West Virginia is the South. To some southerners, like Bowden, West Virginia is the North. Bowden wasn't sure what to make of his new surroundings, and West Virginians weren't certain what to make of this young Alabama boy. "My coaching had been living in Alabama for thirty years, living in Georgia for four years, and living in Florida for three years. That was my life," Bowden said. "Then all of the sudden I go to West Virginia, which is probably a thousand miles from here at least and West Virginia is not south. I think we were fifty miles south of Pittsburgh, and we were eight miles south of the Pennsylvania state line."

There was another issue. From the homey campus of Howard, the scene at West Virginia was a drastic step up for Bowden in size and class. Initially, Bowden's lack of exposure to far more intense pressures, such as hard-core boosters with unrealistic expectations and segments of a fan base who in some cases didn't just act cruelly but criminally, left him unprepared. "I have to admit I made some rookie mistakes," Bowden said. "In the six years I was there I made a bunch."

At smaller programs, a coach can make those mistakes and few will notice. It was drastically different at West Virginia. "The biggest challenge when an assistant coach becomes a head coach is all of the sudden he gets blamed for everything," Bowden said. "All the responsibility falls back on him. If the defensive line fails it's the head coach. If the offensive line fails it's the head coach. If the quarterback fails it's the head coach. Therefore criticism is going to jump up."

There is no better example of that difference than the game on October 17, 1970, in Pittsburgh during his first year as head coach.

"Probably the darkest day of my entire career," Bowden says.

Bowden's Mountaineers started the year 4–1, and they were on their way to a nice season. On that afternoon West Virginia was playing a bad University of Pittsburgh team the Mountaineers had beaten three consecutive years. Pittsburgh was also a fierce rival, and the first-half play of Bowden's Mountaineers reflected the animosity. West Virginia jumped to a huge 35–8 lead over the Panthers. Every person in the stadium thought the game was over. So did Bowden. He pulled his quarterback, Mike Sherwood, aside as the team was heading into the locker room. They had a brief and ominous conversation, stemming from Sherwood's success in the previous two games against Pittsburgh.

"Mike, you've really got their number," Bowden told Sherwood as the two men made their way off the field for the halftime break.

"Well, for two and a half games anyhow, Coach," he told Bowden.

. . . .

The Great Bowden Collapse actually began earlier in the week. The Pittsburgh coach, Carl DePasqua, had recently taken control of a troubled and loss-riddled football program that had won only three games from 1966 to 1968. While Bowden spent time up-grading West Virginia's archaic passing game, DePasqua focused on getting the Panthers to do the basics: blocking and tackling. Pittsburgh's preparation for the game has been well chronicled by writer John Antonik, and it's clear that Pittsburgh might have taken the game far more seriously than Bowden's Mountaineers did. DePasqua, blunt and grounded, was part of the reason. Dick Polen was the sports information director at the time and told Antonik of an incident that occurred during a press conference with Bowden and DePasqua several days before the game. When one of the West Virginia beat writers asked a question that irked DePasqua, the Pittsburgh coach responded sharply. "That's the damned dumbest question I've ever heard," DePasqua said.

DePasqua was already angry with West Virginia long before the game began. One year earlier, in 1969, West Virginia's Carlen decided to run up the score on Pittsburgh. Afterward, DePasqua approached Carlen and said such a blowout would not happen again under his regime. DePasqua had no idea how telling a state-ment that was. By the end of the 1970 rematch, that prediction had come true. But the first half seemed a disaster for Pittsburgh. Mountaineer running backs pummeled the Pittsburgh defense, and Bowden found no need to use the air game as his team opened a 27-point halftime lead. In the press box, beat writers and col-umnists had already started to write their stories. Inside the West Virginia locker room, Bowden attempted to control the utter joy the Mountaineers were feeling about manhandling their rival, but he failed to do so. The team was laughing and joking. To them, the game was already over.

In some ways, there was a similar feeling in the Pittsburgh locker room. DePasqua said little to his team (and by some re-ports he said nothing). While Bowden—afraid of being accused of running up the score—decided to go to a more conservative offense, DePasqua, ironically did the same. In doing so, the Pittsburgh coach made a decision that would change both his fate and Bowden's.

"He ran the ball and I ran the ball," Bowden remembers. "I should have kept dadgum attacking. Shoulda kept attacking."

DePasqua had spent the first half attacking the perimeter of West Virginia's small, fast defense. It was a gross tactical error. West Virginia's inside linebackers possessed the quick legs to make tackles on the outside. What they didn't have was bulk, and DePasqua switched in the third quarter to an inside power running formation. His larger offensive linemen swamped West Virginia's. It worked perfectly. Very early in the third quarter the Panthers scored in rapid fashion. A touchdown and two-point conversion made it 35–16. Bowden called for three straight running plays and punted. Pittsburgh, again running the football directly into the West Virginia abdomen, scored and converted on the two-point conversion again. The Mountaineers kept punting, and Pittsburgh kept scoring. Suddenly, it was 35–30 with ten minutes remaining. Mountaineer fans were getting agitated—and angry. "There was a lot of rumbling in the stadium with the West Virginia fans," Bowden said. "Everyone was getting nervous. I was dang nervous."

At this point it was too late. There was little Bowden could do to stop the bleeding or halt Pittsburgh's hurricane force momentum. The real mystery was why after the Panthers scored—to take a one-point lead with less than sixty seconds remaining—DePasqua didn't go for another two-point conversion that would have given the Panthers a three-point lead. In the end, it didn't matter. Pittsburgh pulled off what Bowden considers his worst defeat ever. The final score was 36–35.

Inside the West Virginia locker room, the atmosphere was alternately tear-filled and terrifying. For one of the few times in his career—hell, in his life—Bowden didn't know exactly what to say. He was as stunned as everyone else.

"You will overcome this," Bowden told the team. Other than

Bowden's few words and the occasional sniffle and whimper, the locker room was coldly silent.

Though the game was at Pittsburgh, a large number of West Virginia fans had made the short trip north, and a mob of several dozen gathered outside the visitors' locker room. Soon some of them began pounding on that door. Others started kicking it. They were screaming expletives and demanding that Bowden come outside.

"Hey, Bowden!" some of them yelled. "C'mon out here, you gutless fucker!"

There was a genuine feeling that if Bowden obliged, his physical safety would be jeopardized. "I had never in my life seen a group of fans act that way," Bowden says. It was so disturbing that the state troopers providing security for West Virginia wouldn't allow Bowden to leave the locker room until the outraged fans—many of whom were drunk—had departed.

Bowden emerged and spoke with a small group of writers. "This is going to be the most heartbreaking loss I've had in coaching," he said. After speaking with the press, Bowden was escorted to the team bus by several state police officers.

When Bowden returned home, he found Ann lying on the bed with tears in her eyes. She'd been listening to the radio broadcast and fans were calling in after the game, savaging Bowden.

Bowden says now: "People have accused me of running up the score. I made a lot of mistakes at West Virginia and that was the biggest. I didn't keep the pressure on. I went conservative. That was a valuable lesson. So when I hear complaints now about me running up the score, I always think back to that game. I wasn't gonna ever repeat that mistake."

The loss was so bad for Bowden he considers it worse than the Seminoles' 17–16 loss to Miami that would come in 1991. That loss knocked Florida State out of national championship contention.

Bowden likely never had a chance for long-term acceptance at West Virginia after such a horrific loss. It didn't matter that his coaching record was respectable there. Indeed, decades following his West Virginia experience, and entering 2008, only two Mountaineer coaches in the previous sixty years had winning records in their initial seasons as head coach, and Bowden was one of them.

After the Pittsburgh defeat, Bowden would finish 8–3, followed by 7–4; in 1972, he went 8–3 again in the regular season (Bowden lost in the Peach Bowl). In 1973, Bowden was 6–5 and suffered a 48-point loss to Penn State. Then came 1974, which would be Bowden's first losing season (and only one of two in over five decades of coaching). As the year unfolded, displeasure with Bowden turned ugly and personal. Tommy, a walk-on wide receiver on the team, attended Mountaineer basketball games when he'd hear sudden eruptions of "Bowden sucks!" Bobby was hanged in effigy in dorm and shop windows across campus and throughout parts of the town. Some put painted "Bye Bye Bobby" in large letters on bedsheets and hung them from dorm windows. One such sign was draped across a window directly across the street from Bowden's office. He saw it every day for weeks and joked with assistants that it was permanently part of the scenery.

"It was ugly," recalled assistant Garrett Ford. "I was too young to realize how bad it was because I was just happy to have a job. But when you look back it was ugly. When you went to the supermarket people didn't talk to you. We all got it. The only people we had was us."

It would get worse. Some of the West Virginia fans were simply animalistic during that 4–7 year in 1974. One put an M-80 firecracker in Bowden's home mailbox. Colored paint was poured on the Bowden family car, and a brick was launched against the front door, causing a significant dent. Perhaps most disturbing is someone phoned Bobby's house and made death threats against the Bowden girls.

(Psychos clearly aren't relegated to the state of West Virginia. In 1990, while coach at Florida State, someone penned a death threat to Bowden and in the letter claimed that during the game against South Carolina, he'd be shot. The letter set off a flurry of police activity immediately before and during the contest. Bowden received extra security, and no attempt on his life was made.)

Robyn Hines remembers those West Virginia days, and they helped shape her feelings about the coaching profession. She was a graduate student at West Virginia in 1974 and saw a large sign attached to a telephone pole, reading LEAVE TOWN BOWDEN.

"I was very angry with my alma mater," she told me. "They weren't putting the signs up, but they weren't doing a whole lot to prevent them from being put up either."

Tommy got into the act of protecting his father as well, even if what he did was inappropriate. When the West Virginia student newspaper ran a column suggesting that Bowden should be fired, it was typical of the media criticism he was receiving. What irked Tommy was one of the central messages of the editorial, which was that Bowden had lost the respect of the players. Tommy should have let the commentary slide off his back just like the rest of the criticisms. But he couldn't. He cut out the editorial, folded it neatly, and stuck it into his wallet.

Tommy was unclear why he saved the article, he just knew he wanted to. Months later, while on campus, he showed it to another student who identified its author as the president of a West Virginia fraternity house. Now, Tommy knew why he'd kept it. He gathered teammates from the Mountaineers—all offensive and defensive linemen weighing over 250 pounds—and proceeded to the frat house. They knocked on the door and were told the man they were looking for was in the house's basement. They proceeded down the stairs in one large mass of intimidating humanity, with others in the house afraid to stop them. Tommy found the president, pulled out the article, and asked a simple question.

"Did you write this?" Tommy asked.

The man sheepishly admitted he had.

"Well, that's my father," Tommy stated. "You said the players don't respect Bowden. Here are some players. Why don't you ask them if they respect him."

The student was so frightened he didn't dare ask even a rhetorical question.

"What you wrote wasn't true. I want a retraction," Tommy said.

And, sure enough, that's later exactly what he got.

The move was out of character for Tommy but exemplified the frustration felt by the family, especially the football-playing sons.

Tommy remained quiet in 1974 during a team meeting called by West Virginia players without the knowledge of Bobby and his staff. As a player, Tommy had to sit through other players complaining about his dad and the excessive hitting in practice and poor play calling.

What hurt Bobby most was the reaction of people he believed were friends. Many times Bowden's home was the epicenter of the West Virginia sports social scene. Actually, the Bowden home has always been that. When Bowden coached the receivers as an assistant at Florida State, on Sundays, the receivers would meet at Bowden's home in the morning, packing their shotguns for hunting later in the day, leave the guns at Bowden's house, then head off to services. Afterward, they'd head back to Bowden's home, have hot dogs and hamburgers prepared by Ann, get their shotguns, then go duck hunting.

Once, after West Virginia's win over Pittsburgh in October 1971, the school president, James Harlow, chose a Bowden postgame gathering at Bobby and Ann's home over other school VIP events. After almost every home game, Ann and Bobby would host a group of boosters and sports journalists, sometimes numbering as high as fifty. As for Harlow, he had a penchant for gadgets and was devoted then to modernizing and computerizing the West Virginia campus. He also had a penchant for chitchat. As Ann dutifully attended to her hosting duties, Harlow slowly approached and cozied up to her. "Tell Bobby it looked like he saved our jobs for another year," he told Ann. When things began to turn on Bowden, the social scene was less social. And less civil. Although Bowden did have strong support from top school officials, that's where much of the support ended. Golf buddies stopped calling. Certain people in the athletic department treated him coldly. The invitations to dinner trickled to a halt. Bowden knew the push to get him out was officially beginning. But in 1975, in what would be his last year at West Virginia, the team went 8–3, and Bowden made a conscious decision. No one was going to push him. He was going to leave before they got the chance.

"I think my father's attitude was, 'We're going to win and then we're gonna get outta here,'" said Robyn.

CHAPTER SEVEN

PAPA 'NOLE

*When y'all started talking about coaching, my attitude was,
"Boys, if you feel that the only way you're going to be happy is
if you're coaching I want you to do it. But if you think you'd be
just as happy in law or medicine or banking, I kinda hope you
go that way. At least then we wouldn't be competing against
one another."*

—Bobby Bowden talking to his coaching sons

He had a booming arm, maybe the biggest in all of college
football, and he had a strong desire to play at Florida State.
His name was Terry Bradshaw.

The year was 1966, a decade before Bowden would become
the Seminole head coach. Bradshaw was heavily recruited by a
number of schools, including Florida State, but he failed to pass
the academic requirements so FSU dropped out of the Bradshaw
sweepstakes. So did LSU. Bradshaw instead went to Louisiana
Tech. When a coaching change occurred after his first season,
Bradshaw was concerned about the direction of the program. He
again considered Florida State, and the interest was reciprocated.
"They didn't just talk about throwing the football, they threw it.
And their offense was as near to a pro offense as that of any college
team in the country," Bradshaw wrote in his autobiography. "I decided to transfer to Florida State for the rest of my college career.

It would mean sitting out my sophomore year but the way things were going at Tech that would hardly have been a sacrifice."

In Bradshaw's mind it was a foregone conclusion. He was going to be a Seminole. He contacted members of the Florida State coaching staff, and they were equally excited. They urged Bradshaw to come to Tallahassee as quickly as possible. Bradshaw obliged and hopped into his car for the lengthy drive from Louisiana to Florida. Then, once he arrived on campus, something strange happened. Bradshaw was basically told to go home by Florida State coaches and athletic department officials, according to him. "The coaches who had seemed so cordial and encouraging earlier didn't act the least bit interested in my plans to transfer," said Bradshaw. Indeed, an academic counselor told Bradshaw to "get off campus and don't come back."

At the time, Florida State had several decent throwers on its roster, so the program didn't feel it needed another. Still, imagine what might have occurred had Bradshaw transferred to the Seminoles. Unfortunately, in the years before, and in the decade afterward, Florida State's horrid luck, bad karma, and the overall state of its program wouldn't get much better after the Bradshaw fiasco. The football program was a laughingstock—not just within its own state borders, but across the nation, the Seminoles were known as one of college football's great disasters.

Florida State's desire to improve its football program and actually compete with neighbor Florida had its roots in more than just pride. There was also intense, personal history. From the years 1905 to 1947, the state had designated Florida State as the Florida State College for Women and Florida as the official men's school. After World War II, in part due to large numbers of returning soldiers who had overwhelmed the University of Florida system, the state made both schools coed and dropped the women part from the Florida State name. But the fact that Florida State was once a women's school stuck for some time and stuck in the gut of the male students. This was like adding gasoline to an already intense rivalry between Florida and Florida State.

That rivalry played itself out on the football field. In the fall of 1973, in Gainesville, Florida, the weather was still warm and University of Florida football players, finished with their pregame drills, met near the center of Florida Field. They jumped excitedly in a circle just a few yards from their opponent, Florida State. The whipping was about to begin. Florida won the game, 49–0, embarrassing FSU yet again. The Gators whipping the Seminoles was not an unusual occurrence. Florida won nine straight games from 1968 to 1976 by a combined score of 267–112. That wasn't a rivalry; that was a wholesale slaughter.

In the 1970s, the Florida State program did have some player and coaching talent. Wide receiver Rhett Dawson overcame a ruptured spleen and shattered knee cartilage to become one of Florida State's most productive players. Coach Bill Peterson inserted a complex passing offense and hired Bowden as well as two guys named Joe Gibbs and Bill Parcells. (In the book *What It Means to Be a Seminole* by ESPN's Mark Schlabach, he wrote that the crusty Parcells was up to his motivational tricks even then. Parcells one day walked up to Dawson and said, "You're a pretty good receiver. You know what your problem is? You can't make the big catch." Then Parcells walked away. That two-second comment motivated Dawson for years.) J. T. Thomas was only the second African American football player at Florida State; he braved racism and threatening letters from the Ku Klux Klan while developing into an All-American cornerback and later earning four Super Bowl rings with the Pittsburgh Steelers. Thomas cleared the way for players like Deion Sanders.

The Seminoles had players and coaches with backbones and talent, but those men were few and far between. The football program was in such disarray it was difficult to determine when someone was being fired or if they were quitting. During the 1974–75 season finale against Houston at Campbell Stadium, head coach Darrell Mudra and assistant Dan Henning differed on which quarterback to play. The difference led to a heated debate; afterward a frustrated Mudra popped off to the press, stating there would be a major staff shake-up and Henning would be a part of it. A short time later, Henning was gone. The school said he resigned, but Henning said he was fired. Not only did Henning depart but Florida State's top recruiter, Mike Pope, left the Seminoles for Texas Tech.

While Florida State struggled with its position inside a football wasteland, the country in the mid-1970s finally saw the end of the Vietnam War and was stuck in a nasty recession. Parts of the South, including Tallahassee, were being hit the hardest. Economists believed then the nation was in its worst recession since World War II: the unemployment rate in Florida had hit 8.5 percent in January 1975. Some of Florida's universities weren't immune from the financial crisis, and many enacted draconian measures to save money. The University of Tampa dropped football in February—a stunning move, considering that a few years earlier the football program had produced John Matuszak, a top NFL draft pick.

Florida State faced its own problems. Discipline waned, as did the talent pool, and there were not an insignificant number of players involved in serious drug use. Indeed, according to two players who were on the FSU team in the 1970s shortly before Bowden's arrival and who asked not to be identified, there were some players who used marijuana on game days. A handful of players on the team, these players said, also used cocaine on game day. The players interviewed didn't believe the coaching staff or the team in general knew about the drug use. "It wasn't rampant, but it was bad enough," said one player. "There were some guys who couldn't control their drug habits." Both players interviewed stressed the drug use was by a small number of players but also said it was a problem that might have cost them games. "We were kind of running wild," said former receiver Mike Shumann, speaking about the lack of discipline within the program in general.

There was a money crisis as well. The school's president, Stanley Marshall, publicly warned of a fiscal disaster. Privately, the news was worse than many knew. School officials, noting the actions by the University of Tampa, seriously considered the unthinkable: dropping football at Florida State.

, . . .

Although such a thought seemed extreme, it was also understandable. Between 1971 and 1975, Florida State burned through two
coaches. During a three-season stretch in the mid-1970s the
Seminoles went 0–11, 1–10, and 3–8. In those years, a quarterback
flunked out, coaches left for lesser programs, and it was not unusual for the 41,000-seat stadium to have only 17,000 fans and on
occasion only 10,000. Perhaps worst of all, much of the top talent
in the state shunned the Seminoles. In 1975, Florida State had only
one player selected in the NFL draft, linebacker Bert Cooper, who
was selected in the twelfth round by the New York Jets.

The lack of fan interest and a dearth of victories led to a fiscal
crisis. The football program was so broke that Florida State was
unable to repair badly damaged equipment or replace scruffy practice gear. When Tampa abolished football, Florida State athletic
officials hurriedly sent a large truck to the school and purchased
Tampa's equipment at a discount.

Many Florida State fans were not shocked when they picked up
their Sunday, January 4, 1976, edition of the *Tallahassee Democrat*
and saw a front-page story speculating that the ouster of Coach
Darrell Mudra was imminent. After all, coaches were always
coming and going at Florida State. There was practically no stability. If that wasn't enough of a signal that yet another Seminole
coach was on his way out, this next issue was. A group of some seventy boosters, pushing for a change, raised $95,000 in funds and
offered it to the financially strapped university as a way of cush-
ioning any potential buyout of Mudra, who had two years remaining on a contract that paid $30,000 a year. Initially the university
was nervous about making a change, because officials feared there
wasn't enough money to pay off a fired Mudra. Now, suddenly,
there was. In effect, the skids were greased for Mudra's ouster. Interestingly, the *Democrat* story provided this little nugget at the
end, stating that the boosters wanted a "name coach . . . several have
been contacted however unofficially by members of this group—
including Texas Tech's Steve Sloan, Pittsburgh's Johnny Majors,

North Carolina State's Lou Holtz, Maryland's Jerry Claiborne and West Virginia's Bobby Bowden. Majors, Sloan and Holtz have indicated they would not be interested. Claiborne has indicated he might be interested under the right circumstances. Bowden, who has worked under a one-year contract throughout his time at West Virginia, said Saturday: 'I'm not planning on going anywhere. I'm happy here.'"

Mudra was fired shortly after the *Democrat*'s story ran. In actuality he never truly had a chance, as Florida State didn't possess the huge money to keep up with other programs. He took over the Seminoles in 1974 after a disastrous 0–11 season and followed that by going 1–10 and 3–8. Mudra didn't help matters with what was seen as a strange, detached style. He literally coached from the press box, rarely setting foot on the field on game day. He allowed his players too much say, too much freedom. Some of those players took advantage of his laid-back style by practicing lackadaisically and not listening to coaching. He left almost every in-game decision up to his assistants, and in a remarkable contrast to the stereotypical, überfocused coach, Mudra was even known to go fishing the morning of games.

As Florida State searched for a new coach, they clearly looked for someone who could take command of the program in a way Mudra never did. University officials continued to speak to many candidates, but after talking to Bowden, it was clear he was becoming the leader. When Bowden spoke to them on January 6, 1976—reversing his seemingly flippant stance earlier about a lack of interest—it was as if he was reading their minds. Bowden stressed that his years at Florida State as an assistant coach from 1963 to 1965 helped him have an understanding of what was needed to spark a turnaround. He also spoke of how Florida State was a sleeping giant that needed a shock to the system. "What you need," he told them, "is someone who can really get people interested in Florida State football again."

"I really did think that the school had a chance to do something," Bowden says now. "I have to admit now it wasn't a strong feeling. There was a lot wrong with the program, but with a break here and a break there, I thought I had a chance to win."

On a chilly Friday January morning—cold for Tallahassee, that is—the former California governor, Ronald Reagan, was surrounded by fifteen hundred adoring onlookers as he made a speech inside a small shopping mall. It was the opening of a three-day Florida campaign tour, and the future president was in full Reagan form. "If there's going to be forced busing in this country," he told the crowd, "it ought to be forced busing of the bureaucracy out into the country to let them see what the problems are." There was loud applause, and after his speech, a smiling Reagan, with shiny dark hair, shook hands with dozens of people as the Secret Service watched closely.

Reagan arriving in Tallahassee was exciting news, but not even the arrival of a presidential candidate could overshadow the biggest news of the week: Bowden had been hired. His appointment led the *Democrat* and quickly relegated Reagan's visit to old news status. Bowden signed a four-year deal that paid him $37,500 a year. Bowden's new salary was a rise of $2,500 over his previous salary and $7,500 over Mudra's.

One quote from a Florida State dean, Coyle E. Moore, demonstrated how comfortable some at the school were with its image as a redneck institution of higher learning. Moore said that Bowden "fits our needs like a glove. . . . He is a Southern Cracker, to the manner born—perfectly adaptable to us Southern Crackers and rednecks of northern Florida. He speaks our language, adheres to our religious faith." The irony is that in the decades to come Florida State would utilize the success of Bowden's program to help elevate the school from "Southern Cracker" and "redneck" roots into a world-class university crawling with top students and big brains.

Florida State arranged for Bowden to meet the press, and Bowden didn't disappoint. He put on the kind of show that few people in the room had seen before. One of the first questioners asked whether Bowden was a strict disciplinarian. The background to the question, of course, was related to Mudra, who didn't know the meaning of the word. Bowden was ready for the query. "A strict disciplinarian?" he said. "Well, I definitely believe in discipline. But if you hold a bird in your hand too tight you squeeze it to death and if you hold it too loose he gets away." When asked about the emerging issue of the lack of black assistant coaches in colleges, Bowden replied, "I can't stand this token black thing. I want a black who can coach . . . there's no way we're going to be a black and white team—we've got to be a team."

"I know a lot of you look at me and ask if I'm *the* big-time coach," Bowden said. "I don't know what a big-time coach is. I know I have been hung [in effigy]. And I know if I beat Florida, I'm a big-time coach."

The *Democrat*'s editorial board in mid-January 1976 giddily remarked on Bowden's press conference, calling it a great success. "The way he tamed a generally pugnacious press corps Monday afternoon during his first press conference here showed a tremendous amount of stage presence," the paper wrote. "But more than that, self-confidence, which is what FSU football badly needs right now."

In his first year, Bowden went 5–6. It would be Florida State's last losing season for more than thirty years.

Bowden still remembers large chunks of the first speech he delivered to the players as head coach at Florida State. He reprinted the speech in his book *Bound for Glory*, but all this time later, he still can recite significant portions of it from memory. It happened on January 16, 1976, and Bowden walked into a crowded team meeting room that was understandably apprehensive. Who was this new coach? Was he going to rule with an iron fist? The Seminole players didn't have to wait long for the answers as Bowden made his intentions clear the moment he began talking.

Gentlemen, let me explain the importance of why we're all here together. First of all, we've got to have a basic understanding of who's in charge around here. There can never be a question of that. Well, I'm the new guy around here. I'm the head coach. And in the past three years, your Florida State football team has managed to win only four games and, in the meantime, lost 29. Ya'll have tried it your way, and where did it get you? Nowhere. Now, I think I know how to win and from now on at Florida State, we're going to do things my way. If you don't like it, then hit the door. Go somewhere else. Because if winning doesn't mean something to you, then we don't need you.

Players in the room started sitting up straighter in their chairs. "From now on, it's going to be an honor to wear the garnet jersey and represent Florida State University," Bowden told the team.

We're gonna win again at Florida State. Now, I think we can turn this program around at Florida State. But gentlemen, it's going to take a big effort by everyone. We're going to have to push ourselves harder than ever before. We're gonna have to make sacrifices, give up individual goals in order to reach a much bigger team goal. But we can do it. We can win at Florida State.

Vince Lombardi, the great coach of the Green Bay Packers, once described that glorious feeling that winners have, that feeling that none of you have enjoyed at Florida State. He said, "I firmly believe that man's finest hour, his greatest fulfillment to all he holds dear, is that moment when he has worked his heart out in a good cause and lies exhausted on the field . . . victorious."

Gentlemen, that will be our goal. That will be the feeling that we all want to achieve—to feel like a winner, to be able to walk around campus with the satisfaction of knowing that, "Yes, we can win." And in order to get that feeling of confidence and to begin winning football games, then things here have got to change. First of all, we've got to develop a winning attitude and that means self-discipline because self-discipline wins football games. And that's our goal at Florida State—to win football games.

Now, in order to build a winning program and develop self-discipline, we've got to make some rules around here. And that means making a commitment to ourselves and to each other that we're going to follow those rules. So let's start with hair. I'm not going to ask you to look like Kojaks but we are going to keep it neat and we are going to look like football players. We're also gonna go to class and get up for breakfast. And there's not going to be any room on this team for individuals who've got to drink or smoke. If you do, then you're gonna be gone.

No part of Bowden's speech to the team was coincidental or unplanned. Indeed, Bowden's speech at his first staff meeting was not so drastically different. He told the coaches he was boss and that, although he wasn't overly punitive, certain rules were non-negotiable. "I will not tolerate cheating," he told the coaches. "I will not tolerate womanizing and I will not tolerate drinking."

The players were now receiving similar warnings. It would be unfair to say that Florida State players pre-Bowden were a bunch of drunken, unprofessional clowns. But there were definitely significant elements that lacked discipline. Bowden was telling them that was going to change.

And certainly none of the previous staff asked Seminole players to do this. "Next, we're gonna ask that you attend church regularly and write your mom and dad. It'll mean a lot to them, and more to you over the years." It was an interesting dichotomy. He was setting the rules and presenting himself as an overall disciplinarian while simultaneously asking the players to stay in touch with their mommas.

"So, gentlemen, what is sacrifice?" Bowden continued.

It's having a little pride in yourself to not be like the average students. You've gotta outwork them—you've gotta have a desire to excel. Sacrifice also means displaying a winning attitude, looking and acting like an athlete, recognizing the attributes of other students, giving them a pat on the back, shaking their hands and looking 'em in the eye while doing it. Sacrifice means "yes sir" and "no sir" to your supervisors. But remember, it takes class to come back in the fourth quarter and win but if we've sacrificed, we can do it.

There won't be too many other training rules, just use your head. Try to eat and sleep good. Be on time for meetings. And try to have a goal every day—try to get better. If you have a bad day, don't lose your confidence. Just try to improve day-to-day.

Now, gentlemen, listen up to this final point. We represent a lot of people . . . our families, our friends back at home and, very importantly, we represent Florida State University. And as a team I want to throw this out to you. You're not ordinary. You're not average. You're something special and I don't want you to ever forget that. And since you are something special, then I know that as a team, we can win if you put something extra into it every day, and a little bit extra into a game.

Gentlemen, we have a tough road ahead, and we've got to be both mentally and physically tough to make it. But if we're prepared in the proper manner, then when the time comes, winning will take care of itself.

And with that Bowden left the room.

CHAPTER EIGHT

MATRIARCH

I n the not-so-distant future in the Bowden family, father would battle sons (and endure more scathing criticism from some psychologically disturbed fans), wives would battle the media, and the family would battle the withering effects of time and tragedy. Yet over the decades there wouldn't be the ostracizing of brother or sister or the succumbing to the weight of intrafamily squabbles so familiar with other high-profile families—in sports, Hollywood, and politics—which are often irritated by fame. The biggest reason why the Bowden clan never fractured into tiny pieces is Ann. While Bobby would become FSU, it was Ann who transformed into the CEO of Bowden, Inc. Elegant, polite, and chatty, she sits at a neat kitchen table, looking much younger than a woman in her seventies. She is the fierce protector of the Bowden family who speaks with prickly bluntness.

When they moved into their home in an upscale, quiet Tallahassee, Florida, neighborhood, Bobby took a walk around the property—and wouldn't do so again for decades to come. Ann often jokes with friends that what Bobby does around the home is from the elbow down to the hand, meaning he might close the pool umbrellas or shut off a faucet. Ann's joked that he won't change a lightbulb unless she asks, and if he does, he'll ask her to lug over a ladder and grab the bulb itself. When they have friends over to grill, she takes command of the grilling and the fire. The coach is no tinkerer and putterer. She is. And she likes it that way. Ann doesn't want a man telling her what color to paint the walls.

Their marriage has worked because each has accepted the other's strengths and weaknesses and adapted accordingly. Ann might have, at times, longed for a more emotional connection with Bobby, but long ago realized it was not his way. Bobby was a dedicated and resourceful father to be certain. When at the end of one of her six pregnancies, Ann had labor pains in the early morning hours, a wobbly and tired Bobby made toast and fried eggs, settled Ann in the front seat of the family station wagon, and then placed a mattress in the back of the car, where the three children were delicately lain and slept through the entire ordeal. But also it was not unusual for him to drop a pregnant Ann off at the hospital, only to return when the baby was born. "I don't think he really knew exactly how to come in and hold my hand and rub my head," she says. "I think some young men now are better about those kinds of things, sharing the birth of their children." She added: "I don't know, it might scare him a little bit. He didn't know how to relate to that."

She's taken the kids to school and lugged them to their games. She's helped with the homework and attended the PTA meetings. She's the prototypical stay-at-home mom. She's also the disciplinarian who believed the best punishment is a good, old-fashioned spanking with the belt . . . or whatever utensil was nearby. Bobby was the softy. Whenever Ann told him to spank one of the children, he'd take them into a room, close the door, and say, "Your mom says I have to punish you. Now when I clap my hands, holler real loud." He'd smack his hands together, and the kids, happy to be accomplices, yelled as if they'd been hit.

Ann's also been a valuable force for Bobby's success by providing a warm welcome to potential recruits or hosting important football dignitaries at the Bowden home. This has been the case at every Bowden coaching stop, particularly Florida State. There are tales of recruits literally considering changing their minds about which school to attend after exposure to Ann's hospitality.

In 2004, troubled high school football player Willie Williams, who was being recruited by every major football program in the country, wrote about his visit to the Bowden home in his diary for the *Miami Herald*. "Coach Bowden was cool," Williams stated. "But Ms. Bowden was the bomb, I swear, she must be related to Betty Crocker or something. When we walked into that house, it was like walking into a Publix bakery—banana pudding, chocolate cake, cheesecake. I had one of everything. I didn't want to leave." He did, however, pick Miami over Florida State. Guess Williams wanted more than banana pudding.

In the Bowden household, there's never been a difference of opinion when it comes to church. All the children were involved. Ann stayed up late Saturdays to iron the clothes and rustled up breakfast the next morning so all Bobby had to do was pack everyone into the car and drive to the service. Ann remarks: "I hear parents say, 'We can't get our kids to go to church.' I say, 'What do you mean? Do you ask them if they want to go to school?'" Sunday morning the family went to church. Wednesday night, they went to church. Sunday night . . . church. Yes, Sunday night too.

And though the Ten Commandments were primary, there was an eleventh commandment in the Bowden house: You shall not make wrongful use of the family name. Bobby and Ann have always been careful about one thing, their kids using the Bowden name to get an advantage. The kids were constantly warned, "No bragging, no name dropping."

At the rear of their home is a large white door that Bobby has used for decades. It used to frustrate Ann that Bobby would return from practice, walk through that door, take a long shower, change into his sleeping clothes, read, then go to sleep. Or he might strip down to a pair of shorts and park on a sectional sofa and watch television.

"Why don't we talk more?" she would ask him.

Then she adapted. She began to worry less about the things she couldn't control and understand that Bobby wasn't going to change his ways. Her trademark bluntness emerges when she says of her husband: "He's a man, and that means he has the shortcomings and faults that many men do. But he is the kindest person I have ever known."

What Bobby has always admired about Ann is her integrity and dedication to the family. What she enjoys most about him is his faithfulness and simplicity. Bobby has used an old-fashioned shaving mug and straight razor for decades (Bowden hates shaving and sometimes does it before going to bed so he's "ahead of the game"). Inside Bobby's closet, all of his shirts are turned in the same direction, and have been since Ann can remember. He only began using a cell phone in 2001.

Their conversations are typical of marriage, rotating between loving and comforting, harsh and blunt. When Bobby came home once and asked Ann why she watches so many cooking shows when she no longer regularly cooks, Ann responded, "Well, you watch football."

Ann's feelings about their relationship are complex but in some ways can be simplified as alternating between feeling blessed for a loving husband and father who has been a great provider and having frustration that many people outside of the family do not completely appreciate how much she has contributed to Bobby's success. "I don't think people understand just how much sacrifice the wives of coaches make so their husbands can be successful," she says. "Coaching is all Bobby has had to worry about."

The couple's schedule has remained the same for so long, Ann recites it with hardly an ounce of thought. Their morning routine, however, is the most meaningful part of the day for her. They often wake before the sun comes up. Bowden rises at 4 A.M., puts on coffee, and reads two newspapers, Bible passages, and several other books. Ann arrives a short while later. That time of the morning is for private discussion, as the couple talks about what certain biblical scriptures mean to them. Many times, they thank God for their health.

"I don't think you would find many women today who did what I did—marry young and raise a big family," she says. ". . . I never once felt like I made a mistake by marrying young. I don't know what I missed. I don't think I missed anything."

. . . .

BOBBY IS OBSESSED WITH history—learning about it, absorbing it, teaching it, treating it with respect. He reads many books—often four at one time—usually associated with great military battles and leaders. There is a book in the bathroom at home ("I don't like to waste that time," he says) and one in the bathroom at his office. There also is a book in his briefcase and a stack in the kitchen. Bowden's Florida State office walls are crowded with row upon row of books.

Bobby's preoccupation with history means he is keenly aware that it often repeats itself. As he watched his sons grow, mature, and enter the coaching fraternity, he knew they would endure the harsh scrutiny that he did.

"You know, I never really wanted you guys to go into coaching," Bobby would later tell Terry. "I didn't know what it would do to our family."

"Dad," Terry told him, "I don't think we ever had a choice. It's in the genes."

Bobby knew he couldn't fight it. But if he could not stop his children, he was going to prepare them. As they grew out of diapers and grammar school into smart kids who started to understand just who their dad was, Bowden told them about the business. All of it—the good and the bad. The talk-radio flak, the newspaper columnists, the egotistical boosters—Bobby made sure his kids had doctorates in dealing with coaching stress.

Bobby preached to his sons what he practiced: always remain composed. To say Bobby is a gentleman is an understatement. He has a sincerity and geniality rarely seen in coaches of his stature. When he meets people, he expresses a genuine interest in them, their family, their jobs. The whole Bowden family, in fact, has that trait. Yet when it comes to certain issues, Bobby is intractable. He refuses, for example, to make close friends in his profession. When asked the names of his good pals in college coaching, Bobby replies, "You know, that's a good question 'cause I don't hardly have any. We coaches don't get real close. I say we, but I never have. It's too competitive. I'm sure some coaches go on vacation together. That's not me. To be honest, I have such a big family, I'd rather be with them." He added: "I don't think I have a lot of enemies in the profession."

Says former Miami coach Larry Coker: "I think he is friendly and a fun person to be around. But he does not socialize as much with other coaches."

AFTER TAKING THE FLORIDA State job, Bowden immediately got to work. If you want to know why Bowden was able to lift Florida State from the garbage heap and transform the program into something radically different, these formative years are remarkably instructive. What Bowden did was simple: he applied elbow grease to push the football program into the modern age. Perhaps more important, he unleashed his nuclear charm on hundreds of moms in the living rooms of recruits throughout the talent-rich state of Florida.

One of Bowden's favorite players to watch was Dick Butkus, the electric linebacker for the Chicago Bears. Bowden loved Butkus's energy and desire, and Bowden wanted his Florida State players to possess that sort of vigor. Talent was important of course, but to Bowden it would take players with great ambition—not just quick 40 times—to overcome Florida State's severe talent drought.

Bowden could in fact talk the devil into returning to heaven, and in those early years his recruiting was key. Later, in the 1980s, while working with recruiting coordinator Brad Scott, Bowden would refine his already impressive tactics. Before an official visit, Scott would prepare a sort of cheat sheet in which he'd write down facts that were important to the families. Bowden would absorb the info the way U.S. presidents do their daily briefings. Families didn't stand a chance. They'd be amazed at how much Bowden seemed to know about them. There was something else: he'd give the mothers of the recruits photos and sign them, "Love you." Mothers would swoon over seeing the intimate note.

In approximately his first thirty recruiting seasons, Bowden

signed sixty high school All-Americans. There were the handful
of big names like Ron Simmons, who arrived at Florida State in
1977, which were the core of Bowden's recruits, but there were
many others, players like Paul Piurowski, who were equally vital.
In 1979, Piurowski had 123 tackles and six sacks on a Florida State
team that went 11–0.

"The biggest thing that swayed me back then was Bobby
Bowden himself," Piurowski said. "By the time Florida State was
really recruiting me heavily, my father had passed away and I was
very vulnerable to any type of a fatherly figure. Bowden just, in
a way, almost filled that void. If that's possible. A fatherly figure
was the way I looked at him. Just in his mannerisms and his ability
to communicate with my mother, and she felt very comfortable
speaking with him. When he visited the house he fit right in like
he had been friends with the family forever. That was important
to us. I had 10 kids in my family. Family is a very strong ingredient
in our life. It was almost like he was a relative we hadn't seen in a
while. We felt like we knew him at great length. Bobby Bowden
has got a great way of making you believe in yourself that you can
do more than you are capable of doing. He's got an uncanny ability
to make you think about things that you wouldn't normally."

Getting Piurowski to commit to Florida State was an indicator
of something else: Bowden wasn't going to be shy in competing
with the more successful programs either in the state or across
the country. Before Bowden arrived, the Seminoles were leak-
ing talent, and Bowden was dedicated to making the leaks stop.
Bowden went after Piurowski hard and didn't care that it seemed
as if the Seminoles were a long shot to get him since the University
of Florida and Alabama were also recruiting him. During one visit
to Florida, the Gator coaches went to Piurowski's hotel room and
the small group started watching game film. Then they told Piurowski: we're not leaving this room until you commit to us. "How
much money do you have set aside for hotel expenses?" Piurowski
responded. "Because we're going to be here for at least four years."

Bowden was even able to beat out his mentor, Bear Bryant, for
Piurowski's services. Bryant made the trip to Piurowski's home,

which was particularly memorable for Piurowski's mother. "As he walked in he took his infamous houndstooth hat off and threw it towards the back of the sofa," Piurowski remembered. "My mother must of thought it was Moses dropping the Tablets as she made her best attempt to catch the fallen crown before it broke into pieces. In a voice that seemed like it came from a burning bush we heard 'Oh, just leave it lay . . .' To this day my mother and I can't remember if anything else was said during the appearance and vision of the Bear." But it wasn't Bryant who closed the deal for Alabama, but Bowden for Florida State.

Bowden viewed Piurowski as one of his first more versatile athletes. "I'm not saying he had this blazing speed," Bowden explains, "but I always believed he could play almost any dadgum position on the field." Bowden tested this theory early on. Bowden recruited Piurowski as a safety, but after just a few days of practice the staff moved him to linebacker. Piurowski had no idea how to play linebacker and struggled in drills. One of the defensive coaches got so frustrated with Piurowski's inability to properly execute the drill he blasted Piurowski as uncoachable and made it clear that Piurowski might soon be an ex-linebacker at Florida State. Piurowski was crushed and considered quitting, but his family, mainly his mother, wouldn't allow it. She told him to keep fighting. "I knew we were hard on him," Bowden says, "but he needed that. The talent was there but he needed to pick up his intensity, you know?" Piurowski was so insulted by being tagged as uncoachable he decided to prove the staff wrong. He would finish his career as one of the most coachable—and talented—players Florida State has ever seen. (Four years after being blasted by the assistant as uncoachable, Piurowski would see that coach again. "I'm flagging a cab after the Orange Bowl and the door opens with coach sitting inside," he remembered. "I get in and asked him if he remembered telling me fours years ago that I would never play for him? He said he did and that was a sign of a good coach. Which I replied, 'No, that was a sign of a full house.' Thank God for the wisdom of moms!" A full house meant it was Piurowski's mother who taught him about perseverance, not the coach.) The man who was almost booted off the team would end up a professional football player and was later inducted into the Florida State Hall of Fame.

Some players met Bowden and were instantly enthralled; Bowden didn't even need to use his power of persuasion. After Bobby Butler's Atlantic High School football team in Delray Beach, Florida, lost by a single point in the state title game, he met with Bowden early the next morning, at eight, on an unofficial visit. Butler was so impressed after the brief meeting he excitedly told his mother Bowden was his coach. "Slow down," she told her son, "you can't make a decision that quick."

There was something else that aided in Butler's decision. Before meeting with Bowden and the Florida State staff, Butler visited Michigan State. On the day of Butler's visit to the Spartans, he failed to bring a jacket and the temperature was a wind-chilled 20 degrees below zero. Butler was elected to Florida State's Hall of Fame in 1987 and had a productive NFL career.

While Bowden was shrewd in evaluating the talent he had, and down home in his recruiting, there's also no question that he got lucky. In Bowden's second year, 1977, he sent Louie Richardson, a fifth-year defensive tackle, to the scout team. A player that far into his college career being on the scout team was akin to Barry Bonds being demoted to the minor leagues. Richardson was despondent, but he continued to drill hard in practice. Bowden didn't feel Richardson had the ability to play on the Division I level but was forced to use Richardson in that 1977 season due to a series of devastating injuries at the position. Richardson entered the starting lineup and never left. After his college career, he became a fifth-round NFL draft pick. The episode demonstrated that Bowden's talent evaluations were not always perfect.

What remained nearly flawless was Bowden's work ethic. The year he was hired, Bowden, who'd become an expert at fund-raising while at his lower-profile coaching stops, decided to begin touring Florida cities to raise interest and desperately needed funds for the program. There were off-season booster meetings with alumni across the state, which included golf in the morning and a banquet in the evening. The problem was no one cared. The initial numbers of fans and boosters who showed up were so small that Bowden was stunned; just a few in Miami, eleven in Orlando (the group met at a golf course), and a handful in Tampa. Actually, Bowden wasn't just stunned, he was embarrassed. Indeed, there was more fan interest at some of the much smaller schools where he coached. (Decades later, Bowden's booster club travels would take him to numerous cities across Florida in front of thousands of Seminole fans and boosters. The trips would become a staple of Bowden's relationship with the Florida State fans.)

In 1976, Bowden's first season at Florida State, the team selected four captains: Joe Camps, Jimmy Black, Rudy Thomas, and Jeff Leggett. Camps had the unique distinction of playing for three different coaches at Florida State: Larry Jones, Darrell Mudra, and Bowden. Camps was entrenched, but Bowden's first team was in flux. By August, just nineteen days away from their season opener against Memphis, two key players were ruled ineligible. Leon Bright faced academic troubles, and Mike Shumann was arrested on drug charges. That was not such good news, particularly since Memphis was proving better than people knew. They had just upset Mississippi the week before.

The team that opened on September 11 was not overflowing with All-Americans. Two freshmen started at wide receiver, the offensive line was undersized, and the defense was slow. They lost to Memphis 21–12. Still, Bowden remained encouraged. He told the media after the contest: "I know one thing. FSU players didn't quit tonight like some people thought they would." He wouldn't feel similarly in the next game against Miami at the Orange Bowl. The Seminoles were utterly obliterated, 47–0. At one point in the game, Florida State was stuffed at Miami's 1-yard line on fourth down. In the ensuing offensive series, the Hurricanes drove 99 yards in eleven plays. A stunned Bowden faced the media and made one of the first of what would become many succinct, honest, and entertaining postgame remarks about his team.

"It's gonna take longer than I thought," he said.

. . . .

It wouldn't get better the following week. The Seminoles played
the fourth-ranked Oklahoma Sooners, led by someone who would
later become almost as well known in college football as Bowden.
Barry Switzer and Bowden were radically different. Switzer was a
bootlegger's son with more than an ounce of rascal in him, while
Bowden was the son of a banker with a virtuous heart. Still, Switzer was gracious to Bowden, praising his team as scrappy. That was
true, but they were also extremely young, and Bowden made the
decision to start five freshmen against the dangerous and highly
ranked Sooners. The decision didn't come back to haunt Bowden.
Before 71,184 people in Norman the Seminoles lost 24–9. But in
some ways, it was a win, since Florida State was expected to lose by
far more points.

Following the Oklahoma loss, the Seminoles beat Kansas State,
20–10. Then came one of the bigger wins against thirteenth-
ranked Boston College, 28–9. After years of apathy, fan support
was slowly growing; when the team's charter flight from Boston
landed, about three in the morning, several hundred cheering fans
greeted the team.

There was interest but it remained tempered. Bowden remembers how in his first season he received ten tickets to football games
as part of his financial compensation package. The Seminoles had
been so bad for so long that Bowden had a difficult time giving the
tickets away to friends. Few people wanted them. Once, he managed
to give away eight tickets but couldn't give away the final two so he
left the two tickets on the windshield of his car and went to get a
haircut. When Bowden returned to his car, the tickets were still
there. He literally couldn't give away tickets to Florida State games.

Despite the still significant lack of overall interest in the program, media members and fans started to signal that the Boston
College win meant Florida State was back. But Bowden knew only
one thing would signal the team was really back. "It ain't turned
around until we beat the Gators," Bowden explained.

That was it. Beating Florida. If the Seminoles could win that one game, the season would be a success. Bowden slowly started to open up the offense as quarterback Jimmy Black matured, and against Florida the Seminoles played their most up-tempo game of the season. Black was brilliant. When the pass protection broke down, he'd simply scramble. The loss of Black to a concussion with seven minutes remaining didn't stop Florida State from continuing to move the ball. His replacement, Jimmy Jordan, kept the offense running. In winning 33–26 Florida State amassed 28 first downs, 507 yards of offense, and 320 passing yards. More important, the victory stopped Florida State's losing skid to the Gators and allowed the Seminoles to establish an in-state recruiting foothold. Bowden could go to the state's talent and tell them: we can finally compete with the Gators.

The remainder of Bowden's first season was solid though not spectacular and full of the highs and lows one would expect from a formerly distressed program with a new coach. The Seminoles fell to Clemson in what Bowden would call "the most uninspiring [loss] I've seen in a long time." In a show of toughness against the University of Southern Mississippi, the Seminoles scored three fourth-quarter touchdowns in a breathtaking comeback to win by a field goal. "I don't know how they won that dadgum game," Bowden said afterward about his players.

Bowden wondered how they even found the field in the following game against North Texas State. A soft, heavy snow fell on the field and the school didn't remove it. By game time there was four inches of snow on the field, circulated by a stiff wind of 15 mph. Many of the sideline markers were buried. Bowden still wanted his team to have fun despite the miserable conditions. "And don't any of you freeze," he told the team, "because I don't know how I'd explain it to your mommas and daddies."

On one fourth-and-short play, the game officials told Bowden they thought the Seminoles failed to get the first down. "What do you mean 'you think'?" Bowden asked one official.

"We can't see the yard line," the official told Bowden, "we'll have to dig to find it."

"Then dig," Bowden said.

Most of the Florida State players had little or no experience playing in those kind of conditions, but they made the best of the moment. Pregame snowball fights erupted, and several players made snow angels. The coaches weren't so jolly. They worried how the cold would affect the team, and some on the staff scrambled for thermal underwear for the players. Florida State was chilled, but the Seminoles were still victorious, 21–20. "We just turned it into something like a street game," Florida State's Jimmy Black told reporters afterward, "really wild, laughing, sliding around, having fun." On the bus ride back to the airport the team started singing Christmas carols.

(The Seminoles were surprisingly proficient at adapting to cold elements. In the 1983 Peach Bowl, the team was stunned by wind chill temperatures below zero. So the trainers went to a local store and purchased the largest-sized panty hose they could find. One player's father went out and purchased batting gloves for the offensive line.)

Florida State finished the year 5–6. But the program had grown exponentially in a short period. They'd beaten Florida. Finally. Bowden had built a top-notch staff. Soon after that season there were fewer penalties and missed assignments thanks to a higher level of discipline. Bowden's offense was clicking. Before Bowden, in three previous decades of football, no play from scrimmage for the Seminoles went over 90 yards. In Florida State's last three games, there were four.

Resources and donations from alumni began to increase. The facilities started to grow (albeit very modestly), and things like the food the players ate improved in quality. Meanwhile, Bowden pressed his players to be meticulous. In film study, Bowden would point to a missed tackle and then show the end result, which was often a big gain or touchdown. He'd stress the basics repeatedly, to the point that players started to believe what he said. "Bobby was big on the fundamentals," says Henshaw. "You could see over the years in those early days that belief slowly take hold." Next year the Seminoles went 10–2.

His coaching style was also crystallizing. Bowden was extraordinarily tough and just as fair. Bobby was running his notoriously strenuous mat drills, which he'd conducted for practically his entire coaching career and were becoming infamous at Florida State, as part of his belief. The softer side of the coach would show at times too. In 1977, wide receiver Phil Williams arrived for camp and became so homesick he left abruptly after one week following numerous drops in practice. Williams would later regret the decision after enrolling at Georgia Southern and wrote Bowden an emotional letter asking to return. Bowden responded in a letter to Williams just three days later. "You know, if you'd stayed, you would have a good chance to be playing already," Bowden wrote. "But I understand how those things work out. I'd love to have you back in January, getting ready for next season." Williams rejoined the Seminoles and became one of the better receivers in school history.

Seminole fans were starting to be sold as much as the players, though there was still some headway to make. For Florida State's final game of Bowden's first season, against VPI, a rain-soaked victory, just 16,148 people showed. It would be one of the last times there was a lack of interest in Florida State football—particularly after Bowden was able to grab the most important player of his early years.

In early 1977, Florida State named a new school president, Bernie Sliger, who was viewed as a tenacious supporter of the football program. Noting the opportunity to welcome the new university president, Bowden sent Sliger a note. "You won the big one!" he wrote in part. Sliger sent back a succinct response: "Luke 10:37." Sliger later explained the reference to Luke's Gospel; a man showed mercy, and Jesus told his followers to "go forth and do the same." Bowden would oblige. In January 1977, the *Tallahassee Democrat* ran a story about the highly sought after recruit Ron Simmons. The story quickly came to the point. "Ronald Simmons, perhaps the most sought after high school football player in Georgia, has signed a letter of intent with Florida State." The *Democrat*'s columnist Bill McGrotha wrote soon afterward: "The signing of Ron Simmons has the appearance of being one of the Seminoles' biggest football licks of all time."

Simmons's effect was immediate. Physically Simmons was likely five to ten years ahead of his time. At that point there were few defensive linemen with his speed and agility in college football. In Bowden's second season opener, this one on September 10 against Southern Mississippi, Simmons blocked a punt that was scooped up and returned for a touchdown. In another game, in the final quarter, he tallied four sacks. Simmons's rise paralleled that of Bowden's Seminoles. Positive press began to trickle in. Both AP and UPI ranked Florida State fifteenth in the nation. It had been years since the Seminoles were in the top twenty, and Simmons meanwhile was named national lineman of the week by AP and *Sports Illustrated*. Bowden remarked to the media that "Simmons is turning the program around." It was of course more complicated than that, but Simmons was one of Bowden's early anchors the way a Warrick Dunn or Derrick Brooks became later. Bowden made a bowl game in his second season, and, more important, he beat Florida again that year. One of the main reasons for both successes was Simmons.

The only thing that slowed Simmons were injuries, and there was just once when he disappointed Bowden. Simmons was no longer part of the team when he was accused, along with a group of other men, of buying stolen televisions. It was one of the first huge scandals of Bowden's Florida State career. Simmons's college playing days may have been over, but that didn't stop Bowden from being upset with his former player's judgment. Simmons pleaded no contest to aiding grand retail theft and was put on one year's probation.

In 1977, the Seminoles played Texas Tech in the Tangerine Bowl. Both Bowden and Red Raiders coach Steve Sloan had demonstrated at various points that season their senses of humor. After Texas Tech barely beat a winless Texas Christian University, Sloan laughed: "I've always said the sun doesn't shine on the same dog every day. But we sure as heck didn't expect a near-total eclipse." Bowden described his five-foot-eight, 155-pound Florida State kicker Dave Cappelen in a way only Bowden could. "When we stick him in the whirlpool, we gotta have a lifeguard there."

Sloan and Bowden generally liked each other. They traveled to a Baptist church to speak and became friends, but that didn't prevent Bowden from throttling his new buddy. In the bowl game, the Seminoles destroyed Texas Tech 40–17; the victory capped off Florida State's first 10-win season. The game was important for another reason. Bowden was wired for the television broadcast and viewers got to hear Bowden say his various dadgums and see the Seminoles throwing the football all over the field. It was positive press for the program. At that time there weren't several million bowl games on the television, so a significant number of people across the country outside of Tallahassee got their first exposure to Bowden and the Seminoles. One person watching was a sixteen-year-old high school quarterback named Mark Richt who would later become Bowden's offensive coordinator.

That bowl win is often lost among Bowden's achievements and championships, yet it shouldn't be. It was the school's first bowl game in six years and the school's first bowl victory in over a decade. "We could have gone to a garbage-dump plant and we would have been excited," said Shumann.

After that year, Bowden was given a new multiyear contract extension through 1982. As Bobby's career rose dramatically, another Bowden was struggling on and off the field.

CHAPTER NINE

TERRY

The phone rang in late 1983, and when Bobby heard Terry on the other line, he knew instantly something was different. Terry sounded tired and there was the palpable tone of regret in his voice. It was as distinct as Terry's normally excitable demeanor. Terry started in the family profession in 1983 when he took the large leap of faith and accepted a head coaching position at a tiny school in West Virginia called Salem College. Although Bobby never wanted his sons to enter the profession, he told them if they did, starting at a smaller school was ideal. "That's what I did," Bobby says now. "It was invaluable. You learned how to do all the small things that make you appreciate coaching." Terry agreed and took the job. In many ways Terry duplicated his father's early coaching years. Salem's budget was tiny. Terry drove the team bus and even cut the grass on the playing field.

That first year Terry started 0–7, and some of the losses weren't close. That's when he contacted his dad.

"I'm not sure how long I am for coaching," Terry told his father.

Bobby gave his son The Speech. "I'm joking calling it The Speech," Bobby says, "but he needed to know that these things happen to all coaches. They happened to me."

Bobby spoke to Terry as a father and a coach. There was the usual Bobby blend of straight talk and comforting words. "You go through four phases when you coach a team that struggles," Bobby told Terry. "You lose badly. Then you start to close the gap and you lose close. Then you win close and then you start to beat teams and win big."

Bobby of course turned out to be correct. Terry won his final three games in 1983 and went 8–3 his next two seasons at Salem. He was on his way.

There was just one problem. Terry didn't know it, but the coaching profession would soon eat him alive.

The anxious moments for Terry didn't stop in 1983. Some fifteen years after that conversation with Bobby, a series of physical pains would follow. They were attacks, really, frequent and unpredictable. This time, for nearly six months, his insides felt as if they had been ripped apart. He couldn't get out of bed in the morning. The times he could, it was nearly impossible to get dressed, so he would crawl back under the covers. Following a chaotic departure as coach at Auburn in 1998, Terry had the wind knocked out of him by intense panic attacks that completely changed his personality. He was physically and psychologically beaten, but he showed a brave face to many in the public, even members of the Bowden clan. For some time, only his wife, Shryl, and his mother knew the truth. "I can't talk to my brothers about this now," he told his wife after the initial symptoms hit. "They won't understand." C'mon, Terry, they might say. Get up off the bed. What the heck are you doing? Stop being weak. Even after landing a new job as an analyst for ABC Sports, the attacks continued. The night before flying to New York for a college football show, he would be unable to pack. He was at times afraid to cross the street and suddenly would have a fear of crowds. There were moments when he lost that gift of gab (a phrase Ann uses to describe Terry) and couldn't complete a full sentence or carry a prolonged thought.

In typical Bowden fashion, once Terry made everyone aware of the extent of his problem, the family was there. There were no wisecracks or snide remarks, just support. Terry was prescribed Paxil, an antidepressant used for, among other things, the treatment of panic and social anxiety disorders. The attacks soon calmed.

"My problem," Terry says, "was just holding in too much of the Auburn stuff."

The Auburn stuff. Few have been burned by the ugly side of the business as badly as Terry was. Although Bobby had his own horrific West Virginia experience, even that doesn't compare to the Auburn stuff. There's almost nothing in the history of big-time coaching that does.

It wasn't supposed to happen that way. Everything Terry did, every aspect of his life, every breath he took, was aimed toward becoming a football coach. In high school, when other kids took extra shop classes, he chose public speaking because he knew coaches spent a lot of time in front of people. He studied accounting at West Virginia, knowing even then that football was big business. On the day he received that head coaching position at Salem, he attended Bear Bryant's funeral with Bobby. While there, he saw a headline in the local newspaper about Bryant's 323 wins. At twenty-six, the youngest college head football coach in the nation at the time, Terry made a pact with himself: "I'm going to get 324." He did the math in his head, figuring out how many games he needed to win over how many years. He told people close to him he was going to get that record. He was going to get Bryant. That was how bold his ambitions were.

None of the Bowdens, not even Bobby, possessed the kind of drive that Terry did. He was driven to succeed at everything. After football season in high school, he'd drop thirty to forty pounds to make the wrestling team. "Terry is very bright," Ann says. "He was the smallest of our guys, so he always felt like he had to over-achieve to make himself come up to the guys when he was little. From kindergarten on up, excelled in every class. Graduated from West Virginia magna cum laude. Went to law school, was a graduate assistant and worked a job at night. Terry is a lot like me because he has the gift of gab."

Yet Terry's almost primordial urge to be the best might be the reason his first marriage failed. "It cost him his marriage because he was young and didn't realize that he had to spread himself a little better with his spouse and all," Ann says.

Ann was so valuable to Bobby because Bobby *could* spread himself thin and she'd be there to fill in the gaps. Terry didn't have that type of marriage (few people do). Although he paid the price with a divorce, his work ethic led to a rapid rise in the coaching profession, far faster than even his father's. At Salem, he won the school's second conference title in eighty years. In 1987, Terry's first year at Samford, he led a 9–1 team that had won six games over the previous three years. Two years later, he took the school from Division III to I-AA. When he was hired December 17, 1992, by Auburn, he was ready to be a major college coach.

His days at Auburn, a traditional southern football powerhouse, actually started off well. University president William V. Muse called Terry the perfect choice to lead Auburn football into the twenty-first century. And Terry didn't wait long to prove the president correct. In his first year, he went 11–0. By the second season, Terry had won twenty consecutive games, and became the first college coach in fifty years to win his hundredth career game by his fortieth birthday. Though some players did not initially know what to make of the man who spoke so fast—they sometimes needed Terry to repeat himself—Terry quickly earned their admiration. Terry was liked for being friendly and charming and was respected for his unwillingness to skirt NCAA rules. Terry would not cheat—not only because it was morally wrong but also because it would've been dangerous. Auburn was on NCAA probation when he took over and another scandal could seriously injure the program.

To the media, Terry was a blessing. He was extremely cooperative with local or national press, once gracing the cover of *American Football Quarterly* magazine, which noted that *GQ* listed Terry as one of the fifty most influential people in sports. Beat reporters hung out at his home for cookouts. There were few secrets; it is part of the Bowden genetic string to be candid. He was always talkative, always good copy, and he was always within hailing range of his dad. Terry in fact kept reminders of his father throughout his office. On the wall were two photos, one with Terry as Samford coach in 1988, holding a clipboard, and the other of Bobby, in the same pose, in the same job (though the college was called Howard when Bobby coached there) some twenty-five years earlier. It all seemed so perfect, a sort of familial symmetry. The situation at Auburn was far from ideal, however. What followed was one of the most convoluted, most bizarre chapters in the history of college coaching.

Terry Bowden was not the right man to coach Auburn. At least that's what some powerful boosters and other Tigers supporters firmly believed. They saw him as merely a stopgap between Pat Dye, the legendary coach who had stepped down before Terry's arrival, and another at the time unknown coach who was supposed to lead Auburn after Terry was fired. Terry is a warp-speed-talking lawyer who studied at Oxford and didn't fit the mold of what those boosters believed an Auburn coach should be. Ironically, they wanted a Bear Bryant clone—genteel to the public and ruthless behind the scenes. "They wanted to move Terry out and get a slow-talking, good old boy in there," one former athletic department official who requested anonymity said. That official and another, who both worked during Terry's tenure at Auburn, requested anonymity for fear of retribution from Auburn boosters and current athletic department officials. Both former officials say they don't have any ill feelings toward current or former Auburn employees or people close to the athletic program.

When Terry began winning and no death penalty sanctions were delivered from the NCAA probation that Terry inherited, critics could do little to hurt him and they certainly couldn't then push for his ouster. Yet that didn't mean influential men surrounding the Auburn program were powerless or that Terry didn't anger them. Athletic department officials and boosters did not object when Terry inserted into his contract a clause that he would receive 50 percent of all football video sales. When the team went 11–0 and eighty thousand videos were sold, Terry made $500,000.

Late into his second year, Terry developed his own clothing line—
Bowden Sportswear—and there was criticism that he'd become
as much self-promoter as coach. The former officials said that as
much as they liked Terry, they believed he had become too cocky
and wasn't putting in the hours he once did. And, they said, Terry
told anyone who would listen that he was running a clean program unlike past coaching regimes, which irritated longtime loyal
Auburn fans. What Terry said was mostly true, but he didn't need
to shove the news down their throats.

Although Terry is a different person now, there's little question
during those Auburn times that he'd gotten somewhat arrogant.
He was feeling bulletproof. When star wide receiver Robert Baker
was accused of trafficking cocaine, Terry stood by him. "You just
don't understand the background some of these kids come from,"
Bowden told people in the athletic department. "What would you
do if he sold drugs to your kids?" one of the former Auburn officials asked. Terry just shook his head and walked away, the former
official said. Terry's defense of Baker was strikingly similar to the
ones launched by his father, and the arguments have strong merits.
But Terry had the same vulnerabilities as his father when it came to
troubled players. The two Bowden men share the inability to dif-
ferentiate between the players who truly deserved second chances
and the con artists who were simply playing them for suckers.

After winning his first twenty games, Terry's record by 1998
had slipped to 26–12–1, which included a 5–11 record against
SEC giants Alabama, Georgia, Florida, LSU, and Tennessee. The
people who did not want Terry at Auburn believed he was slipping.
And one of those people was Bobby Lowder, a powerful Auburn
trustee who, according to the *New York Times*, was appointed by
Governor George Wallace after Wallace received a substantial donation from Lowder just prior to his appointment. The Jerry Jones
of college football, Lowder's influence on the football program has
been well chronicled by news organizations and Auburn faculty
but tolerated because of his deep pockets and power. The *New York
Times* reported that Lowder gave a onetime donation of $4.2 mil-
lion to the athletic department. In 2003, he donated $600,000 to

Auburn's booster club; and at one point, six of the fourteen Auburn trustees have had financial ties to Lowder or his business, The Colonial BancGroup, Inc., according to the *New York Times*. In 2001, the president of the university, William Muse, resigned, saying the board of trustees made it impossible to do his job. Tired of what that newspaper described as "obsessive meddling," the Auburn faculty in December 2004 overwhelmingly passed a resolution asking Lowder to resign over conflict of interest issues. (Nevertheless, Lowder still serves on the board of trustees and, in fact, has recently been involved in questions about the Reverend Chette Williams, director of the Fellowship of Christian Athletes and chaplain to the football team and their secrets, who receives payment from a nonprofit in his name, to which Lowder donates liberally.) An Auburn history professor wrote in an op-ed piece for the *Decatur (Ala.) Daily:* "Whether because of his obsession with football—as some critics claim—or his determination to recast the school according to his own inaccurate and myopic understanding of what a land grant university ought to be, Lowder has used his political influence to pack the board with trustees beholden to him."

Even though Lowder had recruited Pat Dye, who later resigned when the NCAA discovered several rules violations, Terry's relationship with Lowder began amicably. "The benevolent dictator," Terry once called Lowder. He initially returned Lowder's phone inquiries about the latest developments at practice and complied with his desire to hear from Terry on a regular basis, the former athletic department officials said. But things changed when Lowder demanded Terry not speak to certain high-ranking university officials about football matters, one of the former officials said, a request the coach ignored. Lowder also wanted a say in who Terry could hire and fire, the former official said. Terry again refused to comply, and he soon stopped the practice updates and daily communication.

Suddenly, Terry could not have the simplest things done. His request for $25,000 to upgrade the weight room was declined by the administration, according to the former official. Two former officials said there were far more curious, if not insidious, things alleged against Terry by the university. However, since the officials declined to go on the record for this book, those allegations could not be discussed for fear of legal action against the author and publisher.

An indication of some of the sordid allegations that surrounded Auburn at the time came to light in 2003 when taped comments by Terry two years before were published in the *Opelika-Auburn News*. The Associated Press also reviewed the tape. The columnist who taped the comments was quoted in an AP story as saying the two-year lag time was because there had been concern that Terry's remarks were off the record. Terry had e-mailed him, encouraging their publication, the AP story said. On the tape, Terry says that before he arrived at Auburn, players were paid thousands of dollars and a monthly stipend in a pay-for-play scheme allegedly set up by boosters. An Auburn player, in 1990, admitted he had been paid. Terry says on the tape that he stopped the payments. Auburn released a statement at that time saying Terry had repeatedly certified to the NCAA from 1993 through 1998 that "he was unaware of any unreported violations of NCAA rules by anyone involved with the Auburn football program," the AP story said. The AP reported that university president Muse stated in transcripts for a book that he'd heard the pay-for-play rumors, but that they were never verified by the NCAA. The transcripts were for a book by an Auburn history professor and made public by the university archives, the AP story said. Muse was quoted as saying that he'd heard of "a network of alums who each had agreed to provide X number of dollars per year for a particular player and that there was a [notebook] that listed all of these individuals and the amounts they paid. There was even a rumor that, at one time, [an assistant coach] was the keeper of the book. In fact, after he left Auburn, Terry even told me that. But that has never been verified. In the NCAA investigation, there didn't turn out to be any evidence of that." The *Opelika-Auburn News* published Terry's taped comments after Muse's remarks were made public.

It wasn't a surprise to Terry that after his Auburn team started 1–5 in the fall of 1998, the athletic director, David Housel, informed him he would have to win four of his final five games to keep his

job, according to the *Atlanta Journal-Constitution*. After the ridicu-
lous ultimatum, Terry once again spoke with Bobby, and Bobby
had one piece of advice for his son. "I think you should leave now,"
he said. Terry then remembered what his father had told him so
many times about how the football business can be an unforgiving
one. "Dad," he said, "you were right about how nasty this business
can get."

Some people close to the Bowden family often remark that
Terry is like his father. Tommy is actually more like Bobby, and
Terry more resembles Ann, particularly in several ways. Ann
believes in fighting injustice even if it comes at great personal
cost. So when Auburn boosters and others began to engineer his
exit, Terry's genetics took over. To him, his response was almost
preordained. He was going to fight back. He would be outspoken
in defending himself against his critics. In late October, Terry was
headed to his weekly radio call-in show, *Tiger Talk*. Minutes before
the broadcast, he told one athletic department employee that if he
was going out, he was going out "guns blazing," the former official
said. Terry stopped by his office and then proceeded to do *Tiger
Talk*. But instead of the expected fireworks, Terry had a drastic
change of heart and on the air was complacent and docile, both
former officials said. The following day, October 23, 1998—and
midway through the season—Terry resigned. What happened in
those last hours? Was Terry about to be fired? "Coach Bowden was
not forced to resign, period," Housel told the *Journal-Constitution*
at the time. "There are a lot of factors and personalities in college
athletics. Any time you're dealing with a complex situation . . .
you can look to a lot of simple answers but they're usually wrong."
One of the former athletic department officials did believe a
firing was imminent. "Terry heard the thunder in the distance
and panicked," the former official said. In response to accusations
that he had engineered Terry's exit, Auburn trustee Lowder told
the *Journal-Constitution* in October 1998: "I did not plan, I did not
plot, I did not conspire or encourage Terry Bowden to resign."

As for Terry, he explained that, in the end, there is nothing
strange about what happened. Though he refused to go into spe-

cifics, Terry did say: "The bottom line is it was just best for me to leave. There is no mystery. I just decided it was time to go." There's little question that what helped Terry's decision was that according to ESPN, Terry received a severance package that included a $620,00 payment, an $860,000 lakeside home, and two cars. In the South, when it comes to football, as one Auburn source told the author, football powerhouses "don't ever fuck around. Even when they fire people they don't fuck around."

It concluded one of the most dramatic—and rapid—ascensions and subsequent falls ever for a major college coach. It took just five years at Auburn to have his coaching career practically annihilated.

The author met with Terry several times, including once at his home. In another meeting, while enjoying a glass of iced tea in a restaurant near his Orlando house, Terry was his usual friendly self, just like his dad. And also like it is with his father, if you underestimate Terry's intelligence, it is at your own risk. Terry was as opinionated as ever about what happened at Auburn. "Here I am at Auburn, and Pat Dye was bitter because he was paid to leave," he says. "My defensive coordinator was bitter because the same guy that promised him the job hired me. It was a dynamic that wasn't going to work. And then there were a lot of other things behind the scenes that I was trying to work with and correct. I went through such a traumatic experience at Auburn where I won so much but then found out really there were a lot of people there that didn't want you there for ulterior reasons. It was a real political problem at Auburn. The more I knew, the more they ripped me and tried to kill the messenger. Ultimately, I was probably hired at Auburn to get through the NCAA investigation. We had a bunch of success, but no one was happy with how this thing worked out. I didn't survive the backroom politics." Terry declined to publicly discuss Auburn in detail for fear that officials close to the program would seek retribution against him by seeking to have him fired from his various media positions. His severance package also forbids such discussions.

Asked if Auburn prevented him from getting subsequent coaching positions, Terry responds, "I don't think Auburn has the ability to blackball me [for another college job]."

One of the things Terry remembers most about his Auburn experience is something Bobby told him soon after it was all over. "This is a test," his father said, "not the definitive moment in your career." Everything changed for Terry after Auburn. Beating Bryant was no longer his dream, because it now meant catching his father. "Chasing Dad ain't fun," he told friends. "So I'm going to go do something Dad's never done before." It was television work. It was analysis. It was radio. It was blogging and writing online. As Terry likes to say, he went different. He had found his antidote to the addiction of coaching, and it was being a media star.

At least, that's what he thought. In 2009, at a press conference in Florence, Alabama, Terry was introduced as head coach of the University of North Alabama. Terry's fifty-two years old, and it turns out his professed passion for television masked his true beliefs.

One of the first things Terry did upon getting the job was to contact his brother Jeff, who had been released by father Bobby several years before. Terry wanted Jeff to coach the receivers, and Jeff agreed.

"I was trying to decide which direction I wanted to go in after leaving Florida State," Jeff said. "Terry advised me to get totally away from football for a year and enjoy being with my family. That's what I did, and I really enjoyed spending that time being a parent and doing things with my kids. It gave me a chance to recharge my batteries."

So in one fell swoop two Bowden men were back in coaching. To the family, it wasn't a shock. "They say you don't go into football because you love it," Terry says, "you do it because you can't live without it."

CHAPTER TEN

"TAKE FIVE MINUTES A DAY TO HATE FSU"

I n the late 1970s, Florida State expanded its Doak Campbell Stadium by some sixty-five hundred seats. Finally, fans wanted to come to games; there was genuine excitement about Florida State football again. Bobby and Ann sensed the change and wanted to develop something that was missing: a tradition. Bill Durham, a 1965 graduate, had long wanted to use his Appaloosa horses and honor Chief Osceola of the Seminole tribe. No one in the administration warmed to that idea until the Bowdens came along. After discussions with university officials, Bobby sent a rider atop a spotted horse onto the field on September 16, 1978, against Oklahoma in the second game of the season. There were 40,338 people present for the game that witnessed the horse, Renegade, careen around the field before the contest, and its rider plant a flaming spear in the end zone. Florida State fans loved it, but the move would later become highly controversial. Renegade's riders dressed in American Indian attire and had painted faces. Some of the riders themselves were American Indians from a nearby tribe, but that didn't stop the criticism. Some saw the crowd pleaser as offensive, something that played on stereotypes of American Indians as savages. Stereotypical or not, as of 2009, a rider still circles the field before games, whipping crowds into a frenzy with the burgundy and gold spear.

It would be unfair to say that Florida State was becoming arrogant as their success increased. They weren't good enough to do that, and Bowden knew it. Some of his players, however, were getting slightly frisky. In the final game of 1978, FSU beat Florida again. Before the game, Seminole players slathered war paint on their faces. Some were infuriated over the words of a Gator assistant who told several newspapers the Gators had more talented players than Florida State. Bowden and his staff of course made sure the quote was distributed heavily throughout the Florida State locker room. Players vowed revenge. Florida State player Willie Jones told the *Tallahassee Democrat* after the game: "Those things he said about us helped fire us up." What also helped Florida State was how they controlled Florida wide receiver Cris Collinsworth, who was held to four catches.

The toughness of that Seminole defense was becoming apparent. In the 1978 opener against Syracuse, the Orange were celebrating "Bill Hurley Day," which was named after the Syracuse quarterback who was also playing that afternoon. In the game, on one play near the sideline, the Seminoles applied a clean but hard hit that broke Hurley's ribs. He was knocked out not just for the game but for the entire season.

The players weren't cocky, but they were enjoying the attention. The national media began to praise Bowden and his burgeoning program. In December 1978, Mike DelNagro wrote in *Sports Illustrated* about how the 8–3 Seminoles deserved a bowl bid despite not receiving one and noted how a coach named Bobby Bowden was changing the school's fortune. "What Bowden has done is build a big-play defense around spectacular 6'4" End Willie Jones and Guard Ron Simmons and match it with a wide-open passing offense that can score from the parking lot. Last year the Seminoles passed for 2,466 yards and 18 touchdowns. This season they let fly for 2,749 yards and 23 touchdowns," DelNagro wrote.

Bowden won that season despite breaking one of football's oldest rules: If you have two quarterbacks you have none—rotating two throwers in and out of the lineup causes more chaos than productivity. Bowden decided to test the axiom with Wally Woodham and

Jimmy Jordan. Jordan had the stronger arm with the slightly faster release; Woodham was more accurate and took better control of the huddle. "That's the sort of thing I needed to do then because our talent was getting a lot better, but it still wasn't top-notch," Bowden explains now. "We just did whatever we had to do."

Bowden made sure alternating between the two men didn't lead to bitterness or a rivalry run amok, but his efforts were mostly unnecessary. The Seminoles were a tight group playing in a different time. Back then, the me-first jerks and wasn't-me thugs weren't overpopulating sports like they do now. It's not that there weren't any criminals in college football then; of course there were. It's just that it was a simpler time. Even the pranks were more wholesome then. On one road trip during the team's undefeated year in 1979, Paul Piurowski phoned the hotel room of one of the Florida State freshmen when the team was in Blacksburg, Virginia. Piurowski concocted a genius story telling the gullible first-year player that a writer for *Sports Illustrated* wanted to do a lengthy spread on him. The player was seriously excited, but Piurowski quickly explained that the writer's deadline was extreme and he needed to speak with the player immediately in the hotel lobby. When the freshman protested that he'd just emerged from the shower, Piurowski pleaded that he just wrap a towel around his waist and scamper to the lobby immediately to meet with the writer. The freshman obliged and waited in the lobby as players and team personnel walked by and gawked at the unusual scene.

As for Woodham and Jordan, they genuinely liked each other; and the rotating quarterback system was doing little to change that notion. They were both members of the same fraternity and even went duck hunting before the Florida game. There was also history there. They'd both grown up in Tallahassee and played football for Leon High School just a few blocks from Florida State's campus. It was Jordan, the following year as Florida State won its first eight games, who appeared on the cover of *Sports Illustrated* as the magazine asked which of several unbeaten teams was actually the best in the nation. That the Seminoles received this sort of media attention was shocking even to Bowden. No one, not him, not even the rosiest of rose-colored-glasses-wearing fans, thought the re-building of Florida State would occur this rapidly. Toward the end of the 1979 season, Florida State climbed to fifth in both the AP and UPI polls—just four spots behind top-ranked Alabama. On November 17, minutes before Florida State was to play Memphis State, the school was told they'd been picked to play in the Orange Bowl. Word spread quickly throughout Tallahassee. Hundreds of cars across the city blasted their horns, and fans who had gathered in the stadium tossed oranges onto the field.

After beating Florida, the Seminoles were undefeated for the season and played Switzer's Oklahoma in the Orange Bowl. Before the game Bowden and Switzer chatted on the field. "You've done a great job with that program," Switzer told Bowden. The Seminoles were crushed by the Sooners, 24–7, proving that though Florida State was good, they still weren't one of the elite. The same defense that stopped the Gators gave up 447 yards of offense. Florida State had no answer for quarterback J. C. Watts (who would become a Florida State nemesis and later a Republican congressman) and Heisman Trophy–winner Billy Sims (that game was Sims's last at Oklahoma), who combined for 291 rushing yards. Switzer's de-fense spent practically the entire game playing with at least one extra defensive back daring Florida State to run the football. They simply couldn't. Bowden was hurt by the loss, but it was clear the Seminoles had come far under him. They were receiving national attention, something Bowden was readily using in recruiting, and the Seminoles had come a long way from 1947 when the school was the Florida State College for Women. Between then and Bowden taking the helm of Florida State in 1976, the school had won a disappointing 150 of its 293 games—a hair more than half. After four years, Bowden had gone 34–12, including 11–0 in the 1979 regular season. The loss to Oklahoma did make Bowden rethink his pass-heavy offense but not too much. Bowden used the forward pass as a crutch. He'd gone from not believing in the passing of-fense in college to relying on it almost entirely. That strategy hurt him against the Sooners. "Oklahoma was so successful stopping us with a fifth defensive back, we made running the ball our goal in 1980," Bowden told *Sports Illustrated* at the time.

If Florida State remained shell-shocked the following year after its demolition at the hands of the Sooners, it didn't show. They opened the 1980 season with a 16–0 shutout of LSU. Several games later Florida State played Nebraska for the first time in school history. The Seminoles were traveling to Lincoln, the Cornhuskers were third ranked in the nation, and Nebraska was averaging 566 yards of offense a game. "I wasn't sure what to expect, to be honest," says Bowden now. "I thought we had a good chance to win, but Nebraska was playing so well realistically I wasn't so sure if we weren't going to get beat by 50." What Bowden did was emphasize the aspects of the game he could control. Nebraska was going to run the ball and probably run it well. Therefore, in practice that week, Bowden emphasized special teams and defending against the Cornhusker passing offense. During the game, Florida State kicked four field goals, and the Seminole defense caused massive disruption along Nebraska's offensive line whenever the Cornhuskers attempted to pass, generating multiple turnovers. The Seminoles' toughness so impressed the Nebraska crowd that thousands of fans gave the Florida State players a standing ovation as they walked off the field.

Florida State's 18–14 win is one of the more underrated victories in Bowden's Seminole career, but it was arguably the most important. The school beat a powerful and imposing team on the road. More than any of the other games in Bowden's career up to that moment, that victory made the nation recognize that Florida State was no fluke. If no one knew it then, they did the following week. Pittsburgh, with quarterback Dan Marino, had replaced Nebraska in the polls as the third-ranked team. The Seminoles won 36–22, again using special teams and defense (kicker Bill Capece made five field goals). By the middle of the season, Florida State was ranked third by the AP, the highest ranking in school history. On November 15, Bowden accepted an Orange Bowl bid and learned soon afterward he'd face Switzer and Oklahoma for a second time.

Before the 1981 Orange Bowl, the Seminoles still needed to play one last regular-season game against their rival Florida. Bowden knew that wouldn't be an easy game, but he still did something highly unusual. Bowden spoke to Florida State's players about the team's chances at playing for a national title. The chances were slim, but the opportunity was there. The Seminoles were ranked third in the country behind top-ranked Georgia and No. 2 Notre Dame. Both schools had committed to the Sugar Bowl, and it was a near certainty that one would end up as the champion. There was one hitch that favored the Seminoles. The Irish, like the Seminoles, had one game remaining on their regular-season schedule. It was against USC in Los Angeles, where Notre Dame hadn't won since 1966.

Publicly Bowden stuck to the script that the Gators were the most important team on the schedule, not Oklahoma, and certainly not any potential championship game. Privately was a different matter. "I throw that national championship thing at my players anytime I think their ears need to hear it," he told a *Sports Illustrated* writer. "Maybe I'll pop it off again right before the kick-off against Florida."

In team meetings Bowden spoke to the players about dreams and how they had a chance to make history. "You're doing things now no one thought Florida State would ever accomplish," Bowden told his club, "and we're not done yet." Bowden was daring his players to think big, which was new territory at Florida State.

It's understandable that Bowden was confident. He was actually starting to inject raw talent into the Florida State bloodstream, and this allowed more flexibility for game planning and strategy. He shifted slightly from his pass-happy machinations and made several personnel adjustments. First, Bowden moved his wide receiver Sam Piatt to running back; Piatt ran for 188 yards against Memphis State, and in ten games overall rushed for 954 yards. Bowden implemented a plan that utilized the speed and agility of quarterback Rick Stockstill, who despite his last name was more mobile than Woodham or Jordan. Bowden allowed his throwers to check off at the line of scrimmage and Stockstill took advantage of the freedom about half the time. If a fierce pass rush came up the middle, Stockstill simply scampered to the outside avoiding the rush.

In the 1980 season, Bowden did perhaps his best work on defense. His need to improve defensive play actually started near the halfway point of the 1978 season when Florida State lost 27–21 to Houston, 55–27 to Mississippi State, and 7–3 to the University of Pittsburgh. Then as badly as the season began, it turned around marvelously. Florida State would go on to win fifteen consecutive contests as Bowden inspired a group of younger players not to lose faith. When that young group gelled into a mature one—with Bowden acting as the backbone—they were dangerous. With the exception of Simmons, and possibly Piurowski, the names weren't easily recognizable across the country (and historically). They were names like defensive backs Keith Jones, Bobby Butler, and Monk Bonasorte and linebacker Reggie Herring. They were talented but not yet on college football's radar, though that was changing slowly, particularly as Piurowski made more than 100 tackles and Simmons started shattering spleens. By 1980, five of Florida State's wins came after the defense held opponents to eight first downs or fewer.

As FSU entered the important game against Florida, only Nebraska ran the ball successfully and the Cornhuskers' 201 rushing yards was 177 below their average. The Seminoles allowed 85 points before the Gator game, the fewest in college football. Bowden was becoming known as an offensive guru, but he was often quick to point to any reporter with a pad and pen the progression of his defense. "People think we're a team that throws the ball, doesn't play defense and just tries to outscore you," Bowden told *Sports Illustrated*. "They're wrong. General Neyland, Earl Blaik, Red Sanders, Bear Bryant—those guys would be proud of Florida State. They always preached defense and kicking. There might be teams with a bit more offense or defense than we have, or one that outkicks us. But nobody does all those things as well as we do." He had a point. The Seminoles toward the end of 1980 were first in scoring defense, sixth in scoring, and first in net punting.

As the magazine noted, Florida State had hit these numbers with a schedule that included some tough victories against fourth-ranked Pittsburgh and ninth-ranked Nebraska. Their lone defeat was a one-point loss to twentieth-ranked Miami, a fierce rival. In that game the Seminoles were missing their first- and second-string centers, leading to five fumbled snaps.

Any shot at a national title rested on the Florida game, and the Gators were in typical arrogant form. Florida was a drastically inferior team, yet they behaved as if they were the ones ranked among the top teams in the country instead of Florida State. Bowden made sure each Gator jab was well chronicled in the locker room. He posted neatly and prominently a quote from Florida tight end Chris Faulkner. "We think about Florida State all year long," he told the media. "Coach [Charley] Pell tells us to take five minutes a day to hate FSU." Bowden, who'd thought he'd seen just about everything, was slightly amused when he was told that Gator coaches hung a stone brick with three holes in it on a wall in the Gators' eating area. Directly near the brick was a sign in bold letters that read: THIS IS A FLORIDA STATE BOWLING BALL. Bowden made certain the team knew that the Gator program was mocking their intellect. "They're calling you stupid," he told the team prior to the game.

As 53,772 people packed into Doak Campbell Stadium (the team's largest crowd to that point), the Gators continued to taunt their in-state rivals. Bowden sent out his three captains for the coin toss: the Gators sent their entire team. It was a cheap but apparently effective ploy. Bell had the Gators ready to play and believing they could ruin Florida State's season. The first half of the game was proof as Florida jumped to a 13–3 lead, mainly by confusing the Seminoles. The Gators normally used an offense where the pass was the focal point. Instead of four wide receivers, Florida used a number of two tight end formations and ran right at that proud Florida State defense. Because Bowden has a sense of humor, he might've thought to himself at the end of that first half: "Maybe the Gators were right about the brick bowling ball." Instead he instituted a sense of calm among the players. He didn't scream or become apoplectic. He asked a very simple question. "Right now they want it more than we do," Bowden told the players. "We're down 13–3. But we were behind 14–3 at Nebraska and came back. Is this worth fighting for?"

The Seminoles fought back. One of Bowden's weapons was wide receiver Hardis Johnson, who had a touchdown in the second half and finished the game with seven catches for 107 yards. Bowden was particularly happy for Johnson's eruption. He'd recruited Johnson and Anthony Carter in-state and dreamed of having the fastest receiving duo in the country. One reality interrupted that fantasy. Carter decided to attend the University of Michigan, where he helped make Wolverine quarterback John Wangler a Heisman candidate. Still, Bowden had Johnson and he destroyed the Gators (the following season he'd become an academic casualty). By the time the fourth quarter began, the Seminole players started holding up four fingers as did many in the Doak Campbell crowd. It signaled the fourth quarter, and Florida State had yet to give up any points in that final period all year. They didn't against the Gators either.

Both UPI and AP ranked Florida State second in the country, and there was a general sense of shock in Tallahassee at just how quickly things had changed. "Once we started winning Bobby was practically the mayor of Tallahassee and the president of Florida State," remembered assistant coach Henshaw.

It was a stark contrast for Bowden from his recent time at West Virginia where he was hanged in effigy. The only thing being hanged at Florida State was the ghost of past failures. Bowden actually noticed his change in stature when he got off the bus at the Orange Bowl earlier in the year before playing Miami. When he emerged, a group of fans approached and asked for autographs. One stood out. "Will you sign this for my mom?" the fan asked. Bowden obliged, continuing to sign as many autographs as he could, and not looking up. Then Bowden noticed the same voice. "Will you sign one for my sister?" the man asked. He kept going down his family tree. Bowden finally looked up and put the man's face in his memory bank. Bowden thought he had to be a collector and would later sell the merchandise. His beliefs were later con-

firmed when Bowden was next in Miami and the same man again
went down the laundry list of alleged family members.

Entering the 1981 Orange Bowl game against Oklahoma—the
second straight time the Sooners and Florida State would meet—
the Seminoles were understandably giddy and a tad Gatorlike. They
were cocky, maybe even mouthy. Florida State was flying high, but
they didn't have the bowl pedigree of the Sooners, who were ap-
pearing in their fourth consecutive Orange Bowl. That didn't stop
a chirpy Seminole team. "There is a little more confidence this
year and definitely less awe," guard Lee Adams said. "Oklahoma
seems more human to us now. Being human, they can be beat."
The quote quickly appeared in the Oklahoma locker room. Adams
might've been correct, but he was better off not making the statement publicly. The problem was, no one on the Florida State staff
was telling the players to tone down the rhetoric; in fact, Bowden
was adding more. "I think we've got a lot better chance to beat
Oklahoma than we did last year," he told the media.

The Seminoles initially backed up their brashness when the
game began. Again Florida State was able to mostly wreck Oklahoma's ground game with physical play along the defensive line,
and the first half score was a shockingly low 7–3. In the second
half, the Sooners won in a way some didn't envision. Watts hit
several big pass plays, including what turned out to be a game-
winning two-point conversion. The Seminoles lost, 18–17. As disappointing as the loss was, Bowden knew the program had reached
new heights. A fat check from the Orange Bowl to Florida State for
$1,288,573.87 also helped to cushion the blow of the loss.

Bowden was happy, but he soon grew concerned. He was worried about Florida State's schedule. Bowden was earning the reputation as a fearless coach who would play anytime, anywhere. That
wasn't any truer than during the 1981–82 season, when between
September 19 and the end of October, Florida State played Nebraska, Ohio State, Notre Dame, Pittsburgh, and LSU—all on the
road. The schedule was composed before Bowden's arrival at Florida State, but he had actually come to embrace it as an opportunity
to put the Seminoles in the national spotlight.

The schedule was so brutal it became the talk of the sport (which is exactly what Bowden had hoped). Bud Wilkinson, the former Oklahoma coach turned broadcaster, called Bowden's schedule "the most difficult in the history of college football." *Sports Illustrated* predicted a losing season, and *Street and Smith's* stated the Seminoles would lose the first four of those games. A writer for the latter wrote: "How tough is Florida State's road schedule? Well, when you consider the Seminoles play—in succession . . . their road trips could turn out to be a reminiscence of the Bataan Death March." As someone who well knows war history, Bowden chuckled at the colorful hyperbole. Bowden joked that the Tallahassee airport was Florida State's home field and labeled the October road horror show "Oktoberfest."

Although Bowden could joke about the road schedule, there was a reason for the suicide gallop through October hell. The athletic department needed the money, and the financial guarantees offered by the opposing schools were enticing and would keep the program from financial ruin. It was a risky, calculating decision that initially seemed like it would seriously backfire. Nebraska beat the Seminoles 34–14 after a six-second, two-touchdown third-quarter flurry by the Cornhuskers. Nebraska accumulated 472 rushing yards—the most ever gained on the ground against the Seminoles. Bowden fared much better in the following game against Ohio State. The Buckeyes were the seventh-ranked team in the nation, and the Seminoles had never faced a Big Ten team before. The Buckeyes featured a strong-armed thrower named Art Schlichter; although Ohio State's athletic department was suspicious of the now infamous gambling habits of their quarterback, there wasn't enough evidence to remove Schlichter from the team. He'd produced a solid college career, finishing among the top ten vote getters in the Heisman race in his final three years at Ohio State. Schlichter played well against the Seminoles, completing 31 of 52 passes for 458 yards; but it was the Florida State offense that truly dominated and was key in winning the game 36–21. Back in Tallahassee celebrations erupted across the city, and fans later eagerly awaited the polls. AP ranked the Seminoles twentieth after the win against the Buckeyes. Bowden's hot streak continued the following week with a victory against Notre Dame.

The schedule that was supposed to wreck Florida State's soul instead produced two wins against several of the most prestigious football programs in the country. Bowden couldn't control his elation following the win at Notre Dame. "To me personally," he told the press, "it was the biggest win I'll ever have." On the plane ride home players barely sat in their seats, instead choosing to celebrate almost the entire way back to Florida. "Everybody was hugging everybody," said wide receiver Phil Williams. "I don't even remember what Coach Bowden said to us I was so psyched. Everybody was going crazy." The *Tampa Tribune*'s Tom McEwen wrote of the win: "In tradition, Notre Dame is years of Hail Mary's ahead of Florida State. Physically, Florida State cannot make Notre Dame's weight. And it could be expected the ball would bounce more favorably for the Irish in Notre Dame Stadium, and Saturday, it did. But those are the only propositions Notre Dame had going for it in the awaited, closely watched meeting with the upstart Seminoles of FSU. The Florida State Seminoles were better offensively when they had to be Saturday, better defensively when they had to be Saturday, better at the punting game when that was needed, as good at the place-kicking game, and better prepared and coached."

The win was impressive, but Pittsburgh quickly ended the euphoria with a 42–14 crushing of the Seminoles. Few teams knew how to stop Marino, and the Seminoles weren't any different. Marino tossed three touchdown passes, and the Pittsburgh offense produced over 500 yards. It was a momentary slap in the face.

Bowden had to regroup what was a depressed Florida State following the drubbing by Pittsburgh. One last tough game remained in the gauntlet. Florida State traveled to 3–4 LSU on October 25, 1981, and although the Tigers weren't the quality of Pittsburgh, winning a game there was still a rough task. To make things worse, injuries forced Bowden to start two freshmen at running back. It didn't seem to matter. The Seminoles jumped to a 17–0 first-quarter lead, and though there were 74,816 people jammed into Tiger Stadium, the entire place was eerily quiet. Another of Bowden's freshmen, Cedric Jones, took a third-quarter reverse and went 70 yards for the touchdown and 38–14 lead, which is how the game ended. It was Bowden's third consecutive victory over LSU.

More important, the brutal road schedule was finished, with Florida State winning three of the five games. "Personally, I have been dreading this road trip for four or five years," Bowden told the press then. "Every year I'd think it's three years away, two years away then one. It was a countdown. I was afraid we'd get destroyed but it didn't happen." That potentially disastrous period remains not just one of the best coaching jobs Bowden has accomplished. It's also one of the best coaching jobs done by any coach across college football's history. Things didn't get too much easier. Now FSU had to face the Hurricanes. The University of Miami, ranked tenth in the nation, had just upset top-ranked Penn State. The Hurricanes were also extremely angry. Several days before the game, the NCAA announced Miami would be put on probation for a number of violations, including improper financial aid, extra benefits, and out-of-season practice. Miami received two years' probation and a one-year bowl ban. "At first the team was hurt," Miami coach Howard Schnellenberger said. "Then it turned into frustration and anger. Now we're not thinking of anything but Florida State."

Florida State also had a great deal to contemplate. They were facing quarterback Jim Kelly, who completed 22 of 41 passes for 273 yards and one score to beat the Seminoles. Miami won the game and not solely because Kelly efficiently ran the Hurricanes' pro-style offense. Florida State's fatigue was also a factor. The brutal schedule was taking its toll; the Seminoles were beginning to tire and ache. The following week against undefeated Southern Mississippi, with five bowl scouts in the press box, the Seminoles were badly beaten, 58–14. Southern Mississippi scored on its first seven possessions, and Florida State was powerless to do anything about it. Bowden was aware of his team's fatigue, and the week of the final game of the season, against Florida, he cut practice back by more than an hour each day. The Seminoles still lost to the

Gators, and a Peach Bowl bid slipped through Bowden's fingers.

The 1980s were a pivotal time for Bowden. They were bountiful and beautiful, ugly and wondrous. Bowden elevated the Seminoles from practically nothing to a nationally recognized power. The Florida Gators would remain a stiff rival, but the 1980s also saw the Seminoles' feud with Miami elevated to a national scale. The Hurricanes would ruin Bowden's national championship opportunities on several different occasions in the decade, grounding the Seminoles temporarily before they became the team of the 1990s.

The 1980s were tumultuous for another reason: Bowden almost left Florida State. The decade also saw the coaching career of another Bowden son start in earnest. And later end in controversy.

CHAPTER ELEVEN

TOMMY

I t hung in front of the library. The library, of all places. Tommy remembers seeing it on his way to church one day in 1974. He was twenty, playing wide receiver for the Mountaineers under his father. Bobby was struggling as attacks from West Virginia fans came fast and vicious. He was being hanged in effigy seemingly regularly, and this day was no different. But the library?

Tommy was infuriated. His first instinct was to run up to the dummy and tear the monstrosity down. Then something strange happened. His sense of humor kicked in. He's joked about how his father sometimes mixes up the children's names. "Sometimes he calls me Terry," Tommy once said. "Sometimes he calls me Steve. Now when he calls me Ginger, that's taking it too far."

So that unyielding sense of humor activated like someone had flipped a switch. So did his memory. He could almost hear his father whispering to him. *This is all part of it. This is what coaches go through, son. If you don't want to see it, stay out of the business.*

So Tommy laughed. He saw his very own father hung in effigy in front of a library and he laughed. He looked at the dummy and thought *Eh, y'all didn't make him fat enough. Throw some more stuffing in there . . . he's got a little more belly than what you all made him.*

Bobby began to see the difference between Terry and Tommy in the late 1950s. He tells the story of when he was coaching at Howard College, which had just built a new swimming pool, and none of the kids had ever gone off a high dive. One day, he took Tommy and Terry to the pool. Tommy was six years old, and Terry was about five. Since Tommy was older, Bobby wanted him to jump first. Tommy slowly walked out, like he was on a plank about to leap into a tank full of sharks, and didn't want to jump.

"Let's go, son, jump," Bobby yelled from below. "It won't hurt."

Tommy wouldn't move. He was frozen. Then Bobby had an idea.

"I'll give you a quarter if you do it," Bobby says.

He jumped.

Terry didn't need to be offered money. Not long after Tommy's splash, Terry had climbed up and dived in, not once thinking about what was below. He was fearless.

The Bowden children always were also hierarchical. They respected the chain of command, the natural order of things. In high school, Tommy was a senior and Terry a sophomore. Terry always tried to compete with Tommy, but, being older, Tommy always won. In the coaching hierarchy, Tommy was supposed to be a head coach, followed by Terry. So when Tommy, Auburn's offensive coordinator under Pat Dye, was passed over for Terry, then the head coach at Samford, it was awkward. Terry kept his brother on the staff, but neither was initially comfortable.

Still, Tommy stayed true to the bloodline. No Bowden has ever turned on another, and he was not about to make history. Tommy buried his frustrations in his job. He became almost legendary for his work ethic. If the light was on late in the football offices, it had to be Tommy.

Tommy was important to the football operation in another way. His dazzling sense of humor is one of the reasons why Auburn players liked him and played hard for him. But Tommy did learn things from his little brother. And he was proud of how Terry never showed panic or fear during staff meetings, even as things turned bad. When Tommy took the Tulane head coaching position in 1997, Terry lost a confidant and a trusted voice, but Tommy could begin to build his own career.

As Terry had done at Auburn, and as Bobby had done at West

Virginia and Florida State, Tommy produced a classic Bowden turnaround. Tulane was 5–28 in the previous three seasons; Tommy took the Green Wave to 7–4, then 11–0 (making him the third Bowden to lead an undefeated regular-season team). At Tulane, Tommy's name is still revered; he played a large role in putting Tulane football back in the national spotlight. Tommy worked with offensive coordinator Rich Rodriguez, who would later become the head coach of West Virginia and then Michigan, to implement the now famous spread offense, which is the trendiest offense in the genre. Rodriguez knew the Bowden family well, long before pairing with Tommy. He used to be a regular at the Bowden football camp in Alabama, and he and Tommy became close buddies.

Rodriguez was to Tommy what Richt was to Bobby. The offense proved extremely powerful, and many coaches stole aspects of the offense for their own use, spreading it quickly throughout football. Tommy also had some talent to deploy there. His quarterback was Shaun King, who became the first passer to reach 3,000 yards in the air and 500 yards rushing in the same season. King's quarterback rating for that season was an obscene 183.3.

The Clemson head coaching position followed closely on the heels of the wondrous Tulane experience, and Bobby's prediction that history would repeat itself with his coaching sons was accurate. Like his father, like Terry, and later like brother Jeff, Tommy would go through The Bowden Process. Tommy heard the ugly calls for his firing as Clemson struggled under his leadership and faced ridiculously überobsessed fans. Once, when he returned from a trip at 4 A.M., fans were waiting in a car in front of his house. They only left after noticing Tommy had a police escort. "I wondered," he says, "what they would have done if the police weren't there."

And like Bobby upon offensive coordinator Richt's departure, there was a precipitous fall in offensive production once Tommy and Rodriguez parted ways. Rodriguez followed Tommy to Clemson and then left after the 2000 season for the Mountaineers. Clemson, since he departed, has lost at least four games each year.

Entering the 2008 season, Clemson's offensive rankings were 31st, 71st, 30th, 110th, 53rd, 15th, and 52nd. Gone was the offensive magic. Although it's true that Tommy suffered from the same two coaching diseases as his father—parity and stratospheric expectations—both men found it difficult to find a new offensive niche once their respective coordinators left town.

Tommy is bold and strong and one of the fittest of the Bowden children. As an adult, he ran a marathon. As a child, though, he could be somewhat introverted. He approached new things cautiously, whether it was gently testing the temperature in the pool with a hand or foot, or learning to drive a car. His mother taught him how to drive, and when he was first behind the wheel, Tommy drove 15 mph and gripped the wheel tightly. Tommy isn't shy anymore. He is opinionated on many different topics, and while Terry is more like his mother, Tommy is almost exactly like his father. "Tommy is like Bobby in that when he can't deal with anything, he makes a joke about it," Ann says.

Tommy might even be more fundamental in his religious beliefs than Bobby. He once changed churches at Clemson because he didn't believe the preacher's message was conservative enough. "It is not my job to convert people to my faith," Tommy says, "but it is also not my job to shy away from it." He's ultraconservative in other ways. A close colleague once described his political beliefs as "way to the right of Attila the Hun."

"Tommy is very much like his father," said Ann. "Conservative . . . straight arrow, very fundamentalist, almost to a fault . . . I don't think he's learned you can catch more flies with honey than you can with vinegar. He tells it like he thinks it is."

Bobby was tough on all the children, particularly his coaching sons, but he might have been toughest on Tommy. All of the Bowden men played football under Bobby, and he was harder on them partly because he didn't want the public's perception to be that they got breaks because they were Bowden men. Tommy experienced this on several different occasions, once in high school. As a senior, Tommy was a good receiver, but so was another player on the team. Bobby gave the other player, not his son, the scholarship

to West Virginia. Tommy was crushed, but he understood. Ironically, after one year, the player Bowden provided a scholarship quit
the team and Tommy, endowed with that brilliant Bowden work
ethic, continued on, outlasting him, eventually forcing his father
to give Tommy the scholarship he'd earlier denied him.

"Out of all my kids, Tommy was the most disciplined," Bowden
says. "The best kid. If you said, be in at eight o'clock, he was in at
eight o'clock. Terry, now, would come in when he got good and
ready. I would say, 'Terry, I'm gonna whip you.' And he would say,
'Hurry up and get it over with, because I'm getting ready to head
out again.'"

Tommy, though, would occasionally wade into the unfamiliar
waters of emotional expression. After Tommy married his wife,
Linda, he wrote a beautiful note to Bobby and Ann. The note
started "Dear Mother and Daddy":

> Now that I am married and on my way, I wanted to write
> a small thank-you note. I have wanted to do this for a long
> time, but when you get right down to it, it always seems hard
> to find the right words. Plus, that mushy stuff just isn't in the
> Bowden blood.
>
> I can't begin to list the things I'd like to thank you for,
> so I'll make it brief. You raised me like I would like to raise
> my children. Anytime I speak or give my testimony, I'll tell
> how much you have influenced my life. I'm just now realiz-
> ing how important it is to be raised by Christian parents in a
> Christian environment.
>
> It is because of y'all that I pray that God will remain
> the Lord of my life and be instrumental in establishing the
> guidelines of my life-style. (Not bad for a P.E. major.)
>
> I love y'all more than anything in my life. I hope I can
> make you as proud of me as I am of y'all. May God bless you.

The letter was typical Tommy: it possessed talk of faith, humor,
and the appropriate number and usage of the word *y'all*.

One thing about The Bowden Process: many times, it finishes

with a Hollywood happy ending. It is because each family member, in his or her own way, is remarkably resilient. After calls for Tommy's firing from Clemson during the 2003 season, he beat Bobby-coached FSU and then Duke. At the end of the year, Clemson traveled to rival South Carolina and pummeled the Gamecocks 63–17. Tommy received a contract extension through 2010. From the way he returned so strongly from the brink, there was no doubt he was a Bowden.

But it's not easy, particularly when it's Bowden versus Bowden. Bobby once stated that when his team used to play Tommy, it wasn't fun "because one of us has to lose. He loses, it could cost him his job. I lose, it's not going to make me too popular." As for his sons joining him in the profession, "It hasn't done anything to draw us apart. It's probably made us tighter because we all have been through crises. Do you wish you didn't get scrutinized the way we do? Yeah, you do wish it, but forget it, that's part of it. They pay us coaches big bucks. I always taught my sons that it's part of the game. If you cannot handle it, get out."

Bowden versus Bowden on the field was a lifetime in the making. Tommy knew he was going to be a coach, and the coach he wanted to be was his father. He admired his integrity and work ethic. Tommy was different somewhat from Terry. Tommy never truly wanted to coach against his father while Terry, at least initially, salivated at the opportunity. Though he would later, as the Samford coach, lose interest in playing Bobby, Terry constantly asked his dad for a game, pestering his father for years. There was no advantage for Bobby and nothing to lose for Terry, since such a game would have been a major risk to Bobby. Terry asked Bobby so many times that Bobby finally wrote Terry a note in March 1991 asking his son to stop being a know-it-all smarty. "You have become too obsessed with playing a I-A school," Bobby wrote to Terry. "For a football coach working to go to the top, your top priority should be winning games. Your priority is not to balance the budget and pay the bills . . . quit telling other coaches and athletic directors what they need to do with their programs . . . I don't want you to come off as a know-it-all." Bobby's message was simple: get victories and don't worry about politics or taking on the larger programs.

The competition in the family wasn't just between father and sons; it was also brother to brother. In 1995, Terry's Auburn Tigers had lost a close game to LSU, and he desperately searched for a way to inject more vibrancy into the offense, so he reached out to his coaching family. He called Jeff, who was coaching under Bobby with the Seminoles. Florida State was using a four wide receiver set better than almost any team in the nation, and Terry wanted to utilize certain elements of it. So he phoned Jeff and asked him to send some Florida State offensive game film. Jeff called him back. "You want our film," he said to Terry, "you've got to send me yours."

Terry was incredulous. Jeff continued, not caring if he committed some sort of family faux pas. "I just want to study it," Jeff continued. "You know we may have to play y'all in a bowl game. If you're looking at our film, I want to look at yours."

"I'll send you the dadgum film," Terry said. Then he hung up on his brother.

Disagreements between family members are about as constant as sunrises, but the Bowden men, despite being in such a high-profile profession, actually seem to have fewer fights—both large and small—than the average family. This disagreement between Terry and Jeff was about as animated as things got once the men entered adulthood, and this one did get slightly heated. Terry, thinking his brother was acting like an ass, decided to give it right back to him. He told one of his graduate assistants to take the Auburn film and make the three-hour drive to Tallahassee and hand-deliver it to Jeff. The package was indeed given to Jeff, who was on the Seminole practice field at the time. He got the film but he also got something else. It was a sarcastic note from Terry. "I hope this helps y'all with Clemson," Terry wrote.

There were no film shenanigans between Tommy and Bobby. Well, at least mostly there weren't. Before Bowden against Bowden, Bobby remembers, they shared plays and game film. That stopped when Tommy took over at Clemson and they started battling each other.

To Tommy, playing his father seemed more like a headache, yet he wasn't going to just roll over for dad. When Bobby and Tommy met on the field in 1999, it was the first father-and-son coaching matchup in major college football history, and the entire family was dedicated to not letting it be a divisive thing. Before that first game, and afterward, the two men declared that at the family outings to the beach in Panama City all football talk was off-limits. "We stopped talking because it got too tense," Bobby says.

Before the game, Ann posed for ESPN, wearing a sweater that was divided in half: one portion being Florida State colors and the other being Tommy's Clemson orange. The Seminoles won the game, 17–14, and after the game, Tommy and Bobby hugged near midfield. It was a tender moment that both men say they'll never forget.

The problem in the rivalry came later. As Tommy and Bobby continued to meet in the years to come, the games became more pressure filled as the Clemson program increased in relevancy and ability and Tommy became not just a nuisance to his father but a serious threat. Several years after their initial contest, in 2003, the then third-ranked Seminoles were utterly shocked by Tommy's Clemson team, 26–10, at Memorial Stadium. The loss destroyed Bobby's national title hopes; worse, there were some Florida State boosters who privately wondered if Bowden had purposely lost the game to help his son gain even more traction at Clemson. Such a task would be all but impossible even if Bobby wanted to do it, but such speculation showed a lack of understanding about how competitive the Bowden coaching men were. Not only that, every action Bobby took with his children when it came to football was tough love. He never wanted them to have it easy so they'd avoid such nepotism charges. Bobby wasn't going to change his ways no matter how much he loved Tommy.

"I never want to lose to anybody," Bobby said. Then he laughed. "I especially don't want to lose to my sons. I don't want them to have braggin' rights."

. . . .

Bobby predicted in an interview months before the 2008 season that he felt Tommy would struggle that year. It was instinct in part honed by decades in the sport, but Bowden also knew that Clemson's rough ACC schedule was destined to take its toll. "This could be a tough year for Tommy," said Bowden. "He needs to be strong because the heat might come again. He's got some pretty high expectations for him." Bobby told reporters at ACC media day a short time afterward: "It's going to be a strain. If he doesn't meet expectations, there's going to be a lot of criticism. But I'd rather have that than not get there or at least get a shot at it. He's got to learn how to live with that. The advantage Tommy has and Terry had [when coaching at Auburn] is they were around me all their lives. They've seen me kicked around, they've seen me hung in effigy, they've seen me nearly fired. That's the way this game is."

Bobby was more than prophetic. In 2008, Tommy's Clemson team started off 3–3. In the season opener, the Tigers were blasted 34–10 by Alabama in a game that knocked the Tigers out of the top twenty-five. It was a humiliating loss, but Tommy refused to sit back and feel sorry for himself or the program. Tommy next did something he's done many times before. He picked up the telephone and called his father for advice on how to rebound from a brutal defeat. It's a topic his dad knew a thing or two about. Bobby believed the Tigers became too entangled in the talk that Clemson was a contender for a national title and overlooked the Crimson Tide. In addition, Alabama was far better than anyone knew. Nick Saban's team would later win at Arkansas and Georgia by a combined score of 90–44 and reach the SEC title game.

Then, in what was not an atypical Tommy move—or a Bowden one for that matter—Tommy called Saban to pick his brain for weaknesses about the Clemson team. Tommy is proud but not overly prideful. In his mind, you get advice from anyone who's smart—even if they just whipped you. He made a similar phone call several years ago to Michigan's Lloyd Carr while searching for a way to generate turnovers. "I'm not one to have enough pride where I've got all the answers," he told Saban. "You had six months to study me. What did you see?"

The *Sporting News* wrote of Tommy in October 2008: "A preseason top 10 ranking in your 12th season as a team's head coach is a death sentence only if you're the sort of coach who enjoys toying with failure, running the program perilously close to the gaping edge of a losing season, and then dramatically rallying in WWE style from a sure submission hold. If this sounds like your football program, then you are a Clemson fan, and your coach, Tommy Bowden, has once again run his career status at Clemson to 'Mostly Dead.'"

Tommy was taking massive criticism. Again. Like father, like son. Again. It didn't look good for him and there was some concern within the Bowden family that another son would experience the coldness of a firing line. "Well, all I can tell you is, don't count my boy short," said a smiling Bobby. "Don't ever count him short."

Bowden's prediction that Tommy would face a brutal season was accurate. In October 2008, Tommy resigned. In actuality, his dismissal was imminent, and he quit before they fired him. "We talked of course," Bobby said. "It was sad, but he was definitely prepared for something like this." Then Bowden chuckled. "He should be prepared. He watched me. Tommy's ready for life after football. He's prepared for it. He always thinks long term. He never let football be his God." The only positive for Tommy was that the financial settlement he received from Clemson was substantial— a $3.5 million buyout with payments in twice-yearly installments through December 2014.

Months after his resignation, Tommy was able to laugh at his situation. He joked: "Life right now is *Judge Judy, Judge Mathis, Judge Joe Brown, Judge Christina, Judge Karen, Judge Hatchett, Divorce Court, People's Court.* That's what life is like. I do a lot of speaking. I still do a lot of church speaking on Sundays. I did some work with ESPN."

When Bobby was asked about witnessing now all of his coaching sons being fired, he replied, "You wish it didn't happen but that's this life. We picked this life. You have to live with the great parts of it and the bad parts of it." Those words have been Bowden's mantra for decades, but perhaps no one in football history has lived this ideal like Bobby. There's great sadness when one of the sons is forced to depart the business, but there's also a matter-of-fact aspect to how the Bowdens deal with this sort of news. It's not apathy by any means. It's just that they've lived with college football's vicissitudes so long their minds and bodies have adapted to the heartbreak.

Tommy's dismissal was thick with ironies. When Florida State and Clemson faced each other in November 2008, it was the first time in a decade that Bobby wasn't coaching against Tommy. Dabo Swinney, Clemson's wide receivers coach at the time, was selected to replace Tommy. Swinney was familiar with the Bowden clan; Swinney's mother had attended Birmingham's Woodlawn High School just as Bowden did, and several years before he took over the Clemson job, Swinney and Bobby met on a 2005 recruiting trip to Tallahassee. While Swinney and Tommy were in town, Tommy surprised his colleague by saying, "Let's go see Daddy." They walked into Bobby's office where he was watching film in preparation for the Gator Bowl and talked football.

Rumors flew before the Florida State and Clemson game that maybe Tommy would leak inside information about Clemson to Bobby. The biggest emotion the Bowdens felt at that point was not revenge but relief. "It was getting where Ann, especially my wife, she just got so tired of—she can't win because she takes a lot of pride," Bowden told the media at that time. "She wants me to win, she wants Tommy to win, she wants Terry, and all of them to win. So when Tommy and I play, she can't win. And of course I didn't like it either, because I didn't like it when he beats me. And when I beat him, I feel for him. I am so happy, this is the first time in ten years I don't have to worry about Tommy being on the other side looking at me, or me looking at him."

He added, "People will think that, 'Oh well, you're going to try to beat them bad because they fired your son.' No I'm not. No I'm not. He had ten wonderful years at Clemson. He will tell anyone that. I really have no animosity toward them. Then of course Dabo Swinney, Tommy coached him at Alabama so he kind of raised him really. I like him, but I'm still going to try to beat him."

Tommy's resignation came just weeks before Bobby's seventy-ninth birthday, which was on the Saturday of the Seminoles' game against Clemson. It was Bobby's 400th game as coach of Florida State. The Seminoles won 41–27, assuring Bowden of his 32nd consecutive winning season. They were also bowl eligible for the 27th straight year, the longest such streak.

In the final moments of the contest, many of the eighty thousand fans at Bobby Bowden Field at Doak Campbell Stadium sang "Happy Birthday" to Bowden. The chorus grew louder and louder: "Happy birthday to you . . . happy birthday dear Coach Bowden."

The Wednesday before the game, Bowden was in his usual spot, up high, in a tower, watching practice. Many players and assistant coaches over the years have wondered what was Bowden seeing or thinking. That day, it seems, Bowden was thinking about his birthday and how he wasn't supposed to live this long. Bowden told the *Tallahassee Democrat*, "I was thinking up there when I was sick back in 1943 and I stayed in bed for half a year and out of school for a year, my doctor told my mother I might not live past 40. So as I approached 40 I always worried about that. And now I've nearly doubled it."

There was another irony. On December 27, 2008, with Bobby's Seminoles playing Wisconsin in the Champs Sports Bowl, Tommy took a seat in the ESPN studios and spoke about his father's Florida State team. The son was analyzing the father. Not the first time in Bowden history, but fascinating nonetheless, because Tommy was back. He spoke fast and bluntly and he didn't have to rip his father because, well, Bobby won the game.

CHAPTER TWELVE

BOBBY'S SONG

The song blared across Florida State's campus out of car windows, at tailgate parties, even inside some campus dorm rooms. Tallahassee radio played it often. At moments, the song was everywhere. It was written by singer Rod Kilbourn and was called "The Ballad of Bobby Bowden."

> *Deep in the land of sweet sunshine*
> *there lives a man and a legend*
> *He goes by the name of Bobby B.*
> *a bad, bad boy, yes indeed*
>
> *Some people call him a riverboat gambler*
> *some call him a saint*
> *But he'll beat 'em all large or small*
> *in the sun or driving rain*
>
> *Sing a song for Bobby*
> *Let his praises ring*
> *Sing a song for Bobby*
> *Long live, long live the King*
>
> *Well, I've heard of Knute Rockne*
> *and the Alabama Bear*
> *But the man with the plan*

lives in T-town, baby
And they know it everywhere

Sing a song for Bobby
Let his praises ring
Sing a song for Bobby
Long live, long live the King

Well the crybabies cry
down with the king
'Cause we ain't seen
number one yet
But this year, baby
They'll be shouting in the streets
Bobby for President!
Bobby for President!
Bobby for President!

In Tallahassee the song became popular soon after its release in 1993 as Bowden emerged as a national coaching force. But before then there was a moment, in the late 1980s, when Bowden almost didn't last until the 1990s as coach of the Seminoles. That's because the University of Alabama came calling. The Crimson Tide wanted Bowden, and he already had one foot out the door. Few people know how close the school came to having a different sort of ballad. One called "Good-bye Bobby."

"You have to understand how much that school meant to me," Bowden says now. "It was home. It was going home."

Alabama had just lost Ray Perkins, who took the gamble of leaving a sure-win program for the NFL. Swiftly following Perkins's departure, news organizations reported that the fifty-seven-year-old Bowden was the leading candidate. Bowden began hearing the buzz, and his excitement built, though there was no question he loved coaching at Florida State. Indeed, Bowden had turned down other opportunities to bolt for potentially more fertile ground. Throughout the 1980s—and beyond—Bowden's name would become a part of almost every athletic director's wish list and a few NFL general managers as well. Can you imagine Notre Dame coach Bobby Bowden? Or New Orleans Saints coach Bowden? The University of Southern California considered Bowden as well. In 1986, Bowden met with the owner of the Atlanta Falcons.

One former high-profile NFL executive said there were far more professional teams interested in Bowden than most people know. "I remember then there were a good half-dozen or more teams giving him real strong consideration for their head coaching position," said the former executive.

"The NFL liked Bowden," the executive continued, "but I'm not so certain they knew what to make of Bobby. I think in the end that's why so few teams made a serious offer to get him. The league saw Bobby as this sort of golly gee guy and country guy. They didn't realize, I think, just how smart Bobby was."

Alabama didn't care if he spoke with a twang. In 1986, the Seminoles had just overwhelmed Indiana University in the All-American Bowl before thirty thousand people in Birmingham. Bowden had been contacted by Alabama officials, but he stuck by his mantra of refusing to audition for jobs. Bowden had done enough of that. "It's not a snobbery thing," he said. "I just didn't want to try out for things. I had enough tryouts." He was unrelenting in that philosophy, even for Alabama. The notorious Alabama governor, George Wallace, phoned Bowden about the job and expressed his optimism a deal could be made. When Crimson Tide boosters called Bowden, they wanted to set up an interview between Bowden and school president Joab Thomas. "No," said Bowden. "With all due respect, if they want me, they can ask me."

And if Bowden was certain of only one thing, it was that Alabama was going to ask. It was only a matter of time.

"The Ballad of Bobby Bowden (Goes to Alabama)" turned into a true blues song. Or a hard-core country one, depending on your perspective. The only thing missing were a wrecked truck, a dying dog, and a wife walking out the door.

In a life full of glorious and painful moments, Bowden's flirtation with the Crimson Tide makes his personal top ten. One of the boosters—or it may have been Wallace, Bowden can't exactly remember—told him that school president Thomas wanted to have a meeting at the school. Bowden reiterated his only edict: no interviews. A promise was thus made to Bowden. If he met with Thomas, an offer would follow. It was a virtual certainty. Bowden was so sure he was headed to Alabama he told his family and others that it was likely the Bowdens would soon be moving to Birmingham.

Ann remembers her own feelings. She was irritated that when news broke of Bowden's possible relocation to Alabama, Florida State didn't move with urgency to keep him. Ann wanted the school to do whatever it took to make sure her husband stayed. That didn't exactly happen. In fact, the school made plans for a post-Bowden football era. In defense of the administration, they were as certain that Bowden was leaving as Bowden was. It was, after all, Alabama.

After being assured that his meeting with the Alabama president wasn't the dreaded interview, Bowden was scheduled to meet with Thomas and a small group of powerful boosters, just a day or so before the All-American Bowl game against the Hoosiers in late December 1986. Perkins's departure meant not only was the coaching position vacant, but the athletic director position was empty as well. As a response, the school organized a formidable search committee composed of former players, trustees, athletic department personnel, and even several deans.

Bowden went to the interview/noninterview with his two sons. Terry dropped his father off on the Alabama campus and then traveled to his own interview (Terry's was definitely an interview) at Samford University.

When Bowden walked into the room, he was practically expecting to be named Alabama coach-elect. Instead, something completely different occurred. The room was jammed with more than a dozen people prepared to question Bowden. It was the interview he dreaded and had been promised wasn't going to occur. Bowden remembers getting up and the president of the school basically saying, "We'll be in touch." Bowden later learned that he was anything but a lock for the job, and, in fact, the school was interviewing other candidates.

"That entire scene," Bowden said, "was truly embarrassing."

It was also infuriating. When Bowden returned to his hotel, Tommy was there. "I was in the room when he slammed the door and said, 'It's going to somebody else.'"

On the drive home, Bobby and Ann spoke about the interview. They drove six hours without once turning on the radio, so they didn't hear erroneous media reports that he'd be the next Alabama coach. When they arrived back in Tallahassee, news crews were camped out on the front lawn of their home. Bowden didn't know why they were there and initially wondered if someone in the family had died. The only thing that had died were Bowden's dreams of coaching the Tide. Bowden went into his home without offering much of a comment, and the school put out a statement immediately saying he wasn't interested in the Alabama job and had withdrawn his name from consideration.

Tommy had just been released from his offensive coordinator position at Duke after Steve Spurrier took control of the program, and both Tommy and his father figured Tommy would be on Bobby's staff. Then came the infamous interview. Ironically, although Bobby wouldn't get his dream job, Tommy would later end up at Alabama as Bill Curry's assistant. Curry stayed three years and was 26–10. Bowden told the *Lakeland Ledger* that Curry was a good coach but "he wasn't popular with the Alabama people. They wanted a redneck like me. He's an Ivy Leaguer."

How did Curry beat out an initially heavily favored Bowden? It's an interesting question, one Bowden admits to still contemplating even today. Curry had an unimpressive 34–43–4 record at Georgia Tech and had just three winning seasons in seven years. But he'd gotten Alabama's attention by beating the Crimson Tide two times in five attempts. "It's a long time ago," Alabama school president Thomas said. "The thing I remember most vividly is that Bill Curry did just a beautiful job in the interview we had and there was very, very strong support for him from the whole committee. The decision was very, very strong in favor of Curry." He added: "Bowden did not do a good job in the interview. He has implied a number of times—I've gotten feedback—that he didn't know it was supposed to be an interview, but that just wasn't true. He was told, and there were a dozen people there."

Another person in the room at the time who asked not to be identified said Bowden appeared to be "heavily distracted. Like something else was on his mind." That assessment rings true. Bowden clearly believes there wasn't supposed to be an interview, and he was visibly irritated that there was. The source also said it was the committee's understanding that Bowden was to be interviewed, though the source admits "there may have been a little misunderstanding and that misunderstanding may have been triggered by us." When asked to explain further, the individual said, "It's possible Bobby may have been a little misled by some people. Not necessarily people on the committee but others around the program." Just possible? "Maybe probable," the source said.

What happened next is a cautionary tale: first, on the dangers of a committee taking over a coaching search, and second, on the problem of a school outthinking itself. Curry lasted three seasons and then departed for Kentucky. *Departed* isn't the right word. He was practically run out of town by an angry fan base because he couldn't beat Auburn.

The Tide did win a national title under Gene Stallings, but it came at a price. The school was hit with repeated scandals and NCAA sanctions. Some of those punishments led to the forfeiture of all but one win in 1993. When Stallings left, the school went through four losing seasons and five different coaches. The Seminoles retained Bowden and their stability while Alabama went temporarily into a black hole.

Of course, Bowden's Florida State was at times no stranger to controversy or off-field issues, but it's a near certainty that the problems Alabama faced wouldn't have occurred if Bowden was the coach. There was another round of severe NCAA sanctions as well as a high-profile admission in 1999 from then coach Mike DuBose of an affair with an athletic department employee. There were also allegations that another Alabama coach, Mike Price, had been seen at a strip club. Bowden, by all accounts, has been extraordinarily loyal to his wife, and the chances of Bowden ending up in a strip club are about the same as President Barack Obama's. Most important, Bowden might have provided the Crimson Tide with decades of stability, the same stability he provided to Florida State. After Stallings, no coach stayed longer than four years; it took until 2007 and Nick Saban for Alabama to have the kind of stability at the head coaching position that approximated Bowden's. "I would assume Bowden would still be the coach," said Roger Shultz, an Alabama lineman from 1987 to 1990. "We wouldn't have had 20 coaches since then. You definitely wouldn't have had him getting in trouble out drinking in strip clubs or sleeping with his secretary. When you look back at it, absolutely it would have been a good thing. It would have been a lot different. You would love to think that all the ill wills that happened to Alabama during the last decade would never have happened."

"It's hard to go back," said Shultz. "When you look back at it, absolutely [hiring Bowden] could have been a good thing, but at the time Florida State wasn't Florida State. He was on the verge of popping things open. The whole time when Curry was here, Florida State really jumped up."

"I think I would've taken that job if it had been offered to me," Bobby says now. "As I told you before, that was my home. Alabama is the only thing that could've taken me from here. Yeah, all they had to do was make the offer."

"Imagine if Paul W. 'Bear' Bryant wasn't the only all-time winningest coach to ever walk the sidelines at the University of Alabama," wrote the *Tuscaloosa News* in 2007. "Imagine if Bill Curry never wore crimson, if Gene Stallings wasn't around to coach Alabama to the 1992 national championship, if the Crimson Tide had never endured the Mike DuBose and Mike Price scandals, if Dennis Franchione had never bolted for Texas A&M, if crippling NCAA sanctions had never been levied. Imagine no Mike Shula and, yes, even no Nick Saban. Imagine if Alabama had hired Bobby Bowden. It almost happened."

"I often wondered what would've happened," Bowden said. "You know things worked out at Florida State. I would've had to follow Bear Bryant. That wouldn't have been good. Who's going to follow a legend like that? He built what he built. What I built at Florida State is what I built. It's mine."

THE LATE 1980S SAW the continuation of Florida State's growth as a football program and Bowden's growth as a coach. Both the program and the coach would face fresh challenges, and one of them had to do with one of Bowden's assistants.

On every staff, there are conflicts. Then there's what happened with Wayne McDuffie, the offensive coordinator under Bowden from 1983 to 1989, who Bowden simultaneously enjoyed having on his staff, but also at times who Bowden became angry with—perhaps like no assistant he ever had.

Several times, during games, when Bowden would call to the press box and ask for McDuffie, another coach would jump on the line. "Wayne's in the bathroom," one of the other assistants would say. The game would continue and Bowden would get back on the line. "Wayne? Wayne?" he'd say. And there'd be no Wayne.

"Wayne's in the bathroom," one of the assistants would tell Bowden.

Bowden became extremely suspicious after being told for the fifteenth time that his coordinator was in the bathroom. Unless the man had a prostate the size of a dime, he couldn't have been going to the bathroom that much. Eventually the staff came clean. On more than one occasion, McDuffie became angered over a play Bowden called—or didn't call—and bolted out of the coaches' box in frustration. What Bowden didn't know was that McDuffie had done this numerous times. In one game, according to Florida State coaches, McDuffie left during the contest and got into a minor car accident several hundred feet away from the stadium as the game was ongoing. It was an incredible situation.

"Wayne wanted more control of the total offense and Coach Bowden didn't want to relinquish that," former assistant Jim Gladden said. "And he thought trick plays were hot-doggy. Wayne McDuffie left the box a bunch of times. McDuffie would leave the coaches' box in the third quarter and go down [to the locker room] and watch it on TV."

Brad Scott, the tight ends coach at the time, remembers, "When Wayne would leave it would be one of two things. He'd be mad or frustrated that the play he had suggested didn't get called, or there was a great game on that night that had already started and he wanted to go to the locker room and watch it."

Henshaw and Richt were Bowden's best two offensive coordinators, but it was Richt to whom Bowden turned over his play-calling duties. Well, at least mostly. Bowden, to this day, feels badly about how he would interrupt Richt in the middle of games and question why he was making a certain call. Richt was humble and respectful of Bowden, but he also needed to take a stand. Was he the play caller or not? And it particularly drove Richt crazy when Bowden would ask him: "Why did you do that?"

So probably twice a season he'd walk into Bowden's office and politely plead his case for Bowden to let him alone when he was calling the plays. "If you would like to take it over again, then I'm all for that so we can run smoothly," he'd tell Bowden. "But if I'm going to be calling the plays, I'm having a hard time keeping my train of thought when you are constantly wanting to make a suggestion . . . in the middle of the drive. If we can have our conversations between the series that would help."

"You just tell me to hush and be tough with me," Bowden responded.

But Richt didn't want to do that. He respected Bowden too much. You don't tell a legend to shut up, Richt thought. "You're my boss, I respect you," Richt said, "and I'm certainly not going to tell you to hush up in the middle of a game."

"As time went by, I stopped doing that as much as I did years before," says Bowden, laughing at the story. But even after the Richt speeches, Bowden couldn't help himself. Then in the middle of questioning Richt's calls, Bowden would remember, "Dadgum, I need to stay out of it. Go ahead, Mark."

Coaching drama isn't what transformed Florida State into a great program. What propelled the Seminoles into the 1990s were three key things: going for a tie in a crucial game against Miami in 1987, snapping a six-game losing streak to rival Florida, and executing one of the best plays in college football history, the puntrooskie, which came against Clemson in 1988.

Bowden is not the kind of person who won't admit mistakes. He does. Just in his own way. In 1984, before one of Florida State's tougher regular-season games, the staff noticed on film how the linebacker for the opposing team prevented tight ends from having big games. Bowden knew this but couldn't resist desiring to throw to the tight end once the game started. Bowden got on his headset and queried quarterbacks coach Art Baker.

"Art, why don't we throw to the tight end?"

"Let me watch the coverage a couple of times," Baker said.

Bowden queried Baker again a few plays later. "How about that tight end?" he said.

"I've watched the linebacker," Baker said. "He drops right where he's supposed to drop. We can try it, Coach. But I'm telling you the guy is in pretty good position."

"Maybe they can catch the linebacker flat-footed," Bowden said.

Baker complied and called the play to the tight end. As he cut across the field the linebacker was in close pursuit. The quarterback didn't see the linebacker in coverage and threw to a spot where the linebacker was waiting patiently. He intercepted the pass and returned it 30 yards.

Bowden got back on the set. "Art?" he said.

"Yes, sir?" Baker responded.

"I see what you mean," Bowden said.

He will also stubbornly stick to his coaching philosophies and beliefs even if he later regrets them. Bowden insists that his coaching staff be morally upstanding and once fired an assistant coach for getting divorced and later said doing that was a mistake. He'll also come clean about a coaching error. That's the case when it comes to the 1987 Florida State–Miami game.

The Seminoles were ranked in the top ten in the preseason and had won four consecutive games before playing Miami in Tallahassee. Florida State took control of the contest early, leading by 16 points in the second half when the Hurricanes initiated a furious comeback. The score was 26–19 in the fourth quarter. It was a shocking turnaround, but Florida State scored with 42 seconds left and trailed by one point, 26–25.

Bowden had a decision. Should he go for a tie or a two-point conversion and the win?

In those seconds, a number of things flashed through Bowden's mind. What occurred in 1980 was one of them. Bowden had gone for two points against Miami that season and failed. That game cost Bowden a chance at a national title. This time was slightly different, but the same aggressive urges took over. It wasn't just that Bowden felt that two-point conversions were far more difficult to complete than the average fan understood (they were). Bowden also hated the idea of tying a rival. So he went for it and again the try was unsuccessful.

The attempt called for quarterback Danny McManus to throw a shallow pass to tight end Pat Carter. The Hurricanes played it perfectly: two Miami players were near Carter and knocked the ball to the ground. Miami players erupted in cheers and bounced off the field to their locker room. Bowden was left to explain his decision, a decision fans would occasionally ask Bowden about for the next two decades.

After the game, Bowden gathered the players around him. "The first thing I need to do," he told the team, "is apologize to you."

Why did Bowden do it? The decision, in retrospect, looks worse, since at the end of the year the Hurricanes finished 12–0 and were ranked first in the nation; Florida State ended 11–1 and ranked second. Bowden explains he of course had no idea how the two teams would have finished at season's end, but it probably still would not have mattered. Taking a risk in that instance fit

Bowden's nature. "Bobby's a gambler," says coaching friend George Henshaw. "He doesn't have that nickname for nothing." Although the "riverboat gambler" moniker is mostly pertaining to Bowden's running of trick plays, it also applies to his coaching philosophy in general; he'll take chances that other coaches wouldn't dare try.

What some people don't know is that Bowden had initially decided to go for the kick, but was persuaded by several players to go for the win, including running back Sammie Smith and Deion Sanders. Bowden relented. But also in the back of Bowden's mind was that Florida State's kicker had already missed an extra point and two field goals during the game. So the suggestion by the players seemed like a good one at the time. It wouldn't be the first time Bowden would be plagued by errant kicking against the Hurricanes. Over the next fifteen years, missed points by Florida State kickers would contribute to losses to Miami in 1991, 1992, 2000, and the Orange Bowl in 2003.

"Going for it was the right call," says former Florida State player LeRoy Butler. "I wouldn't have changed a thing."

"There is not a player that I played with, still to this day, that regrets going for it," Florida State's Pat Carter said. "Coach Bowden did exactly what we wanted to do as a team and you know unfortunately the play just didn't work."

Again, however, Bowden isn't a completely stubborn ass. "Knowing what I know now," he says, "I'd kick it."

One of the most compelling aspects about that game was the abundance of talent on the field. It's quite possible no single game featured more great college players and NFL prospects than that one, beginning with wide receiver Michael Irvin going against cornerback Deion Sanders. And that includes national championship games. "I've never been involved with a game where there was more talent on a college football field," says Bowden.

Ten future first-round picks played in that game, and many more made it to training camps and pro football rosters. In all, there were fifty-seven total future NFL players dressed for that contest. Jimmy Johnson was the Miami coach and he'd go on to a Hall of Fame career in Dallas.

But the caliber of players . . . it was stunning. Miami quarterback Steve Walsh threw against arguably the best college secondary ever assembled, which included Sanders, Dedrick Dodge, Martin Mayhew, and Butler, who was only a sophomore at the time but would go on to a Pro Bowl career in Green Bay. The teams were so flush with talent that at the time Brad Johnson was a backup thrower. Later he'd lead Tampa Bay to a Super Bowl. The punter for Miami was Jeff Feagles, who would also later play in a Super Bowl. Irvin that day, despite having Sanders covering him for much of the contest, had two touchdowns and 132 yards on just four catches. Irvin won multiple Super Bowl rings and just recently made the Hall of Fame.

The loss was painful for Florida State, but there was an unintentional benefit. The rivalry with Miami intensified tenfold. "You can talk about any rivalry in sports you want," said Butler. "But Miami–Florida State was as nasty as any. We really truly hated one another. It wasn't an act."

"It seemed like every time we played Miami," said Warrick Dunn, "the games got more violent with each passing season."

But despite the intensity and extreme violence of the games, Bowden was always careful not to get his teams too agitated or excited too soon. Some of what Bowden did to achieve this was purposeful and planned, while other moments were not. Before the game against Miami in 1989 in Tallahassee, the stadium was electric and Seminole players were so fiery it bordered on frenzy. Florida State fans were yelling and screaming and the game was still some minutes away. After the players were done with what was an intense pregame warm-up, they excitedly ran back into the locker room, waiting to hear Bowden's speech. When a group of them entered the room, Bowden was in a corner of it taking a nap. The team's trainer, Randy Oravetz, and Bowden's head of security, Billy Smith, stared at each other. It was a highly unusual scene, but it was also typical of Bowden. He grabbed catnaps whenever he could, and his naps were nonnegotiable—even if they came just minutes before one of the biggest games of the year.

Smith and Oravetz continued to wonder what to do. "I'm not

going to wake him up," Oravetz said. The first dozen or so players entered the room, saw Bowden, and were equally initially puzzled. Then suddenly Bowden woke up and gathered the team together. The bewilderment of the players was replaced by confidence. They saw Bowden's laid-back, sleepy demeanor as a sign that everything would be fine. The Seminoles beat the Hurricanes, 24–10.

Although the 1987 loss to Miami was brutal, the year did see Bowden end a six-game losing streak to another rival, the Gators. The rivalry was at times painful for Bowden to endure, but like his rivalry with the Hurricanes, the Gators increased the competitive flow inside Bowden. In 1983, Bowden was driving back from Gainesville after the Seminoles had been hammered by Florida, 53–14. In the car was the team chaplain, Ken Smith, who watched an infuriated Bowden make a promise to himself. The Gators had physically manhandled the Seminoles, and Bowden vowed there'd never be a repeat performance of his team getting outmuscled. "Florida may beat me again," Bowden told Smith, "but they'll never out-physical a team of mine again."

No, Bowden's team would rarely get physically punished again as a dominating stretch for Florida State would soon emerge. That doesn't mean there wouldn't be trouble for the Seminoles. To some—fairly or unfairly—Florida State was elevated by critics as one of several symbols for college football players run amok.

CHAPTER THIRTEEN

LAW AND ORDER

B obby Bowden's recruitment of LeRoy Butler began with a stabbing.

Butler grew up in a crime-plagued section of Jacksonville, Florida. In 1986, Butler, an outstanding high school football player, began receiving letters from universities across the nation. They wanted Butler, but there was only one problem. Butler didn't academically qualify for some schools; others were scared Butler didn't have the capabilities to survive the academic rigors of college. Many schools eventually stayed away from Butler. Bowden didn't.

Florida State's recruiting coordinator, Brad Scott, was scouting Butler's neighborhood with a police officer he had befriended when they witnessed a man knifed a few blocks away from Butler's home.

When Butler first heard Bowden was coming into his neighborhood, he was stunned. "I think a lot of coaches were afraid to," Butler remembers. "They sent letters but they didn't show up. Bobby showed up. That meant a lot to me." And Butler, well known and respected in his neighborhood, a sort of folk hero, actually, wanted to make sure nothing happened to Bowden. Butler told his friends to look out for Bowden, and he asked recruiting coordinator Scott to phone when he and Bowden were within two to three blocks of Butler's home. When Bowden arrived, a crowd gathered around Bowden's car; everyone wanted to get a close look at the coach. In the background Butler was screaming, "They're with me!" It was Butler's way of letting the neighborhood know not to lay a hand on the coach.

Butler was one of five players admitted to Florida State that year as a Prop 48 candidate, meaning he was on an academic trial run and was forced to sit out of football for one season. "Not only did I have the problem with my legs when I was a child," Butler once said, "I came from the projects and I was a Prop 48. No way I was supposed to be in school. They didn't have to take me."

"I was the only one of the group who made it through college," Butler says.

When Butler arrived at Florida State, he entered a different world. Something as simple as seeing the massive amount of food available for players was mind-blowing for a young man who grew up impoverished. Butler once stacked his plate high with multiple slices of pizza, chicken, and other food. It was as if Butler believed he would get only one shot at the buffet. Bowden would occasionally eat with the players and noticed Butler's overloaded plate. "You know, son," Bowden told him, "you're allowed to go back for seconds."

"Coach Bowden taught me how to be a man," Butler says. "He sat me down and taught me how to study, how to maximize my time, how to take responsibility for my actions and life. I don't know where I'd be today without Coach Bowden. I might be in jail or I might be dead."

Butler is one of the great success stories. He would become an All-American at Florida State and go on to a Pro Bowl career in Green Bay. Butler has grown into a civic leader and role model.

Butler, Warrick Dunn, Derrick Brooks—those FSU players have gone on to live exemplary lives. Peter Boulware played under Bowden and then had a prosperous NFL career. Bowden once told Boulware, "Don't go to the grave with life unused." Boulware heeded that advice and ran for one of Florida's House of Representatives seats in 2008 and won. Boulware used the power of the Florida State football brand to his distinct advantage. Despite being a Republican candidate, Boulware won his seat during an election dominated by Barack Obama and the Democrats. After the election, Florida's Republican governor, Charlie Crist, appointed Boulware to the state board of education.

Terrell Buckley, upon leaving Florida State in 1991 as a junior for the NFL, made a promise to Bowden that he would one day earn his undergraduate degree. Buckley did and after a fifteen-year NFL career, he returned to the Seminoles as an assistant coach on Bowden's staff. Then there's the story of Myron Rolle who in high school had a 4.0 grade point average, was an editor at the high school newspaper, and played the saxophone in the school band. He graduated from FSU after only two and a half years and in 2008 was awarded a Rhodes scholarship. His intention is to study medical anthropology at Oxford.

It is fair to say that for each problem player Bowden has coached, he's coached twenty like Rolle or Butler. But not all of his players have been angelic. The biggest criticism Bowden has ever faced— and it is criticism that may injure his legacy—is that Bowden lost control of the Seminole program and allowed troubled players far too much leeway when what they needed was extreme discipline. It is not a completely unfair criticism.

The troubles truly began in the early 1990s, as Florida State was chasing a national title; nine Florida State players violated NCAA rules by allowing agents to bankroll a hefty shopping spree at a Foot Locker store. In October 1999, Florida State All-American wide receiver Peter Warrick and wide receiver Laveranues Coles were arrested and pled guilty to petty theft of clothes and shoes at Dillard's department store. Warrick and Coles received $412.38 worth of clothes and shoes for only $21.40 from a Dillard's clerk with whom both young men had become friends. They were charged with felony grand theft. Warrick was suspended for two games. Coles was thrown off the team. Both players later pled guilty to petty theft and were placed on one year's probation.

Florida coach Steve Spurrier called rival FSU "Free Shoes University." It is a moniker that would stick to Bowden's program until this day (and in Bowden's craw as well). More recently Bowden's players have been called not Seminoles but Criminoles. That was again the case shortly before midnight on April 21, 2008, when

Palm Beach, Florida, police arrested a man they said was carrying a concealed .45-caliber handgun and a small amount of marijuana. It was Preston Parker, a player for Florida State.

The arrest was a major irritant for the Seminoles because this wasn't Parker's first encounter with the cops. In 2006, Tallahassee police held Parker for allegedly swiping a $10 DVD from an electronics store. He received probation for the DVD incident and pleaded guilty to two misdemeanor charges for the gun, receiving probation.

Guns and drugs are not exactly new to college campuses. The problem for Florida State was the timing of Parker's arrest. Florida State had just barely recovered from a massive, schoolwide cheating scandal in which some half-dozen starters were involved and thus suspended for the first several games of the 2008 season. There was also the academic suspension of another football player.

Parker's trouble with the police again raised questions about Bowden's disciplinary tactics. After Parker's arrest, the award-winning writer for the *Orlando Sentinel*, Michael Bianchi, penned a column that likely reflected the views of many outside the Florida State family on Bowden's perceived disciplinary skills with his players.

You wonder if Bobby Bowden was able to keep a straight face or did he laugh along with the rest of us when he released the following statement about star wide receiver Preston Parker's penalty for being arrested on drug and weapons charges.

"Preston made a very serious mistake," Bowden said in the statement, "and there are consequences when one of our boys gets in trouble."

And when Ol' Bobby says there are consequences, dadgummit he means it. Parker's penance? He will miss FSU's first two games against Eastern Louisiana Cake-Decorating College and Bruce's Hair-Styling Academy.

And if he commits another crime, word is Bobby will consider making Parker give up his semiautomatic .45 caliber handgun and downgrade to a double-action .38 caliber revolver.

Bowden didn't make the situation much better when he told the media, "I hate to say this, but if you are in certain neighborhoods, you better have a gun. You have to protect yourself and your family. I really hate to say that, but it's the way things have gotten." In essence, Bowden was excusing one of his players for illegally carrying a concealed weapon. The danger of athletes carrying guns—concealed or otherwise—should be apparent. New York Giants wide receiver Plaxico Burress accidentally shot himself in the leg while carrying a handgun in his pants in a New York nightclub.

Critics who maintain Bowden doesn't take the discipline of his players seriously are mostly wrong. Bowden does and has. Bowden has kicked players off the team for violating rules, including Parker, who was dismissed from the team in February 2009. Bowden isn't the strictest, but there have been penalties for some of the troublemakers who have traversed through his program.

But Bowden's disciplinary tactics have not always been effective, and Bowden (as well as many other college coaches) refuses to acknowledge what has to be an undeniable fact. In some, if not many occasions, there is an uncomfortable and sometimes unspoken symbiotic process in college sports. Coaches exploit troubled kids to win and excuse this exploitation as support for the player.

Meanwhile, the possible breakdown of the African American family has had a trickle-down effect. A significant number of black kids, raised in homes without fathers and sometimes mothers, use sports as an escape, yet they are unprepared for the rigors of college and public life.

Colleges use poor, physically talented black youth as a sort of farm system. Universities profess an altruistic nature, but in many cases their concern is selfish. They want to win and make money. If they do both in great amounts, few care about the arrests. The only time boosters and fans seem to closely examine this process is when programs lose.

Race is an important element in this discussion. The situation at Florida State is similar to that at many top football schools in that the vast majority of Bowden's players have been African American.

In 1989, the NCAA financed a study of the racial composition of its member programs and found that 37 percent of Division I football players, 56 percent of men's basketball players, and 33 percent of women's basketball players were black. In 2006, 45 percent of all Division I football players were black. The 1989 report also stated that some half of the football and basketball athletes came from the bottom 25 percent of society financially.

"Black students aren't given athletic scholarships for the purpose of education," says sociologist Harry Edwards. "Blacks are brought in to perform. Any education they get is incidental to their main job, which is playing sports. In most cases, their college lives are educational blanks."

Edwards said those words to *Sports Illustrated* in a story called "The Black Athlete—A Shameful Story." That story was written in . . . July 1968.

The article also stated something that—like Edwards's remarks—remains true now. "With rare exceptions, the American college coach expects his Negro athletes to concentrate on the job for which they were hired," the story says.

> The aim is neither graduation nor education. The *sine qua non* for the Negro athlete is maintaining his eligibility. At the end of the last second of the last minute of the last hour of a Negro athlete's eligibility, he is likely to find himself dumped unceremoniously into the harsh academic world. Tutors who wrote his themes disappear; professors who gave him superior grades for inferior work rigidize their marking standards; counselors who advised courses in basket-weaving and fly casting suddenly point out that certain postponed courses in English and mathematics and history must be passed before graduation. . . .
>
> These shortcuts, of course, seldom lead to a degree, and that is the second fundamental fact about the Negro athletes in American colleges: they rarely graduate with their classes, and the majority of them do not graduate at all. They are wet-nursed in their courses long enough to remain eligible, and

after all the corner-cutting and duplicity and outright cheating, they return to the Negro community as "leaders" and "college men," when in fact they have done little more than hire out as Hessians [a term that refers to eighteenth-century German regiments in service with the British Empire that fought against the American colonists during the American Revolutionary War] for four years, or long enough to bring a conference championship to dear old Si-wash. Yet their fame is such in the black community that other black children are eager to follow the same futile course.

Bowden sees himself as a savior of some of these young athletes, not an exploiter. Many in the college establishment bristle at the idea that athletes are—to borrow a phrase from journalist Bill Rhoden—million-dollar slaves. Actually, considering college athletes aren't paid (and the value of a college scholarship pales in comparison to the massive billions top athletes generate for colleges and networks), they are ostensibly not even million-dollar slaves. If you take Rhoden's analogy further, they're just slaves. Well, maybe indentured servants, if they make the NFL.

The NCAA hasn't hit Bowden's program specifically with a large number of violations. There'd been only a handful during his three-decade tenure, one in 1996, in which the NCAA cited the school for failing to monitor agents, and the other in 1984 for improper recruiting inducements. The NCAA stated that in addition to failing to monitor agent activity, Florida State failed to object to the testimony of an unfriendly witness during the initial review, among other things.

One of the more recent problematic issues for Bowden was that, according to the NCAA, sixty-one Florida State athletes cheated on an online test for a length of almost two years, and a significant number of the alleged cheating players were on the football team. This was more than your average scandal because it meant the possibility that the school would be forced to vacate up to fourteen victories, which would eradicate Bowden's chance of passing Paterno for the all-time victories mark. As of the summer of 2009 the school had appealed the NCAA's ruling, and no final decision by the NCAA on the appeal had been made.

The chance that Bowden could lose the race to Paterno set off a debate around the country with even Paterno publicly giving his opinion on the matter. "I don't think he was much involved in what happened with Florida State," Paterno told reporters during a Big Ten coaches' teleconference in April 2009. "I'm not even sure what happened. Knowing Bobby, I'm very, very fond of him and admire him very much. I just don't want to see it happen. I think it's fool-ish to take those games away from him. I've thought about it. I just think it would be a shame. Bobby has won all those games and coached all those kids who were out there. He and his staff did the job they had to do to win them. To be honest, I would hate to see them take the wins away from him."

ALTHOUGH THERE IS NO official tally of player arrests in college football, the perception exists that too many Florida State players, particularly in recent years, find themselves in trouble with the law or team policy. During a single four-week period in late 2002, quarterback Adrian McPherson was kicked off the team following a stolen check scam and gambling probe (to which he later pled no contest), quarterback Chris Rix was suspended from the Sugar Bowl for missing a final exam, and defender Darnell Dockett was also suspended from the same bowl game for violating team rules.

Certainly, Bowden is not alone in this problem of disciplin-ing players. Across the country major college football programs have witnessed a pandemic of arrests and troubled athletes. You don't even have to leave the state of Florida to see it. Although Bowden has been highly criticized for the perception that he has no control over his program, Gator players, just several hours away down the interstate, have also felt the cool steel of handcuffs. In an alleged highly despicable act, a Florida player was arrested and subsequently kicked off the team in 2008 for knowingly using a dead woman's credit card. The player faced four misdemeanor counts, the state attorney's office said, for using the credit card of a woman who was a Florida Gator student and had died tragically in a motorcycle accident. Meyer allowed a troubled lineman, Ronnie Wilson, back on the team after Wilson discharged an AK-47 automatic weapon in a parking lot in an attempt to intimidate a man who phoned police after Wilson punched and spat on a far smaller man in a nightclub. In a plea deal, Wilson was given two years' probation and ordered to complete a hundred hours of community service and undergo a mental health evaluation.

When Meyer first took the Florida job, he claimed that his players would be "the top one percent of one percent," meaning they would not only be gifted athletes and solid students, but they would also have excellent character. Between the time Florida won a national title in January 2007 and October of that year, the football program had nine players arrested or charged with at least a misdemeanor. By 2009, Meyer's Gators were arguably the most troubled program in the country.

Meyer's program isn't alone. The University of Miami in October 2006 was involved in a massive, embarrassing bench-clearing brawl with Florida International University. The fight made national headlines and led to the suspension of thirty-one players from both schools. An Alabama player in June 2008 was charged with dealing cocaine in the *parking lot of the Alabama football complex.*

From the University of Tennessee to USC to Nebraska, the problems are pervasive. The University of Georgia had seven players arrested in the 2007 off-season and eight arrested in the off-season one year later. In 2008, Iowa football faced a spate of troubles, including an ugly sexual assault case and a recruit who allegedly led eight police officers on a foot chase that lasted twenty minutes (the recruit later transferred). Penn State is among the more arrest-plagued programs today. Various media reports, including one by ESPN, stated that forty-six Penn State players between 2002 and 2008 were charged with 163 counts (some of them were later cleared). In 2007 alone, seventeen players were charged with seventy-two crimes resulting in nine guilty pleas.

Part of the issue has little to do with the coaches themselves. Society in general and the African American community in particular have to take some responsibility for the rise of troubles facing young black athletes. The disintegration of the African American family, particularly the absence of fathers, affects male athletes significantly. It may be decades before we fully understand the total effect of this social concern on big-time sports, but coaches, more than ever, are acting like surrogate fathers to large numbers of young African American men.

John Calipari, the Kentucky basketball coach who has a reputation for recruiting players with problematic pasts and sticking by them if their names appear on a police blotter, offered a similar defense to the one Bowden does.

"Do they screw up sometimes?" Calipari said days before his then Memphis team played in the 2008 title game against Kansas. "Yeah. I've always been about access and opportunity. Whether I was at UMass or at Memphis, I was at two schools that were about access and opportunities. So every once in a while a kid will do something that's just dumb, like my own children, and I deal with it. I don't throw them under the bus the first sign of trouble. When I need an intervention . . . I had an intervention. A family that understands what I'm talking about, an intervention, you can't be a part of this anymore. Don't come home to our family unless you're willing to change. They're not coming all the time from families and cultures where they're on third base. They're starting in the dugout, and they're gonna make some mistakes at times. The good news for all of us [who grew up before the new modern media world], there wasn't the Internet [like there is now], there wasn't phones with cameras on 'em, there wasn't cameras at every establishment we went into when we screwed up and did dumb things."

A relevant question is, why are African American families putting such a drastic emphasis on sports in the first place? In the late 1980s, there was an important but largely ignored examination of the causes and consequences of race and class in sports by University of Southern California professor Michael Messner. One of Messner's conclusions was that the high value African Americans put on sports participation was in the end self-defeating because the emphasis on sports led to a lack of emphasis on academics and job advancement.

"It is now widely accepted in sport sociology that social institutions such as the media, education, the economy, and (a more recent and controversial addition to the list) the black family itself all serve to systemically channel disproportionately large numbers of young black men," writes Messner, "into football, basketball, boxing, and baseball, where they are subsequently 'stacked' into low-prestige and high-risk positions, exploited for their skills, and, finally, when their bodies are used up, excreted from organized athletics at a young age with no transferable skills with which to compete in the labor market."

It is a difficult problem. Young African American men are herded toward sports with many possessing no alternative if that path fails, yet many in the African American community view athletics as the lone way to get out of impoverished circumstances when that isn't the case.

"At least the colleges, following Robin Hood's example, are redistributing money from the relatively rich to the less well-heeled," wrote Allen R. Sanderson, associate chair of the Department of Economics at the University of Chicago, for the Library of Economics and Liberty, "while the NCAA takes money from financially poor African-American athletes—Division I football and men's basketball players, who generate millions of dollars for the parent cartel and member institutions every year—and redistributes it to middle and upper-income white students (who have grants-in-aid to play on non-revenue sports teams, which are funded largely by football and basketball receipts and are overwhelmingly non-black in composition)?"

Holly Swyers, an anthropologist who has studied sports issues, challenges the assertion of the troubled black family as potential media hyperbole at best and something more nefarious at worst. "In many cultures, it is a very common pattern for grandparents to raise children while parents work to support the family," writes Swyers, an assistant professor of anthropology at Lake Forest College, in an e-mail to the author. "The whole nuclear family deal is an incredibly inefficient way to raise a family and has always been a privilege reserved for the middle and upper classes. About 20–30 years ago, grandparent child-rearing came under fire, and I suspect this move to de-legitimate a traditional family structure is part of a more generalized trend of criminalizing African Americans. The breakdown of the family, in as much as it is a consequence of highly racialized patterns of imprisonment, is an issue, but it's not so much the absence of fathers and sometimes mothers (to my mind) as it is a dominant culture that A) argues that such families are 'broken' and B) keeps imprisoning family members, contributing to a sense of futility and frustration with the system."

One of the bigger problems could be, Swyers argues, the entire "acting white" phenomenon. Too many African American athletes see sports as cool (and even going to jail as being cool) and education as something white kids do. This phenomenon was raised by scholar John Ogbu, who stated some black kids do poorly in academics because that kind of success is seen as "acting white."

"I know the idea that black culture self-destructs by ridiculing academic success as 'white' behavior is controversial, but I've seen enough students under-perform because of peer pressure that I don't want to dismiss it out of hand, at least for some students," writes Swyers.

"I think it's important to sort out race and class here," she says. "I briefly taught summer pre-school in inner-city Detroit where my students were primarily African American kids in foster care. At four many of these little ones could sing the alphabet song but had no notion that the song attached to letters. Some did not have a sense of how to open a book. I did what I could but you know that a child at that point is already a couple of years behind when he/she starts school. This leaves a student feeling stupid, subject to mockery from his/her peers, and turns him/her off the school experience. I think this connects well to Messner's point that low status males tend to turn toward sports as a means of gaining respect, and it should come as no surprise that once a kid demonstrates talent in a sport and gets acknowledged for it, he/she is going to focus on that to the exclusion of school work. So this goes back to the family in as much as book learning is not valued by the family."

And if kids aren't learning at home, the job falls to the schools to deal with students who aren't prepared. The president of Florida

State, T. K. Wetherell, was asked about admitting academic risks. Wetherell was an excellent player at Florida State, once returning a kickoff 83 yards for a score against Miami in the Orange Bowl. But as a student and athlete he also witnessed how some students from across the academic spectrum needed assistance, and he rightly pointed out that it isn't just the athletic department who allows students on the academic margins to enter universities. "Well, sure, that happens in athletics. It happens in every institution," he said. "Every president is faced with it. Most of us have a limited admission program for certain students. Many people in the public think that's [just] athletics. Most of those limited admissions aren't in athletics, they're in music or art or drama or other types of programs.

"It's not uncommon for a coach to come over and say, you've got to let this one in. He can go to Washington or Ohio State or wherever, and I'm sure somebody at Ohio State is saying you've got to let him in because he can go to Florida State. Well, that's probably true on any one given, but Bobby (Bowden) has got a list of 25 of them that he wants. I say, 'Wait a minute, we can't handle 25, we're talking one or two here.'" Wetherell was joking of course.

He continued, "But once you make that commitment to admit that student, I think that student deserves every opportunity that any other student would get, including while they're in high school. Now, that violates a number of NCAA rules. We have a program called C.A.R.E. (Center for Academic Retention and Enhancement) at Florida State. You look at *U.S. News & World Report*, you'll see we're actually graduating African American students at a higher rate than we are white students at one of the highest rates in the nation. [The report from which the statistics came was published by Education Sector, an independent think tank.] The reason we're doing that is the programs we put in place before they get to Florida State. But if I send those same counselors out [to a student's high school] to talk to a football player, I'm going to be slapped with some kind of a violation. That doesn't seem right to me. But you've got to take the chains off of us if we're going to deal with those students."

. . . .

BOWDEN HAS MAINTAINED THE belief for decades that football coaches can't abandon the players they recruit when the cops start showing up at his office. To him, unlike when he grew up and played football, there is now an entire generation of fatherless children matriculating through college sports who have already been abandoned once and he doesn't want to make it twice. He constantly reminds people where some of these kids come from. Bowden tells the story of going on various recruiting trips and before arriving in a recruit's neighborhood receiving detailed instructions about where not to go. Avoid certain streets, watch that corner, avoid that block.

Bowden uses religion—a core theme in his life—as a sort of counter to the issues that a fatherless household presents. Before he signs a prospect, Bowden tells the parents, "I want to take your son to church two times. I'm gonna take him to a predominantly black church and then to a predominantly white church. That way, kids know there is no discrimination before the eyes of God." Bowden believes the Bible tells him "Thou shalt not steal" (or write bad checks or cheat on exams), but it also says that God will forgive all sins. That notion is the basis of his faith.

"The question comes," Bowden says, "have kids changed? No, kids have not changed. Parents have changed. In other words, your parents taught you this, this, and this. Most kids today don't get that. Most of 'em don't have parents. Where's the daddy at? Where's the daddy to teach him discipline? The overall thing is our prisons are full and we just keep building 'em bigger and bigger. So many kids are on the streets with no home life.

"In a lot of cases, the parents have quit raising them. Half of our kids [FSU players] can't tell you who their daddy is. Sometimes the coaches are the only father figures in their lives. You turn on the TV and the father's having children with three different women. Or the mother says, 'I don't want the baby.' These boys walk into my office and they're the same little, ol', sweet boys they've always been. Their hair may be a little longer, their pants may hang a little lower, they may have an earring or a tattoo, but they're still good kids. What's changed is that they don't have a dad and don't have someone to teach them the Ten Commandments."

Bowden later told the author: "I think a lot of my kids have been good kids, but not every kid can be a LeRoy or a Warrick or a Deion or any number of my other boys, you know?"

There is also the simple fact that Bowden believes suspending a player or a group of players injures the entire team; the team, he believes, shouldn't be punished for the mistake of one person. In short, the team is greater than the individual. He learned this lesson as a senior at Woodlawn High School. The coach of the team suspended seven players (Bowden wasn't one of them) for a game after discovering the players went to a city fair the night before. Woodlawn lost by two touchdowns to a team they should have obliterated in what was Bowden's last high school game (he was a graduating senior). That moment stuck with Bowden for decades and shaped his disciplinary beliefs once he entered coaching.

Many of Bowden's beliefs have merit. Yet Bowden is loyal to a fault to some problematic players. He also stubbornly refuses to accept even the possibility that he is too gentle with the more hardheaded elements. There is an interesting dichotomy working within Bowden. He sometimes fails to administer stern discipline partly because he simply wants to win (like every coach) but also because of a belief that the carrot can work better than the stick.

In some cases Bowden has been played by slicksters taking advantage of his too-trusting nature.

Bowden won't change his ways on this topic, however, and he staunchly defends his methods. On occasion Bowden will receive letters from angry alumni challenging him on why he isn't sterner with his players. Bowden says he once wrote back: "If your child came to FSU and got into trouble, would you prefer that I assist your child in whatever way I can until you arrive or would you rather I join the mob who wants him lynched? I have influence either way. Please advise."

CHAPTER FOURTEEN

WIDE RIGHT

The worst rap song of all time begins with video of the Florida State team dancing in stadium stands in the off-season of 1988. "Hey, we are the Seminoles of Florida State," the players rap. "We know we're good, some say that we're great." The smooth lyrics continued: "Our goal is simple, best in the land, rocking to the beat of the Marching Chiefs band."

It was called "The Seminole Rap" and may have been one of the most disastrous ideas in the history of college football. Think it's an exaggeration? Consider the repercussions.

The rap was recorded inside the Flamingo Studios in Tallahassee, but shots of Florida State players rapping from various parts of the athletic building were part of the video. Released just weeks before the start of the 1988 season, the rap was a mix of arrogance, testosterone, and the blind stupidity of youth.

The Seminoles had reason to believe they were good, if not indeed great. They'd finished the previous season ranked second in the nation behind Miami and entered the season opener against those same Hurricanes ranked No. 1 in the country.

What the Seminole players decided was to take the Chicago Bears' Super Bowl shuffle song and morph it into their own. Let's just say the video wasn't exactly Michael Jackson's "Thriller." The rapping was off-key, melting the ears, and the production was *Wayne's World* quality. In one of the unintentionally funny scenes, one of the Florida players put his mouth around the edge of a 45-

pound weight like he was going to snack on it—"we eat steel for lunch," was the preceding lyric.

The problem was that while Florida State was channeling its inner LL Cool J, the Hurricanes were working solely on stopping the Seminoles. It was a classic example of one program focusing solely on the football field and the other believing the positive press about itself. Almost every newspaper in the country was swooning about the Seminoles and penciling them in the title game. The Florida State players started to believe the hype while the Hurricanes believed they could crush the Seminoles.

Bowden was in Europe on a family vacation when the players made the decision to film the rap. Would he have stopped it? "I probably would've tried," he said. "But the players really wanted to do it. When I got back to campus, it was basically done. But I told them, 'You make this and we lose, you'll pay the price.'"

Florida State was hammered 31–0 by the Hurricanes. Florida State's drives ended in a punt, interception, punt, missed field goal, fumble, punt, interception, three straight punts, and then three consecutive interceptions. It remains one of the worst losses of Bowden's career. "I'm no rapper," Bowden says, "but even I know that rap didn't work."

The loss stung, but the pain was short-lived. Bowden soon experienced a high—because of a single play, not a single rap—that would help propel Florida State into the 1990s, the decade of the Seminoles.

IT WAS SEPTEMBER 1988 and Florida State was playing Clemson in Death Valley stadium before 82,500 people. They'd rebounded from the disastrous drubbing against the Hurricanes and pounded Southern Mississippi, 49–13. The Seminoles, playing on a rain-soaked field, were tied with Clemson at 21 and facing a fourth-and-four on their own 21-yard line with 90 seconds left in the game. Bowden decided to call a play that was impossible, improbable, and historic. It was the puntrooskie.

"Twenty years later I still can't believe that play happened," said LeRoy Butler.

"The greatest play since *My Fair Lady*," analyst Beano Cook once said.

"I remember hearing the call and going, 'Wow, we're really going to do this,'" Butler said.

"Might be the best play I ever called," said Bowden.

Bowden had asked his assistants if they wanted to run the play and there was no disagreement. Not even a modicum of dissent. So Bowden called it. When Butler heard, he was stunned. Butler trusted Bowden, particularly tactically. After all, Butler and other Seminole players had noticed how Bowden was the only person on the staff who could coach the entire team; that is, he could coach every position well, a rarity in the profession on any level. Still, there was a trace of doubt. Butler remembers his final words to Bowden before running the play: "Are you sure you don't want to punt?"

"I'm sure," Bowden said.

The play had its roots in a place far from Tallahassee. A graduate assistant named Clint Ledbetter had brought the idea to Bowden's coaching staff. Bowden had developed into a connoisseur of the trick play and loved Ledbetter's idea.

The first trick play of Bowden's coaching career came in 1972 when he was at West Virginia. He used a wideout, Harry Blake, on a reverse against Stanford. It lost 17 yards. "I was afraid for a long time to use the reverse again," he joked. It took Bowden two years to build the moxie to run it after that game. He ran the reverse three times on a sloppy field at Virginia Tech. Bowden would later call for a fake field goal in 1982 against Southern Mississippi, a play perfectly engineered by assistant Henshaw. The Seminoles had a fourth down and short at Southern Mississippi's 2-yard line with the score tied at 17. Bowden was slightly nervous because if Florida State scored a field goal, there was still enough time left on the clock for Southern Miss to win the game on a touchdown. So Bowden called for the fake, the football was snapped to the holder, quarterback Kelly Lowrey, and Lowrey ran the football up the middle for a touchdown.

The media asked Bowden afterward about the fake field goal

and he replied with a typical Bowden quip. "You gotta know when to hold 'em and know when to fold 'em," he told the press. The comment brought a chuckle from reporters.

The fact that Butler was the catalyst of the puntrooskie is one of the greater ironies in college sports history. He was born into the Blodgett Homes projects in Jacksonville, Florida, as bleak an inner-city wasteland as any in the nation. Don't be fooled thinking that because those projects were in a sleepy north Florida town that they didn't have the same draining sting as those in New York City or Los Angeles. They did. And Butler faced other challenges as a kid in Blodgett. He was born with a serious deformity in his legs—his toes turned in dramatically—which meant he was unable to run. "There were times when I was very small that I felt sorry for myself," he said. "But if my mother ever saw a tear in my eye, she'd tell me to wipe that tear away because God put you here and God has a plan for you."

Thus the groundwork was laid for the puntrooskie, and it was poetic justice that a kid who once could barely walk was instrumental in running it.

The fake got its name from the Cornhusker program. They labeled any trick play a "rooskie." Bowden kept the nickname and expanded on it.

The puntrooskie against Clemson is considered one of the gutsiest calls in major college football history, mainly because of the situation. No coach would ever call for a trick play deep in his own territory. At least, until Bowden. He called for the puntrooskie, where the punter fakes a kick and then hands the ball to the upback. Eventually the football ended up in the sure hands of Butler, who raced 78 yards to the Clemson 1-yard line. A game-winning field goal was kicked after that. "I was running for my life," Butler remembers. "I ran out of gas."

The exact play went like this. There were two upbacks, Butler and Dayne Williams. The latter lined up behind the line of scrimmage some five or so yards, right behind the center, and took the snap, which normally would go to the punter. When the ball was snapped by the center, punter Tim Corlew jumped high into the air like he was chasing a bad snap. His splendid acting would've made Denzel Washington jealous. The Clemson defense was totally fooled and chased a football they thought had been snapped over the punter's head.

By the time Clemson defenders realized they had been fooled by a magical punter with the sleight of hand worthy of David Blaine, it was too late. They focused on Williams after discovering that he actually had the ball, but Williams then covertly handed the football to Butler. He literally stuck the football between Butler's legs. After that it was off to the races.

Butler remembers he'd been instructed by the coaching staff to count "one Mississippi, two Mississippi, three Mississippi" before running. Butler was so nervous before the snap he described butterflies in his stomach as "the size of pterodactyls." He made it only to the first Mississippi before his trek downfield.

"Coach Bowden really trusted me for that play," said Butler. "You don't ever want to let Coach Bowden down. He inspires that in you."

The play was so chaotic it caught the sideline reporter for the game, the everlasting Pat O'Brien, completely by surprise. He began asking then sports information assistant Rob Wilson just what the hell had happened. After the game, Bowden had the press corps laughing hysterically when he shuffled several chairs to create an instructional demo of how exactly the play had worked.

One irony from the play is that Clemson knew about it and still couldn't stop it. The coach for Clemson, Danny Ford, told the media afterward he suspected such trickery was coming. Ford's words weren't just hyperbole. Although Bowden never instructed his players to keep word of the puntrooskie as quiet as possible, he might have assumed they would; but there was still a leak. A few days before the game, Butler was so elated about his role in the upcoming play he excitedly called his old high school coach, Corky Rogers, a legend in Jacksonville, Florida. The call came just several days before the game. The evening after Butler unintentionally spilled the puntrooskie beans, Rogers had a small party at his home, which included friends and former players for Rogers.

The host was making simple small talk when he discussed with his guests what Butler had told him. A Clemson graduate in the room relayed the information to a friend, who then provided it to the Tiger coaching staff.

"Isn't that something?" Bowden told me. "Isn't it strange how things work out?"

The next few years were chaotic and in many ways typical Bowden. Florida State's season records were remarkable with the Seminoles going 22–2 in a two-year period from 1987 to 1988. The 1989 season saw Bowden open 0–2 and lose to a Brett Favre–led Southern Mississippi team by four points. Clemson avenged the puntrooskie loss after that.

The Clemson loss caused a crisis among some of the Florida State recruits, particularly, as the *Lakeland Ledger* newspaper reported, a small group of freshmen. After the horrible Clemson defeat, many players in that freshman class gathered at a pool near the dormitory on campus. There were actual questions about whether or not the Seminoles were headed in the right direction. They were legitimate thoughts: Can we win?

"The freshmen class got together at the pool at the dorm in Tallahassee and we started to question whether or not we belonged there," said safety John Davis. "We thought maybe we needed to transfer because this program is not quite where we thought it was."

In that class were players key to Bowden's future, including Charlie Ward, who would go on to win a Heisman Trophy and engineer one of the great college offenses of all time.

Over the next decade, Bowden balanced the program on the shoulders of a handful of core players. He injected not just youth but professionalism into Seminole football, though he certainly also had his fair share of troubled players. Ironically, upon his program entering the 1990s, and with Bowden poised at the beginning of a dynasty, there were questions about Bowden's age. He turned sixty in 1989. Think about that for a moment. People were wondering if Bowden was too old to coach *in 1989*.

The question about Bowden's age actually came from a church member one Sunday that year. "I'd like to coach as long as the good Lord allows," Bowden told the parishioners. "I'd like to get Florida State one national championship before I hang 'em up, and if I do, I'd like to get 'em two."

CASEY WELDON GREW UP in Tallahassee but was a University of Georgia fan. His choices for where he would play college football came down to Georgia and the Seminoles; few quarterbacks are ever going to pass up the opportunity to play for Bowden's high-scoring offense.

When Weldon arrived, the field at quarterback was remarkably crowded, with players Brad Johnson, Chip Ferguson, and Peter Tom Willis. "Things stayed very friendly between all of us," Johnson once told the author. "The situation could've gotten very bitter but [Chip and Peter] were good guys." When it looked like Johnson and Weldon would be competing for the starting job in 1990, Weldon once approached Johnson on the team bus. "No matter what happens," he told Johnson, "I hope our friendship will never be affected by it."

It wasn't. Both Johnson and Weldon would go on to NFL careers and both players—especially Johnson—would become known for their calm and friendly demeanors off the field as well as their skill. Unlike Weldon, Johnson was an excellent basketball player, and he played basketball in his first two years at Florida State.

When Weldon was eventually named the starter, Johnson thought about transferring or even leaving Florida State altogether for Canada or the NFL. "I decided against it," Johnson told me in 2008, "because I wanted to play in the NFL and staying at Florida State gave me that chance."

"Brad could've made a real stink about things," Bowden says, "but he was classy about it."

Weldon would suffer through several stupendous and satisfying moments as well as horrendous losses and wide rights to Miami. Weldon started for Florida State for most of the 1990 and 1991 seasons and as a senior finished second in Heisman voting to Michigan's Desmond Howard. His importance to Florida State remains, to this day, extremely undervalued. Weldon was a stabilizing force at the position and acted as a bridge between the past players at the position and Charlie Ward, the best thrower in school history, who led the Seminoles to their first national title.

"Casey was a great athlete," Bowden remembers. "He was able to make almost any throw. Really one of the more underrated leaders I've coached."

Deion Sanders changed everything for high school cornerbacks across the country. If you played cornerback, you wanted to be Deion. You tried to run like him, you tried to move like him, you high-stepped the way Deion did. Most young football players wanted to be Deion, and Terrell Buckley was no different. Buckley even used to talk smack the way Sanders did. In high school Buckley used to joke that he could cover a receiver with an ice cream in one hand, a Coke in the other, and on one leg.

When Buckley arrived at Florida State in 1989, Sanders had just departed to begin his NFL career. Buckley went to high school in Pascagoula, Mississippi, and some in the media were calling him "Baby Deion." Buckley had big (and fast) shoes to fill. Although Sanders was known for his flamboyant style, he was also one of the hardest-working players Bowden had ever seen. Sanders never missed a single practice in his entire Florida State career and played with biting injuries. "I don't think people understand just how tough Deion is," Hall of Fame wide receiver Jerry Rice told the author.

He wasn't perfect, however. At the time, Sanders cared little about his academics and knowing that he was on his way to fame and fortune in professional sports, he skipped some of his classes and final examinations in his last season. In doing so, Sanders had angered some of the school's academics, who viewed Sanders as someone raising his middle digit to the university system. So the school struck back. The school's board of regents enacted what would be known unofficially to this day as the Deion Sanders Rule, which requires student-athletes to attend class and take tests or face significant suspensions.

Despite those faults, Sanders remains a favorite of Bowden. Bowden says he isn't sure he coached a player who had more love for football than Sanders, and that likely contradicts the opinion of many fans. In his last season with the Seminoles, he played for the New York Yankees in their minor league system, and Bowden would sometimes excuse Sanders from some spring practices so he could play for the Seminole baseball team. But it wasn't often because Sanders was intent on making as many football practices as possible, and he went hard in practice on each play.

Sanders is among the top ten NFL players ever and certainly the best defensive back in professional history, but Buckley wasn't too far behind, both as a college and professional player. Something Buckley did in a 1989 game against Syracuse led to one of Bowden's great lines. In that game, Buckley took a long and high punt and faked as if he had called for a fair catch. He actually didn't. Buckley caught the punt and then just stood there. The Syracuse coverage team *assumed* he called for the fair catch. Buckley then bolted for a 69-yard score. After the game, Bowden called Buckley the "Foolah from Pascagoula."

Florida State cornerback J. T. Thomas opened the door for players like Sanders, and Sanders led to players like Buckley. Actually, it might have been Buckley, not Sanders, who helped initiate the nickname "Cornerback U" for Florida State. High school defensive backs watched Buckley the way Buckley once watched Sanders. The cycle had repeated itself.

Only dedicated Florida State fans know the name Kez McCorvey.

In a testament to how flush Bowden's program had become with raw talent, McCorvey wasn't truly on the Seminoles' radar. They knew about McCorvey, he'd been invited to their camp, but he wasn't a top-tier recruit. Far from it. Then something happened. McCorvey ran the 40-yard dash in 4.5 seconds. Speed is something Bowden always looked for and McCorvey had it. The Seminoles offered him a scholarship.

You know a team is deep when someone who runs a 4.5 can drop out of the sky and end up being a star. McCorvey finished with 189 catches and 16 touchdowns, and it's not an exaggeration to say that Bowden might not have won the 1993 national title without him.

Bowden still remembers a talk he had with McCorvey when the wide receiver was a junior. McCorvey was going to marry a woman he'd been dating and went to Bowden for advice. "I wanted him to get married for the right reasons," Bowden remembers. "I told him, 'Marriage is sacred.' He understood what I was sayin'."

"The thing I really needed at that time," Warrick Dunn says, "was a place that was like a home. I needed a home after what had happened to my mom. Bobby gave me that. He gave me a place that felt just like home. When people say some players looked up to Bobby like he was their father, that's not an exaggeration. I'm a perfect example of that. I still talk to Bobby as much as possible and all these years later he's still like a father to me."

It's a common refrain often heard from Seminole players when speaking of Bowden—he was like a father. Kurt Unglaub played wide receiver under Bowden from 1976 to 1980, and while there Unglaub's parents divorced. Bowden practically adopted Unglaub and counseled him through the rough times.

In January 1993, Betty Smothers, a Baton Rouge police officer, was driving a grocery store manager to a bank in the dark of night. She was ambushed by two men and murdered. The murdered woman was Warrick Dunn's mother, who was working her off-duty job. Dunn was eighteen at the time and accepted legal guardianship of his younger siblings. The accused shooter is on death row in a Louisiana prison, and later Dunn would meet with the man as a form of closure in his own life. "Most people who would go through that would be crushed, just crushed," said Bowden, "and they might not be able to recover. That tells you about Warren's strength. You could see it when you first met him."

After the murder, Dunn thought seriously of staying in Louisiana and playing football close to home. He changed his mind when Bowden paid a visit. They sat in Dunn's home and Bowden told Dunn's grandmother: "I promise you I will take care of him."

"My neighborhood was not the greatest neighborhood," said Dunn to the author. "Here was Coach Bowden, coming to my neighborhood. That meant a lot to me. You didn't see people like Coach Bowden coming to my neighborhood. You mostly saw people who looked like Coach Bowden leaving my neighborhood."

Bowden and his staff saw Dunn's character, but interestingly the Seminoles almost miscast Dunn. Several schools—including the University of Florida—wanted Dunn, an option quarterback in high school, to play defensive back. Florida State also initially made that mistake. Dunn was told he could be the next Sanders or Buckley, but Dunn stuck to his convictions. Bowden relented, and Dunn became a running back. After he blew by the first-team defense with several big runs during a scrimmage, there was no longer any discussion about Dunn playing defense. He led the team as a freshman with 10 touchdowns. He also drove home more than 440 miles in six hours to see his siblings every weekend once the season ended.

"He's about as lovable a guy as you'll ever see. You know how some guys, you just want to hug 'em? That was Warrick," Bowden says. "He was as close to a son as any player I've been around. But don't get me wrong. He wasn't soft. He was confidently shy. He spoke up when he needed to, and when he did everyone listened. I just respected him so much. He practically raised his siblings on his own after his mom died. How many people would have the strength to do that?"

Dunn would do more than that. In the years to come after the murder, Dunn had one question: Why? Why was his mother killed? So he visited Angola State Prison and met with the man, Kevan Brumfield, who murdered Smothers. After speaking with Brumfield, Dunn had his answers and some degree of peace of mind.

"I sacrificed my own happiness. I sacrificed; making sure other people in my life came first because Warrick didn't come first anymore. I was so depressed," Dunn says of growing up without his mother. "I was content being in the four walls in my house. I was content not going outside, watching TV all day. For so long I felt like these guys were taking so much away from me. This one incident has made me so hard and so closed that I wanted to continue to progress and move forward. To not hear [Brumfield] admit to doing it was tough. But, he got teary eyed also by the statements that I made. I just really expressed how this one incident affected so many areas of my life. How I was searching for answers. I think it's the right guy . . . he did it. Why would you really care? I didn't ask him the question—did you do it? But, he just said it wasn't him. If you didn't do it, then I don't know why you're here, but I forgive you or whoever did it. I think that showed him I was coming to peace with everything. [My mother] already knew what I just accomplished going to see the guy that shot and killed her. I know she's proud. She's proud that I hadn't gone crazy, I hadn't gone down a wrong path, I've done something positive with my life."

One of the best pass rushers in the history of college football was a walk-on from a high school in Miami with just one scholarship offer: from Division I-AA Stony Brook on Long Island. There was a moment when Andre Wadsworth thought he'd never play college football, so instead he prepared to focus on academics.

During his senior year in high school, Wadsworth crafted a response to an English assignment requiring the class to write a paper explaining where the students thought they'd be in life five years in the future. His answer was nothing like what would occur. In his real life, Wadsworth would finish at Florida State with 23 sacks, at the time fifth most in school history, and be drafted third overall in the 1998 draft. That draft positioning is the highest ever for a Seminole player.

So how did Wadsworth answer that high school assignment? He wrote nothing about football and instead discussed his desire to earn a master's degree in business from Florida State.

He went to Florida State without a scholarship, walked onto the team, and endured the humiliating life of a player on the rim of stardom. Not long after arriving, when Wadsworth was being fitted for his equipment in the locker room, one of the lead trainers cursed at a group of assistants who were helping Wadsworth. "You need to be helping players who are going to be playing around here!" the trainer screamed. Wadsworth was basically seen as cannon fodder, and few were counting on him to make it past his first few months, if that long.

Then came one remarkable burst that caught the attention of the players and coaches. Wadsworth was strong and quick, but he was extremely light for a pass rusher at 211 pounds. The Seminoles had defensive backs who weighed more, so what happened one day in practice shocked everyone but Wadsworth. In pass rushing drills, he lined up against one of the starting linemen from the 1993 championship team, Marvin Ferrell, who weighed a staggering 315 pounds. With coaches watching keenly, Wadsworth stoned Ferrell, knocking the lineman backward onto an immobile dummy serving as a quarterback. Coaches were so taken aback they asked him to repeat what he had just done. Wadsworth complied, beating Ferrell again.

Bowden doesn't remember seeing the play, but he remembers other coaches talking about it. Mostly, Bowden remembers how Wadsworth made one of the quickest impressions on the staff of any player he's ever been around. "He came out of nowhere," Bowden said. "He gave you that 'wow' thing. We knew we had to keep him." They gave him a scholarship, and Wadsworth grew both in size and impact. Ten years later his story remains one of the more remembered in Florida State history.

There were other memorable players. Some served as bridges from the good times to the championship years. Others were anchors for Bowden when the program started beating everybody. Some players went on to the NFL; others became professionals entering careers in law and medicine. Later, one would become a Rhodes scholar. Some would get into trouble with the law; many would simply earn their degrees.

If you were to try to quantify what type of player came to Florida State, it would be difficult. Bowden uses two words: "Fast and hungry." The description is appropriate. In the 1970s and

1980s, college football still emphasized power. Bowden build Florida State on the backs of players who could outrun and outquick their opponents. Their strength was important, but their speed was critical. It was no accident the Seminoles built several of the fastest championship teams in history and players like Sanders found their way to Tallahassee. Of course there was speed in other programs like Miami, USC, and Nebraska, but not from the top to the bottom like at Florida State.

There is one other word that Bowden left out—grounded. For all the problem Florida State players, there were just as many intelligent football players like Charlie Ward, LeRoy Butler, Chris Weinke, and Warrick Dunn. That's always been the problem with the players who created the ugly headlines. The punks and bad guys nearly obscure—and this is the case with many programs— the accomplishments of the smart players who studied, absorbed the Seminole system, and never felt the steely pull of a pair of handcuffs.

The talent Bowden assembled was astounding. "He took full advantage of the goldmine that was the state of Florida," said Ernie Accorsi.

"If you could rank all of the great college teams in history by talent alone," said Pat Summerall, "a bunch of those Florida State teams would be ranked pretty high, and I'm not just talking about the championship teams."

Of all the criticisms leveled against Bowden—some fair, some not so much—one that rarely is mentioned might be the most valid. With all that talent, Bowden should have actually captured one or two more titles.

At least.

The reason he didn't, at least partially, was through no fault of his own. Two programs stood in his way: Miami and the University of Florida. If not for the former, in particular, Bowden might have won at least two more championships. "I say this with great respect for Bobby," said former Miami coach Larry Coker, "the Hurricanes were a thorn in his side and he was a thorn in our side."

"We were a pain in Florida State's ass," former Miami great Michael Irvin said.

Warren Sapp said to the author in 2002: "Winning national championships was Miami's first goal. Ruining Florida State's season was probably second. It was right up there." When Sapp was with the Tampa Bay Buccaneers, we spoke about the Florida State–Miami rivalry and Sapp was, well, Sapp. "You can't really hate Bobby Bowden," said Sapp. "He's too nice a man. But I hated their program. I hated Florida State. I wanted to bash in the head of every Florida State player. I wanted to hurt them, and they wanted to do the same to us." Sapp joked that he wanted to change his first and last name to "Wide Right."

There was a time when Bowden could've changed his name to that as well.

The puntrooskie was soon followed by a birthday. As Bowden turned sixty in 1990 both the local and national media began wondering if Bowden was too old to coach. The university was extremely sensitive to the talk and jokes about Bowden's age and made a bold move to cease speculation about how long Bowden would stay. Bowden was earning a hearty salary at the time, about $300,000 a year. Bobby and Ann lived comfortably in a Tallahassee house they'd owned for years. Life was good and was about to get better. Not long after rival Steve Spurrier received a multiyear deal to coach the Gators, the Florida State athletic department decided Bowden should earn more than Spurrier. Bowden signed a new deal that was to pay him $600,000 a year. The salary also included media appearances and speaking engagements, but it was a significant step for both Bowden and the school. At the time, Bob Goin, the athletic director, said about Bowden: "We want to have him here until the day he decides not to coach anymore and his contract shows that."

Bowden's epic battles against Miami and his multiple near misses actually started with one of his vaunted trick plays. But this one didn't work. Early in the 1990 season, Bowden played Auburn and the Tigers knew the play was coming. This one was the "fumblerooskie" and Bowden called it when facing a long third down at the 41-yard line of Auburn. Bowden had the team practice the play all week, and he was certain it would fool the Tigers.

Playing Auburn was significant for Bowden. The Tigers, like Alabama, played in his home state. So when they called, Bowden listened. Auburn became interested in hiring Bowden after his fifth season with the Seminoles; the rejuvenated Florida State team in the previous two years had lost only one game, to Miami, of course, by just a single point.

Bowden met with a group of Auburn officials at his uncle's home in Childersburg, Alabama. After initially offering the job to Georgia's Vince Dooley, who declined it, Auburn went to Bowden. He turned them down too. "If you had said to me years earlier, 'Bobby, someday you are going to be offered the head coaching job at Auburn and you are going to turn it down,' I would have told you, 'There's no way I'd turn that one down. You'd better get your head examined.'"

A few short seasons later, here he was, playing the Tigers and running the fumblerooskie. The play called for the center to snap the football but instead of the football going into the hands of the quarterback, the center makes the snapping motion, and the football is covertly put on the ground. As the entire offense goes in one direction, the guard sneakily picks up the football and runs in the other direction, away from the defense.

It's a smart play, but Bowden called it with Florida State ahead 17–10 with just under seven minutes remaining. That moment called for Bowden to run the ball and wind down the clock. Instead, Bowden got too clever for his own good. It might have been a case of Bowden trying to show the team that nearly hired him what they were missing. Perhaps it was simply being Bowden. Whatever the motivation, the play didn't work. Just seconds after center Robbie Baker put the ball on the grass, an unfazed Auburn defensive lineman, Walter Tate, scooped it up. What Bowden didn't realize was that Auburn had prepared for the play. They'd seen it before on film and thought Bowden would try it.

Tate grabbed the football and had a strange reaction. "I just laid there and giggled when I got it," he said.

The Seminoles weren't laughing, particularly the Florida State players. Most, if not all of the players, had come to trust Bowden implicitly. But some of the offensive players knew the fumble-rooskie was doomed. Before the rooskie was called, Seminole safety John Davis remembers several offensive players warning the defense to get ready. "I recall a couple of offensive players running down the side to where we were and saying, 'You guys get ready to go on the field. The play we just called isn't going to work.'" Why didn't they believe it would be successful? Call it gut instinct. The players were right. The play failed miserably, and Auburn took the turnover. On their ensuing series, Auburn tied the score at 17. The Tigers ended up winning the game 20–17.

Losing to Auburn ended the Seminoles' chance at a national championship, and it helped supplement already persistent thoughts—thanks mostly to Miami—that the Seminoles were destined to never win a title. "We start to think we're cursed," Davis says. "Everything had happened for us to position ourselves to be the No. 1 team and we didn't take advantage of it."

"No, we were never cursed," Bowden says to me, laughing. "We weren't cursed. It was that dadgum Miami. The curse was they were on our schedule."

That dadgum Miami.

What Bowden accomplished in the 1990s is astounding and will likely never be duplicated. In that decade, Bowden went 109–13–1 and was 49–1–1 at home. The former record is the best of the decade, and during that era, Florida State spent just five weeks out of the top ten.

The problem was Miami. That dadgum Miami.

The Seminoles had legitimate chances to win national titles in the years 1987, 1988, 1989, 1991, and 1992. Of those five years the Hurricanes knocked Bowden's teams out of the title picture four times.

One of the things forgotten by many is just how good Miami's teams were. In the 1987–88 season the Hurricanes went 12–0, and seventeen players from that team were either drafted or signed as free agents in the NFL. Eight made their teams and four became starters.

"He would've been a lot more dominant if it wasn't for us," Sapp said.

"That dadgum Wide Right stuff too," Bowden said, still laughing. He added: "Yeah, I can laugh about it now."

"When I missed my field goal against Miami in 1992," said former Florida State kicker Dan Mowrey, referring to his infamous 39-yard attempt that sailed wide right, "I wanted to crawl into a hole. I thought my life was over."

The 1991 season saw the first Wide Right. Entering the year, Bowden thought his program was ready to finally win a championship. The Seminoles entered the year ranked first in the country—the second time in four years that occurred—until another Miami clash. "Before the game, during the game, I felt pretty good about our chances," said Bowden.

When asked why he felt confident despite the Seminoles winning only once in the previous six meetings, Bowden explained, "That was one of my best teams."

The date of the game was November 16, and the Seminoles were ranked first and the Hurricanes second. The night before, Bowden opened his talk to the team with a quote from Winston Churchill. Everyone was gathered at a local Holiday Inn and they listened intensely. Churchill's quote that Bowden read was: "To every man there comes in his lifetime that special moment when he is tapped on the shoulder and offered that chance to do a very special thing that is unique to him and that is fitted to his talent."

In the media the contest was called the "Game of the Century," and Bowden had a reason to feel good about his chances. Entering the fourth quarter Florida State led 16–7. The Hurricanes generated a furious comeback. Miami was led by quarterback Gino Torretta, and it was this game that cemented his Heisman Trophy win. The Hurricanes led 17–16 with 3:01 left in the game.

Casey Weldon was able to guide the Florida State offense to the Hurricane 17 with under one minute left in the game. He spiked the football with 29 seconds left, and Bowden made a critical decision. He decided to kick the field goal instead of risk another play. Although some in the media have criticized Bowden for not attempting to run another play, the criticism is misguided, because without any timeouts, running another play would have been perilous.

"My kicker had been perfect that day," Bowden said of Gerry Thomas. "I felt very confident he'd make it." In fact, Thomas had made all three attempts and as the kick left the ground and sailed toward the uprights, Bowden started slowly jogging along the sideline as if he was about to celebrate. Bowden was actually preparing to hold back the team from running onto the field and garnering a penalty for excessive celebration. "I thought the kick was good, it was good," Bowden says.

A depressed Thomas had to be consoled by teammates. Bowden made sure to tell the kicker it wasn't his fault and they lost as a team. Thomas, however, took all of the blame. "This team is a bunch of great guys," he told the media then. "They deserved to have me make it. I hit it real well and I thought it was good for a second but then it kept fading right."

It missed by inches. Miami, not the Seminoles, went on to the national title game. Bowden was crushed. After the game, but before he met the press, Ann hugged her husband. "She's always there telling me it'll be fine after a tough loss," said Bowden. "She's great and she was right. But at the time it was tough. You really start to wonder, 'When am I going to beat these guys?'"

"He was definitely very hurt by losing," said Butler of Bowden.

After the game came a surreal scene. Many of the sixty-four thousand people stayed in their seats, shocked at what had just happened. In the Florida State locker room, some players tossed their helmets in anger and kicked over stools. In the days following the loss, Bowden received an outpouring of support and sympathy from fans as well as the obligatory mail from a minority of extremists angry over the end result. One alumnus sent his Florida State crimson-colored cap back to Bowden with a note: "I've finally given up on you and Florida State ever winning a national championship.

If it ever happens it will be because FSU didn't schedule Miami, because it appears that we'll never beat them when it counts."

It wasn't just that Bowden was losing to the Hurricanes, it was how he was losing. That game was the fourth time Miami had knocked Florida State out of the title picture, and in three of those losses, unbelievably, Florida State lost by one point. The second Wide Right, WRII, didn't help with the belief by some Florida State players that the program was cursed. Dan Mowrey didn't believe in curses, but he knew about what had happened to Thomas, who left the team following spring practice after the inaugural Wide Right. Upon arriving at Florida State, Mowrey developed into one of Bowden's hardest workers. He'd turn that work ethic later into a law degree as he became a prosecutor in the state of Florida.

When Mowrey arrived at Florida State, he was extremely self-assured, even cocky. That changed somewhat after Wide Right II. In the 1992 Orange Bowl, Bowden again faced the Hurricanes and a field goal was again the difference. When Mowrey, only a sophomore at the time, pushed a potentially game-tying field goal wide right, the Seminoles lost the game 19–16; two field goals in two years crippled Florida State's chances at two national titles. "I really felt bad for the kickers more than myself," said Bowden. "It was rough on them." The kickers received harassing phone calls and even notes left on their cars by angry fans. Mowrey's car was decorated with a note that read: "You're the worst kicker in America."

Kickers at Florida State were also causing off-field troubles. In May 1994, kicker Scott Bentley pleaded guilty to a misdemeanor crime of prohibited interception and disclosure of oral communication. What Bentley did was videotape a sexual encounter he had with a young prenursing student from Florida A&M. If that wasn't enough, Bentley then showed the tape to several of his friends.

After the conviction, Bowden probably should have kicked Bentley off the team, but Bowden likely kept Bentley because he was a highly important recruit. *Sports Illustrated* put Bentley on the cover of its 1993 college football preview issue under the headline

"A Sure Three." Bowden only benched Bentley after he struggled with his field goal tries and even his extra point attempts during the regular season. Eventually Bowden sat him down. "Son," Bowden told Bentley, "have you ever failed in an athletic endeavor, ever come in second?" Bowden knew what Bentley would say before the kicker opened his mouth. Bentley said no and Bowden responded, "Then this will be good for you."

It was the missed field goals in big moments, not kicker video-taping debauchery, that caused the Florida State program the most pain. The failed attempts would stick with the kickers for years, becoming a sort of tattoo that was difficult to remove. Long after the failed kick, and after he'd moved on to an entirely different life, Mowrey, in his job as a prosecutor, was offering a plea bar-gain to a petty criminal. The man being offered the deal looked at Mowrey and there was a gleam of recognition. Then the man asked Mowrey: "Hey, aren't you Wide Right?"

At times, some years after the kick, friends or even strangers would walk by on the street and say, "What's up, Wide Right?"

"I have to admit," he says, "it bothers me."

Wide Right III came in October 2000 when kicker Matt Munyon missed a 49-yarder. That's a terribly long attempt for a college kicker, and Munyon had made three extra points and a field goal earlier in the contest. None of that mattered. He was officially a part of Florida State Wide Right lore. Munyon was viciously taunted as he walked out of the Orange Bowl and upon returning home to Tallahassee received nasty phone calls from Florida State fans.

In 2002, the Seminoles had a chance to knock Miami from its top-ranked perch, but kicker Xavier Beitia missed a 43-yarder in the final seconds wide left. That missed kick was creatively called Wide Left I. After the game, Beitia was in tears and practically inconsolable. He received a number of supportive messages and e-mails but also some cruel ones. One, Beitia said, read, "Nice choke, kicker." Munyon had actually followed the plight of Beitia and phoned the kicker after the miss and told him the true chal-lenge wasn't the kick but dealing with the aftermath of the miss.

Mowrey explained that when he watches an NFL playoff game or bowl contest, he always prays that "some poor kicker doesn't end up the goat. But you know it's going to happen."

Mowrey would bounce back from the miss brilliantly and has been able to deal with his infamy with a gorgeous sense of humor and smile-inducing sense of perspective. "I was successful in everything I had done in my life," he said about the time before the kick. "It was a terrible blow to my ego. I was a cocky kid. I went to Florida State to be on the center stage and I blew it. But the kick allowed me to get a perspective on my life I might not have otherwise gotten. I grew up very fast."

He added, "Believe me. There is life after Wide Right."

CHAPTER FIFTEEN

CHAMPION

It's hard to say who was my favorite player," says Ann, who met some of Bobby's top recruits and players. "Charlie's right up there. He was such a gentleman. He was quiet. When I met him he was soft-spoken, but he was always polite. It was always, 'Hello, ma'am' and 'How are you, ma'am?' He was a pleasure to be around."

"Charlie wasn't a big talker," says Bobby. "He spoke when he needed to. He never embarrassed any of his teammates by calling them out or making a lot of noise. He did most of his talking with his play and if he ever needed to say something, he'd just walk up to you and say it matter of fact."

Warrick Dunn remembers one Florida State practice where he was running a wheel route and Charlie Ward tossed him a pass. Dunn dropped it. Ward approached Dunn and said, "You can never let that happen again." Dunn wouldn't drop another pass in practice at Florida State, and he and Ward established a close relationship on and off the field. They collaborated on a brilliant 79-yard score against Florida in 1993 that helped to catapult the Seminoles into the national championship against Nebraska. The game was in Gainesville, and the Gators made what looked to be a Florida State blowout into a competitive 27–21 game. Florida State was on its own 21-yard line and was stopped on first and second down. Then came third and ten. If the Seminoles were forced to punt, the Gators would have likely gotten the football back in excellent field position. The third-down play was supposed to be a simple 5-yard out pattern, but after catching the ball Dunn beat his man with a brilliant fake and broke open down the left sideline. There was no dropped pass.

Bowden has maintained that the togetherness of his 1987 team, the one that defeated Nebraska in the Fiesta Bowl, is likely unprecedented. That may be true, but the most physically daunting Bowden team is his 1993 version. That team is unmatched in Florida State history in terms of its sheer athleticism.

ESPN's Ivan Maisel writes in his book, *The Maisel Report: College Football's Most Overrated & Underrated*, where he ranks the 1993 team the fifth most underrated football champion ever: "The 1993 Seminoles dominated in ways that many national champions never do. They won their 11 regular-season victories, including five against ranked teams, by an average margin of 37 points."

Ward wasn't your typical Division I college quarterback prospect. At large college programs in the late 1980s, African Americans were still being shuttled away from the position and toward either defensive back or running back. Ward also didn't fit other quarterback molds. He was quick, which allowed him to eventually become Florida State's starting point guard and later a player for the New York Knicks. But he was barely over six feet and weighed only 190 pounds; other top pass throwers were much bigger.

There was something about Ward, however, that intrigued Bowden. He even once mentioned Ward to Ann, saying, years before it would come true, that he thought Ward could be a phenomenal player at quarterback. It was the athleticism that piqued Bowden's interest. Bowden envisioned an offense with Ward at the helm that was drastically more up tempo and quick. What intrigued Bowden most was how, potentially, Ward could be a weapon that a defense would find almost impossible to account for. "What truly frustrates a defense," Bowden said, "is to play great pass coverage and then that quarterback breaks free."

Bowden had one hesitation. Centering an offense around Ward, Bowden believed, was potentially problematic. Not because of Ward but because Bowden had long resisted building any offense or defense around a single player. Bowden liked diversity and multiple options, not just one.

There were other problems. Ward needed work in the classroom; in 1988, however, he studied at Tallahassee Community College where he raised his grades and Bowden's confidence. Bowden was convinced and made a deal with Ward: keep your grades up and you'll be my quarterback in the future. It was a promise not unlike ones Bowden made to previous players and his assistant coaches, and like those former instances, it's a promise Bowden would keep. In the 1991–92 season, Ward led the Seminoles to the NCAA basketball Sweet 16 and Bowden made Ward the starting quarterback.

On November 7, 1992, Ward, as a junior, for only the second time that season, went into the shotgun and no-huddle offense and overcame a 14-point deficit to defeat Georgia Tech 29–24. It took a game against Virginia, a 13–3 squeaker, for the Seminoles to change their offense and make history. Assistant Brad Scott proposed to Bowden that the Seminoles start the game with the no-huddle, basketball-style offense. Bowden had envisioned Ward running this type of offense, but doing it from the beginning of the game would take some convincing. It just seemed so unusual to Bowden to utilize the scheme for the entirety of a contest, but after watching Ward so much in practice and games, Bowden relented. (There are actually several different versions of how the offense entered the Seminole system. Even Bowden has told several different ones.)

Bowden adapting should have been easily predictable. He'd initially believed in the 1960s that the passing game wouldn't be an effective tool in college football until he was convinced otherwise. This was similar. As stubborn as Bowden can be about certain things—his morning routine and beliefs about religion haven't changed in decades—when an educated argument is made to Bowden, he doesn't always remain entrenched, particularly when it comes to football.

There were also more personal reasons to believe in the fast break. Terry was at Samford, and Tommy was an assistant at Alabama learning the intricacies of the shotgun. Terry learned from

Tommy, and Bobby learned from Terry. It was a fascinating evolution. The concerns Bowden had about the blocking schemes were also soon eliminated. The problems the offense faced was that when receivers were spread out five wide, it left Ward vulnerable to unaccounted-for attackers. During the early use of the shotgun, assistants Brad Scott and Mark Richt traveled to NFL shotgun hotspots like Buffalo and Tampa Bay to watch how they protected passers. The Bills were particularly skilled at running the offense. Quarterback Jim Kelly used the "K-Gun" to make four Super Bowl appearances. Bowden also pilfered a play from the Bills, and the Seminoles called it "direct." It was basically what has now become called colloquially the "wildcat" offense. In it Dunn would take a direct snap from the center out of the shotgun and scamper. The play would pay huge dividends in critical moments of the championship season.

After the Seminoles went permanently to the fast-break offense, and with Ward playing the role of basketball player Steve Nash, the Seminoles won their final three regular-season contests by an average score of 61–17. Bowden destroyed the rival Gators by three touchdowns. The fast-break offense and one of the top ten athletes in college sports history were born.

So was Bowden's first national title. It was finally here. But of course it didn't come easy. It wouldn't be a Bowden moment if it did.

The comparison of Ward to Steve Nash is an apt one. What Ward did was coordinate the chaotic offense with supreme skill and patience but what's often lost—and this is where the Nash comparison comes in—is that Ward made the offense especially dangerous with perfectly skilled scrambles. The way Nash runs a devastating point guard and then, when needed, sinks a perfect jump shot. Ward looked to throw first and run second, but when he did run, it devastated a defense. And Ward did this against the sport's best athletes on that side of the football.

The Seminoles again opened the 1993 season ranked tops in the nation, and Ward was spectacular. The Seminoles started the season 9–0 and destroyed teams by a walloping average of 44–6, and the Seminoles weren't beating tulips. Bowden beat the Miami program that had given him so much heartache by a comfortable score of 28–10 and amazingly, afterward, the words *Wide Right* weren't mentioned at all.

The challenge to Bowden winning his first title didn't come this time from Miami. It came from Notre Dame. When Florida State played them in 1993, the Seminoles were ranked first in the nation and the Irish second. Notre Dame, known for its alleged forthright approach to college sports, demonstrated the Irish weren't above cheap tricks to get an advantage. McCorvey remembers taking a pregame walk on the Notre Dame field just a matter of hours before the game and the field sprinkler system was active. The players were flabbergasted. "Who would turn a sprinkler system on before a game?" McCorvey asked himself. The reason why was simple. The Irish thought a slick field would slow down Florida State's speed.

The media, rather unoriginally, again used the "Game of the Century" moniker. It started as the blowout of the century. The Irish were one of the few teams that possessed the athleticism on both sides of the ball to handle Florida State. Most important, the Irish defensive line was massive and strong, and they gave a tremendous push up the middle, which disrupted Florida State's running game.

Meanwhile Notre Dame's runner, Lee Becton, ran for over 100 yards and a score. The Irish defense not only shut down the passing game by corralling Ward but also by crushing the Seminoles with huge runs. At least, all of that remained true for over a half. The problem for Notre Dame—which is why the sprinklers were on—was no team could account for FSU's speed, and that fact showed as the game wore on. In the third quarter, trailing 24–7, Seminole receivers who had been slipping on the field had adjusted to the slick footing and began making catches. When Bowden went to a four-receiver set, McCorvey starred. He was greatly helped by a pair of long spikes for his cleats sent to him by his high school coach. In Florida State's momentous second half, McCorvey grabbed 10 passes for 124 yards.

The offense started taking hold, and Notre Dame's lead was only 31–24. The game ended with a Ward pass being knocked down with just seconds left.

Bowden was dumbfounded. He thought, again, his chances to snag a national title were dead. "Some will say the big one got away from Bowden again," he told reporters after the game. "Well, it took me six years to figure out what the big ones are. The big one is the one you lose."

"We thought we deserved to be in the national championship game," said Dunn. "But we thought that loss ended our chances. We were wondering how far we'd drop in the polls. We didn't drop far."

Pollsters correctly figured that the game was so close the Seminoles didn't deserve a precipitous fall, and Florida State went from first to second place in the polls. Then, finally, some of the breaks started going Bowden's way. Just a week after that loss to the Irish, a kicker would again play a crucial role in Bowden's life. Boston College jumped to an early lead against Notre Dame and held on to it for three quarters, only to watch Notre Dame score three touchdowns in eleven minutes. Dan Gordon, the kicker for the Eagles, made a last-second field goal to beat Notre Dame. When Florida State players heard the news, some shouted and screamed in joy.

Bowden was happy, but he knew they had to beat Florida, so his joy was tempered. But he made it to the title game against No. 1 Nebraska thanks to perhaps the greatest play in Florida State history, Dunn's 79-yard screen pass for a touchdown.

He did it. He finally did it. Now all he had to do was win the game. Easy, right?

The week of January 1, 1994, Bowden faced a litany of questions from the media and it would be one of the few times he'd get cranky with the press. He'd heard for years how he couldn't win the big game and now he was hearing it in triplicate. And, frankly, though he was able to smile about the questions and joke about them, Bowden was wholly irritated.

In Miami several days before the Orange Bowl game, Bowden had a question for the assembled press. "Men, let me ask you something," he said. "What is the highest honor in ya'll's profession?" There were several responses, with at least one being the Pulitzer Prize. Bowden seized on the opportunity. "How many of you have ever won one of those awards?" he asked. None of the writers raised his hand.

"Well, is the fact that you've never won driving you crazy?" Bowden continued. "Does the fact that you've never won mean you're no good at your profession? Are ya'll failures? Are you obsessed with winning one of those awards? I'll bet you don't give a darn whether you ever win one of them or not. Now, if you win one, good. But I'll bet it ain't driving you crazy. That's about the way it always was with me about winning a national championship. It was not driving me crazy." Bowden, with a smile and a laugh, was able to turn the tough questions back on the press.

But was it true? Did Bowden really feel that way about winning a championship? "He wanted to win a national championship," says Ann, "but it didn't keep him awake at night."

"My dad is big on his place in history," said son Terry. "Of course he wanted to win. He wasn't obsessed though. More important to him was building a program that could consistently win, year in and year out."

What frustrated Bowden, in his mind, was the inability of people to appreciate how difficult it was to do what he'd done at Florida State. In seven consecutive seasons, the Seminoles had gone 11–1, 11–1, 10–2, 10–2, 11–2, 11–1, and 12–2. Couldn't people dadgum see, Bowden thought, how difficult it was to do that?

Bowden remembers that he could only be so frustrated, because shortly before the game Ward traveled to New York for the Heisman Trophy ceremony and won the award by the second-largest margin ever with 2,310 points versus Heath Shuler's 1,622. Miami's coach, Dennis Erickson, called Ward "the greatest college quarterback I've ever seen," and Bowden called Ward's winning the Heisman one of the proudest moments of his life. Ward would go on to a splendid NBA career and then become a high school football coach, all the while being a great sports ambassador. (Ward did have one moment of horrid judgment. In 2001, the *New York Times Magazine* quoted Ward saying in a bible-study meeting: "Jews are stubborn . . . tell me, why did they persecute Jesus unless he knew something they didn't want to accept. . . . They had his blood on their hands." After a huge firestorm of criticism, Ward said: "I want to truly apologize to everyone who was offended by the *New York Times Magazine* story. I will say again that I would never criticize any group or religion.")

Ward's winning the Heisman did have an unforeseen negative consequence on the Seminoles and the national championship. "Charlie was dead tired from the Heisman and all those dadgum distractions [surrounding the ceremony]," Bowden explained. The traveling and numerous interviews took its toll, especially early in the game as Ward missed several throws that he normally easily made.

In the fourth quarter—ironically a field goal battle—Florida State trailed 16–15 with 1:16 left in the game. Bowden then turned to his freshman kicker, Scott Bentley, who made a 22-yard field goal with 21 seconds remaining in the contest. It looked like Bowden was finally going to win a championship. "I thought that was it," Bowden says.

It wasn't. There was still drama to come. After the made field goal, a significant number of Seminole players ran onto the field celebrating what they thought was a win. After the coaching staff got the players back behind the sideline, a chill went across the Seminoles and the celebrating players stopped their guffawing after Cornhusker quarterback Tommy Frazier threw a 29-yard pass to Trumane Bell that put Nebraska at the Florida State 28-yard line. For a moment, the Seminole sideline was eerily quiet, then everyone looked up at the scoreboard and saw that time had expired.

The game was over and players dumped a bucket of ice water over Bowden's head. The cold ran through his body like a shot of electricity. He shivered and laughed and thought: the cold never felt so good. He started to make his way to the other sideline in search of Tom Osborne, the Nebraska coach. As Bowden started walking (he'd just taken a few steps) he was approached by one of the game officials.

"Coach," he told Bowden, "we have to put one second back on the clock."

Bowden was stunned. He could barely talk. The combination of the ice bath and incredulity left one of the most talkative men in football almost speechless. Almost.

"Why?" Bowden asked the official. "Ain't the game over?"

"No," Bowden was told, "they called a timeout."

"I was just dadgum shocked," Bowden said.

So Bowden did the only thing he could. He moved his drenched figure back to the sideline and quickly, after a few seconds, recovered from the awkwardness of the moment and started coaching again. He queried the game officials about where the football would be spotted; after checking the video replay, they put the football at the 28-yard line, which meant Nebraska had a makable 46-yard field goal. Bowden thought for certain the field goal would be good and he'd lose the big game again.

When the kick missed, Bowden didn't exactly see it go wide left because of where he was standing, but he knew it had missed when he heard Florida State fans cheering loudly. Bowden relaxed and knew, finally, he had done it. He likes to joke that he's the only coach in history to win the same championship game twice.

"It's hard for me to believe we won the thing," Bowden told reporters after the game, still smiling. "Seems like every time you turned around, someone else was winning the game." The big game, that is.

Bowden was also asked, now that he'd won a title was it time to retire? He was incredulous over the question. "Retire?" he said. "Heck no. Now that I've got one, I want two. Next season I want you writers saying, 'Did you know that Bobby Bowden is the oldest football coach who ain't never won two national championships?'"

Some of the more humorous stories about Bowden focus on his inability to remember the names of players. The name gaps are not a function of age either. It's been this way for years. The *Lakeland Ledger* newspaper did the best job of assembling the examples, like when Bowden was at West Virginia and he called one of his players named Greg Dorn "Phil." After Bowden constantly called him Phil, others on the team did as well. He called quarterback Danny McManus "Fred" and thrower Thad Busby "Brad." Warrick Dunn was "Warren" (close enough). In 1978, the Seminoles beat Cincinnati, 26–21, and the game was won after a 54-yard bomb from Jimmy Jordan to Sam Platt. The play came on a fourth down and long 22 yards. On his television show the following day, in which Bowden breaks down the game with a host, he saw the play and could hardly contain his excitement and his recollecting of names was at its humorous worst. "Sam, oh my goodness, Merriwell, whatever the heck your name is," Bowden said. "Sam, I never loved you so much in all my life as I did then. Fourth and 22 . . . I could've hugged your neck."

Where his memory isn't fuzzy is with general or specific details about the past, particularly games and eras during his tenure at Florida State. Actually, during his tenure at any school. They remain crystal clear, even the games from decades ago. "When people ask me about the 1990s," Bowden says, "I sometimes think about the 1970s."

He remembers what Florida State was like when he took over. The football program was practically bankrupt. There was no enclosed weight room, just wire surrounding a room under the stadium. Bowden's office was once only eight feet by twelve feet with three of the walls being only concrete and gray with no paint. The players had one helmet only for both practice and games, not separate ones for each as with most big programs. So the helmets, on the Friday before games, would be painted and a Florida State decal attached. Practice pants didn't fit on some players, but there was nothing the school could do because they couldn't pay for better. The school couldn't afford Astroturf cleats so when they played at schools that had the surface, the trainers had to borrow Astroturf cleats from other schools that weren't using theirs. They were once stomped on yearly by the rival Gators. No one wanted to play for them. Florida State football was a joke and then came Bowden.

There are a handful of moments in sports when the success of a program or team can be traced directly to one person. Michael Jordan and the Chicago Bulls, Babe Ruth and the New York Yankees, Paul Brown and the Cleveland Browns, Tom Landry and the Dallas Cowboys, and Bill Belichick and the New England Patriots are some of those instances. Bowden's time at Florida State is another one of those moments.

For Bowden it didn't come without heartache but now he had the title, and a visit to the White House in the months following the national championship game; the theme was how Bowden had finally won it. It was an impressive sight. The Seminole football program that was once just an arm's length away from elimination was next to the president of the United States. Bobby and Ann stood next to President Clinton as the team and others formed a semicircle in the background.

Clinton opened the ceremonies with a Bowden-like humorous tale. "It seems that sometime in the distant future, his sons, Terry and Tommy, arrive together at the Pearly Gates, and they're startled to find that their name is not on the register," Clinton said. "So Saint Peter tells Terry and Tommy they'll have to take the elevator down to the other place. When the elevator opens at the bottom, instead of fire and flame, they're shocked to find bitter cold, icicles hanging from the ceiling, the whole place frozen over, at which point Tommy turns to Terry and says, 'I guess Dad finally won a national championship.'"

Clinton continued, "There have been so many years when so many people thought that the Florida State Seminoles at the end of a given season were the best team in America. It was really rewarding for those of us who follow football year-in and year-out to see this day come. But what this season really teaches is a lesson that Coach Bowden and I both understand, the power of perseverance. You and your team didn't quit when the sportswriters said you couldn't win the big one. You didn't quit after you lost a tough game to a great Notre Dame team. You didn't quit when you were trailing Nebraska with a minute and sixteen seconds left on the clock in the Orange Bowl. And in the end, when everything was on the line, you believed in yourselves and stayed together as a team, and you got the job done."

Bowden couldn't resist making a joke at his own expense in front of the president. "After getting so close for the previous six years," he said, "I was beginning to wonder if I would ever get to come here, after forty-one years of coaching, which means if that rate keeps up, I'll be 106 the next time we get to come here." The moment wouldn't be the last time Bowden swapped one-liners with Clinton. When Clinton phoned Bowden after the coach won his second national title, Bowden asked the president: "Hey, buddy, why aren't you working tonight?"

The mood was festive and the quips were flying, but inside Bowden felt a deep sense of relief and accomplishment. He did it. He really, finally did it.

AN ILLUSTRATION OF JUST how far Bowden's image had changed in both the eyes of the media and the coaching community, from one where Bowden was seen as someone who couldn't win the championship game to one who was on the verge of building a dynasty, was the phone call Bowden received from Tom Osborne not long after Bowden had just beaten Osborne's Huskers in the title game. Osborne had a curious request. He wanted to spend time with Bowden's staff during the spring of 1994 and simply observe. Osborne had replaced—temporarily at least—Bowden on the hot seat as the coach who was struggling to win a national title and Osborne had just witnessed Bowden beating him. So he decided to see how Bowden did things, and for a week in March 1994 Osborne spent every minute possible with Bowden by attending practices and team meetings as well as watching how Bowden ran his staff meetings. When Osborne returned to Nebraska at the end of the week, the only thing he could determine that Bowden did differently was that Bobby held deeply intimate devotionals at the beginning of staff meetings; Osborne implemented his own devotionals in 1994. The Cornhuskers won the title in 1994, 1995, and 1997; and Osborne was the national coach of the year in 1994. ESPN named Osborne coach of the decade in 1999.

Osborne wrote of his meetings with Bowden in his 1999 book, *Faith in the Game:* "The common perception of football coaches is that of hard-driving, profane, callous individuals who care little about spiritual matters. Often people engaged in highly competitive enterprises believe that matters of faith hinder effective performance. My experience has led me to believe that spiritual preparation contributes to effective performance no matter what the arena."

Questioning someone's faith is a profane act, particularly with Bowden, who is sincere in his religious beliefs. Yet there is a fair point to raise with coaches who openly discuss their religious beliefs and the dichotomy between those beliefs and their actions when it comes to some players on their teams who repeatedly commit crimes and violate team rules. Osborne is a pertinent example. Although his religious beliefs were and are sincere, he coached some of the most notorious scoundrels in recent college football history. One was Lawrence Phillips, who was accused while at Nebraska of dragging a woman down a flight of stairs by her hair. Phillips pleaded no contest to misdemeanor trespassing and assault. Osborne was widely criticized for what was seen as a mild punishment of Phillips, suspending him briefly, when Phillips likely should've been kicked off the team.

Christian Peter, like Phillips, was a key component of Osborne's great Nebraska teams in the 1990s. While there Peter was arrested eight times for a variety of ugly offenses, including threatening to kill a parking attendant, grabbing a woman by the throat, public urination, and trespassing, among other violations. His alleged rapes of then Nebraska student Kathy Redmond—who would later emerge as a prominent activist—were buried by the Nebraska coaching staff. Osborne would later apologize to Redmond, but it took years for him to do so.

So the question is: Are the religious beliefs espoused by coaches compromised by their actions with thug players? Are they, in effect, hypocrites? Redmond, who like Bowden is deeply religious, has thought about this question often. Redmond started the National Coalition Against Violent Athletes not long after she was attacked by Peter. She has respect for Bowden and his faith, and she's actually had extensive communications with Osborne.

Perhaps the biggest problem Redmond has is not solely with how some coaches handle problem players but also how some fans, purported to be Christians, handle female victims who accuse an athlete of a violent crime. The faith Christian fans preach, she believes of some fans, isn't what some hard-core fans actually practice if their college hero faces criminal accusations. She was attacked personally and viciously by Cornhusker fans once her case became public.

Redmond wrote to the author, in part:

It is very difficult in many situations, to follow a Christian path because simply, a human being cannot know another human being's heart. However, coaches faced with athlete misbehavior cannot judge the heart of a victim, either. And so, by accepting the role as judge and jury over a very private matter involving only a few people, it could be said that they are seizing control and power from God in order to create an outcome that benefits their end. That situation in itself presents a contradiction to the Christian faith which asks that followers surrender themselves to God, trust God and allow Him to control their lives. As it stands with many Christian coaches, the coach becomes God to the player, instead of God becoming God to the player.

Personally, the most difficult and traumatizing part of being victimized was having my Christian integrity questioned by those who did not know me, but purported to be fellow Christians . . . the betrayal was the most painful part of my entire journey and one that created my bitterness, hostility and ultimately, my own control issues as it relates to God and my own personal Christian journey.

"I could accept an evil man doing an evil act," Redmond said, "but not a Christian man condoning it."

Bowden himself would endure his own problems with the discipline of his players. They would become so notorious, they'd threaten his image and legacy.

The cover of the May 16, 1994, *Sports Illustrated* featured the Florida State helmet in the center under a bold headline that read: "Tainted Title." The subheadline minced no words: "Florida State won the 1993 national football championship, but because of unsavory agents; rule breaking players and its own lack of vigilance, it ended up a loser." And, with that, the Foot Locker scandal was born.

It was an exhaustive and thorough story. The article began and read in part:

> The most brazen episode was a midseason, two-handed, shelf-clearing, 90-minute shopping spree by members of the Florida State team that would go on to win college football's national championship. Running shoes galore. Team jackets of all colors. Dozens of hats, T-shirts, shorts and gloves. Winter coats that the players could wear to South Bend for the big game against the Fighting Irish. Some $6,000 worth of merchandise in all, armloads and armloads, large cartons crammed full, every item purchased on the credit card of Raul Bey, a Las Vegas businessman who was in a loose partnership with a street agent named Nate Cebrun.
>
> "We had about seven boxes of stuff," says Corey Sawyer, a Seminole cornerback, describing the buying binge that took place last Nov. 7, six days before Florida State was upset by Notre Dame, the Seminoles' only loss of 1993. "Big boxes. We were fitting about 12 winter coats in one box. We just bought out Foot Locker. Period." Sawyer, though only a junior, made himself available for last month's NFL draft and was chosen by the Cincinnati Bengals as the first player in the fourth round. "Half the football team was there," says

Sawyer, one of seven sources who told *SI* about the after-hours expedition to the Foot Locker store in Tallahassee's Governor's Square Mall. "We had four carloads of people. When we stopped, they [Bey and Cebrun] asked, 'Are y'all finished?' Everything was fine. That was the purpose of them coming to Tallahassee: to buy." To buy not just clothing but also the honor of Florida State, whose national title is now tainted.

To this day, Bowden says he didn't know about what the agents and players were doing, but in some ways it doesn't matter what Bowden believes. What matters is that Bowden was seen as a coach who didn't maintain an acceptable level of discipline. Again, Bowden vehemently denies this, but the evidence from that and other examples shows a coach who while caring about his players deeply sometimes allows them far too much leeway, and some of those players take gross advantage of that leeway.

Some of the problems Bowden faced soon after the national title game, and in the years after it, though not on the same felonious level as some of Nebraska's players in that era (as well as other schools) were nevertheless troubling. They included:

- The team's kicker, Sebastian Janikowski, was known for his brawling at campus bars in the late 1990s.
- Another player was accused of soliciting sex from an undercover female police officer.
- Wide receivers Peter Warrick and Laveranues Coles went on a discounted shopping binge in 1999 that led to a charge of theft. Warrick was a Heisman Trophy candidate at the time and was suspended by Bowden before rejoining the Seminoles. Coles was kicked off the team. He'd had previous run-ins, including a suspension for a misdemeanor battery charge and academic issues. "It's not like I killed the president," Warrick told the media then. Warrick initially was charged with a felony, and Bowden joked at the time that he was "praying for a misdemeanor."

- In 2002, quarterback Adrian McPherson was being investigated on gambling and theft charges. Bowden dismissed him from the team. "When they recruited me, the coaches came and told my parents that they would be my parents away from home," McPherson said. "I went to the coaches, and they turned their back on me." However, later, McPherson pled no contest to theft, forgery, and gambling charges. He was sentenced to forty days of work camp, thirty months' probation, and fifty hours of community service.

- In 2003, quarterback Chris Rix, far from handicapped, used an unauthorized handicap parking tag on campus and was fined $100. The year before he'd been suspended for Florida State's Sugar Bowl for sleeping through a final exam. He'd also been benched for being late to team meetings and missing classes. Bowden quipped when asked about advice he'd give Rix, "Stay healthy, park in the right place, and if any teacher even mentions an exam, take it."

  (That one-liner was reminiscent of another Bowden line when he was asked by a reporter about Florida State linebacker Reggie Herring, who played for Bowden from 1978 to 1980. When describing Herring, Bowden said, "He doesn't know the meaning of the word 'fear.' In fact, I just saw his grades and he doesn't know the meaning of a lot of words.")

Rix's relationship with both Bowden and Florida State fans typified the complexity of this issue. When Rix first got to Florida State in 2001, he was one of Bowden's favorite young players, and the feeling was reciprocated. Bowden awed Rix even when he saw the coach disrobed. Rix played well in his first game as a Seminole beating Duke and after a round of postgame interviews, Rix headed to the shower. For many away games, coaches and players in college use the same showers at the same time and that was the case with the Florida State coaches and players. A few minutes into his shower Rix turned and suddenly there was Bowden showering too. "Good game, boy," said a bathing Bowden, "not a bad start." Rix had come to idolize Bowden and seeing Bowden in his birthday suit was almost surreal. "Thanks, Coach," was all Rix could think to say back. But Rix thought: *Coach Bowden is congratulating me while naked in the shower. What a strange world.*

Rix's tenure at Florida State would be mixed, full of great highs but also missteps, and this is the point where it gets complicated. Rix made mistakes born of arrogance and the garden-variety immaturity every teenager faces, but there were also extenuating circumstances few people knew. According to Rix, part of the problem was that his father was a serious alcoholic who had traversed into a frightening state of depression. His father's alleged severe alcoholism and mental state affected Rix deeply, on and off the field. "At times I admit that I brought some undue negative attention on myself as a teenager in college growing up in front of the whole country," Rix said. "At other times, I felt that members of the media acted like they were in the know about everything in my life. The one that sticks out the most is when I missed a religion exam my sophomore year and was ineligible for the Sugar Bowl. The media made it sound like I didn't care and blew off the test when the truth was that my father was very ill. Actually, the real truth is that my father was in a deep depression and was drinking himself to death. Believe me, I felt the impact of this and was hurt more than anyone else because of this. Football and class was the last thing on my mind the night before that test." Rix explained that only one member of the media, a writer for the *Tallahassee Democrat*, knew about the situation with Rix's father. Rix says that his father is now sober.

One person who knew the entire story was Ann. Bowden's wife told several friends and family members that Rix deserved sympathy, and she pleaded with Bowden to be understanding of Rix's dire issues. Bowden was except, Rix maintains, just once. "I would have to say that Coach Bowden was always fair with me, with one exception," says Rix. "When I was ready to come back after getting hurt against Clemson in the third game of my senior year," Rix didn't get his starting job back, he said. "I did not feel it was fair," explained Rix. "I am sure that Coach had pressure on him from different angles, but I didn't think that you could lose your job due to injury."

The media once fixated on Bowden's inability to win national championships and now there were writers questioning if Bowden had full control of his program. "At major programs across the country," wrote former *New York Times* columnist Selena Roberts in 2002, "where the perp walk has become the unofficial sack dance, accused players have been propped up by their coaches' unconditional love. And Florida State, as much as anyone, has laid out the welcome mat for misfits."

Competitors took advantage of the scandal. One in particular was Spurrier. Bowden wouldn't be the sole target of Spurrier's wit. He'd spend a coaching lifetime mocking rivals. Spurrier once called Georgia coach Ray Goff "Ray Goof" and said of the University of Tennessee, referring to the fact that Spurrier's Gators often beat Tennessee and sent them to the Citrus Bowl, the resting place of second-place teams in the SEC, "You can't spell Citrus without 'U-T.'" He later added that Tennessee quarterback Peyton Manning, who would win a Super Bowl with the Indianapolis Colts, returned for his senior season at Tennessee because Manning wanted to be the three-time Citrus Bowl most valuable player.

As mentioned earlier, Bowden has implemented discipline at times, and those instances have actually been meaningful. One was in 1995. Randy Moss was a high school wide receiver in West Virginia who had been contacted by numerous colleges infatuated by one of the fastest players some college scouts and coaches had ever seen. Moss was a *Parade* magazine All-American who was physically perhaps the most gifted player in the nation. In high school, he weighed a sturdy 200 pounds and was six feet five inches tall. In leading his team to state titles in 1992 and 1993, Moss returned kicks and was the team's punter as well as wideout. Moss was also the state's basketball player of the year. Notre Dame's coach, Lou Holtz, believed Moss was the best high school football player he'd ever witnessed, and the Irish won the battle to get Moss. The problem for Notre Dame came late in Moss's senior year when a close friend was called several racist remarks by another student. Moss defended his friend and pummeled the offending student, sending him to the hospital with injuries to his spleen, head, and kidney. Moss pled guilty to battery and received a suspended jail sentence along with probation. Moss avoided serious prison time—he spent three days in jail and had the remaining twenty-seven suspended—but the incident caused Notre Dame to revoke his scholarship.

"Having been an athlete [in high school] and a big star of the state [West Virginia], I think that put an extra eye on me," Moss said. "A lot had to do with me being black and not staying in the state to go to college. I did get myself in trouble, but in all honesty I was given the raw end of the deal. To this day, I still hold a grudge."

After losing Moss, Holtz called his friend Bowden. "You won't believe the speed of this guy," Holtz told Bowden. Bowden didn't have to wait long to see it. Moss was accepted into Florida State and sat out his freshman year. When the Seminoles timed Moss in the 40-yard dash, their jaws dropped when he ran a blistering 4.25, which had surpassed the mark of Sanders.

"I've said this before," Bowden said. "I compare all great athletes to Deion and Randy was a bigger Deion."

"When I met him, he was just the nicest kid," Bowden said. "He was kinda quiet. While he was here, he never caused problems. Not a one."

Bowden sat down with Moss and warned him: you have one strike left. If you get in trouble, you'll be gone. Moss was home in West Virginia when Bowden read in the local newspaper that Moss had violated the condition of his parole by testing positive for marijuana use. Bowden didn't hesitate. Moss was gone. Thus, over a two-year period Bowden had dismissed Moss and Coles. Coles was almost as fast and talented as Moss. If Bowden had not initiated those dismissals, he would've had Moss, Coles, and Warrick on the team. With that kind of firepower he might not have lost a game over a two- or three-year period.

So, yes, Bowden will discipline his players, just not as much as he should, not as fast as he should, and not as consistently as he should.

"I discipline my boys the way I think I should," he said, "not the way the media or anyone else thinks I should."

. . . .

THE WEEK OF FLORIDA State's national championship game against
Virginia Tech in January 2000, the quarterback for the Hokies,
Michael Vick, enjoyed his fair share of the New Orleans nightlife.
According to two former teammates, Vick did what young men do
in New Orleans: he drank and partied. Teammates say they were
amazed at Vick's performance in the Sugar Bowl title contest—he
passed for 225 yards and rushed for 97 more—because, said one
teammate, Vick appeared to be severely hungover for the game.
"He made Sebastian Janikowski look like an AA member," the
player said, referring to Alcoholics Anonymous, and the former
Florida State kicker. No one except Vick will ever know about the
veracity of those claims, but they don't seem completely absurd.
Vick's judgment would be a constant topic as his football career
continued into the professional ranks. There would be numerous
incidents with none worse than Vick serving a federal prison sentence for running an elaborate dogfighting ring.

If Vick was indeed suffering from a week of drinking on
Bourbon Street, he needed to do it more. He put up one of the
more gutsy performances in title game history. He also wasn't the
only player drawn in by the allure of the New Orleans party scene
(far better people than Vick have fallen victim to its charms). For
that reason, Bowden was extremely concerned the effect New
Orleans might have on the pregame preparation. He nicknamed
the Big Easy "Sodom and Gomorrah" after the biblical cities
destroyed by God (though Bowden obviously gave that nickname
before the devastating storm that was Katrina). Bowden made
certain the team knew that excessive partying wouldn't be tolerated. For the first three days of practice he instituted a 1 A.M.
curfew, and after that the curfew was moved up to 11:30.

"There are so many distractions in that city for young kids,"
said Bowden. "There are so many distractions for adults, let alone
kids. We needed to keep them focused."

Most of the Florida State players abided by the curfew and were
indeed focused. In many ways, what happened before and after

that game was typical of a Bowden team. Most of the players bordered on professional in their preparation, and most took Bowden's curfew elective seriously. They even went further. A group of seniors on the team called a players-only meeting and agreed that all of the starters and other vital players were to avoid the partying scene and catch up on their REM sleep. "We told the guys who weren't going to be playing in the game to have a good time," says safety Sean Key, "do whatever they wanted to do. We told everybody else to stay in their hotel and sleep."

But it wasn't perfect curfew attendance and angelic devotion. Two players missed the 1 A.M. curfew by several minutes, and bad boy kicker Janikowski missed the 11:30 curfew by almost two hours. Bowden punished the three curfew offenders by making them run extra laps after a Sunday practice.

The majority of Florida State starters, however, followed the advice of the seniors. There was barely any partying, just hard work. The Seminoles have always been one of the more mentally tough programs and this game proved it, though it came one year after Florida State showed a moment of arrogance and vulnerability. The year before the Virginia Tech game, Florida State lost in the national championship to Tennessee. There's little question that this was one of the few Bowden teams that lost its poise in a big game. There may have been missed field goals, but there was rarely hubris and large amounts of sloppiness in those moments. Against the Volunteers, the Seminoles generated less than 300 yards of offense and had a dozen penalties for over 100 yards. Bowden remembers that after the game, he walked into the locker room, and there were a number of players openly crying. He can't remember a team being more emotionally crushed after a loss and that included some of the "Wide Right" games.

The Tennessee game was a jolt to the Seminole program. Afterward, there were questions Bowden had for himself and his coaches, and there were, for a brief moment, pangs of disgust at losing what might have been. Months after the Tennessee game, Bowden and Ann were sitting in their house when Bobby suddenly blurted, "We should have beaten Tennessee, you know that? We should have beaten those boys." Ann has heard Bobby make such exclamations before, but something was different about this one.

The game against the Volunteers was Bowden's third title game appearance, losing two. Some in the media began calling the Seminoles the Buffalo Bills of college football. "Oh, yeah, my legacy is terrible," Bowden responded several weeks before the Virginia Tech game, sarcasm dripping from his words. "Thirteen years in the top four in the country, 13 straight years with at least 10 victories. It's just terrible because I haven't won but one national championship." His comment said a lot about what Bowden had accomplished at Florida State. There was a time in Florida State's history when winning one title would have led to a decade-long party in Tallahassee.

Bowden and the Seminole players used what happened against the Volunteers as motivation against the Hokies. The embarrassing performance was a constant topic in the days leading up to the Virginia Tech game. The discussion was so well worn that Bowden mostly stayed away from it as the game got closer. He instead focused on some tactical changes in his bowl preparation plans. As Bowden told the media at the time, he believed the biggest reason the Seminoles lost to Tennessee was due to massive inactivity. There were forty-four days between Florida State's last game and the title contest versus the Volunteers. That lapse was forty-five days for the Sugar Bowl, and Bowden wanted his team physically challenged in the layoff. He ran the Seminoles through a series of rugged full-contact practices and scrimmages. When some of the practices got extremely chippy, Bowden knew it was time to pull back. *We're ready*, he thought.

So was quarterback Chris Weinke. It had been a brutally long road for Weinke. Weinke was an All-American high school player from St. Paul, Minnesota. He was drastically different from Ward. Both were smart and adaptable, but Weinke was taller and bulkier and had a far stronger arm. He also wasn't half the scrambler Ward was (though not many quarterbacks were). Weinke was nevertheless a gifted athlete, and Bowden thought Weinke could be practically the apotheosis of the drop-back thrower. Bowden told some of his assistants that Weinke was the best pure quarterback prospect he'd seen in many years, if not ever.

The problem for Florida State was that the Toronto Blue Jays thought just as highly of Weinke as Bowden did. Weinke was a star baseball player in high school as well as a gifted quarterback. When Blue Jay scouts saw Weinke, they made plans for him to be with their organization just as Bowden was making plans for Weinke to be a Seminole. In the end, the Blue Jays were able to capture Weinke because of a $600,000 offer, given to Weinke if he gave up football. It is impossible to expect a teenage kid to turn down that kind of money. Weinke didn't.

Bowden was disappointed but he understood. In January 1991, soon after hearing the news that Weinke was going to baseball, Bowden wrote Weinke an emotional letter.

Dear Chris,

Thanks so much for your Christmas card. Coming from you it really means a lot to me. I think of you often and your family and the great visit we had a year ago at this time.

I sure hated to lose you to baseball, but if that is what you wanted, that is what I wanted. Chris, I do want you to keep one thing in mind. If baseball does not work out for you, I hope you will come back here and play football. I have had a lot of quarterbacks in my 38 years of coaching but I have never had anyone that I thought would be a better prospect than you. I really think you have all the tools. With about 3 1/2 years of college football you could be a No. 1 draft choice. Probably be worth many millions and millions of dollars. Now knowing you and your quality, you might do the same thing in baseball, but if it ever does not seem what you want, I hope you will get in touch with me immediately and we'll get things worked out. Now I'm not trying to talk you out of your commitment. You have got to do your best in reaching your present goal. I am just saying that if your elbow, shoulder or

something knocks you out of baseball, I still think you can be a
great football player and we would love to have you here.
  Give my love to all the family and I will always consider
you one of mine. Thanks again for your note and have a
wonderful 1991. I will be keeping up with you.

Sincerely,
Coach Bowden

There was of course a self-interest aspect to the letter. Bowden
was planting the idea in the mind of Weinke that he'd be welcomed
back at any time. If Weinke returned, that was good for Bowden
and the program. Yet Bowden also meant what he said. He cared
about Weinke, and the letter serves as an excellent example of why
Bowden was able to not just reach many of his players but engender
their loyalty long after they departed the school.

The Seminoles moved on without Weinke. Years passed, and
while Bowden's program continued to grow Weinke was beginning
to think he'd selected the wrong sport. Weinke struggled as a third
baseman in Toronto's farm system and never made it beyond Toronto's AAA level, failing to hit above .284 in his five seasons with
the Blue Jays. It was a frustrating time for Weinke, and eventually
he decided his baseball career had run its course. He contacted
offensive coordinator Richt, following up on Bowden's letter and
offer that he could return to the program if something happened
with baseball. Richt went immediately to Bowden.

"Guess who I heard from?" Richt said. "Chris Weinke wants to
come back."

Bowden wondered if Weinke could still play after some six years
away from the sport. So did Richt. There was one other complication, and his name was Drew Henson. Bowden had become almost
as intrigued with Henson as he had with Weinke (though not
quite). It was easy to see why. Henson was a three-sport star at a
Michigan high school and attracted both NFL and MLB scouts.
USA Today named him its baseball player of the year, and there was
at least one scout that compared Henson with John Elway.

As Weinke had attracted the attention of the Blue Jays, the New

York Yankees were becoming infatuated with Henson. During his junior year in high school, Henson desired to sign with the Seminoles but wanted a curious, if not overly demanding, guarantee: he asked Bowden not to commit to any other quarterbacks. Bowden was going to agree. That is, until he heard from Weinke.

Bowden made a declaration to Richt. "We're gonna keep our word to Chris," Bowden said.

What Weinke gave Bowden was a coach on the field and what Bowden gave Weinke was rescue from a baseball career that had gone off track. Bowden believed baseball had given Weinke poise, though there were initial doubts if the correct decision had been made after Weinke tossed six interceptions against N.C. State. Those doubts would quickly subside. When Weinke returned to the Seminoles in 1997, he was an extremely mature twenty-four years old. That allowed Weinke to lead Florida State to an undefeated year in 1999 and a national championship. Weinke also became Bowden's second Heisman Trophy winner.

Weinke's toughness impressed Bowden particularly in November 1998 during a game in Tallahassee against Virginia. When Weinke was sacked, his head and neck were dangerously compressed. The team's trainer and director of sports medicine, Randy Oravetz, knew immediately something was badly wrong and his instincts were correct as later examinations revealed that Weinke had a ruptured disc in his neck. Weinke was operated on almost immediately and miraculously, after a long and painful recovery, was able to start again in the following season.

In the national championship game, Weinke's calmness was on full display. Despite Vick's night of alleged heavy drinking before the game, he and the Virginia Tech offense presented an unexpected challenge to the Seminole defense. Vick and the Hokies returned from what seemed like an insurmountable 28–7 lead by the Seminoles some eighteen minutes into the game to take a 29–28 lead late. "We could have fainted right there," said center Eric Thomas to the media after the game. "Last year we would have."

Weinke was twenty-seven years old in that game, and after Virginia Tech took the lead, he engineered an 85-yard, eleven-play drive in which he connected on all seven passes. The experience in New Orleans was in sharp contrast to when he traveled with the team to the national title game the year before in Arizona. He was still recovering from the neck injury and suffered from waves of pain and migraine headaches caused by still present leakage of spinal fluid.

Weinke wasn't the only hero of the game. Warrick had recovered from his Dillard store discounted shopping spree to emerge as one of the best players in the nation. As spectacular as Vick was, Warrick was better. He scored on a pass from Weinke, a punt return, and then on the game's final score. "Y'all want me to finish them?" Warrick asked before that last touchdown.

After the win, as Florida State players, families, and fans swarmed the field, and there was raucous jubilation. Bobby remembers seeing Ann in a corner of the Superdome, near the end zone. When they spotted each other, they both smiled; and Ann greeted Bobby with a great hug.

"When you win a second national championship," Bowden tells me, "it puts you in a pretty unique group of coaches. I was proud of that, but I was most proud of my boys. Goin' undefeated. That's something special. It was a real feeling of accomplishment."

It was his first undefeated team in three decades. The high from that game, Bowden says, lasted years. It's easy to see why. That team became the first in college football history to go the entire season—from the first poll to the last—ranked first in the country. At the close of the decade, Bowden had accomplished everything a coach could do. He turned around the Florida State program, went undefeated, won multiple titles, and had established the Seminoles as the program of the 1990s.

What put Bowden on a similar and likely higher plateau than almost every other coach in history was how Bowden had won at many different places with many different styles. At small colleges in Alabama, his teams ran the football extensively. As an assistant at Florida State, he learned the intricacies of the passing game, and expounded on them, running a pro-style offense when few teams even tried. As head coach at West Virginia, he ran a more varied offense, taking advantage of all the previous stops and lessons. As head coach at Florida State, he first ran an offense that resembled the Magic Johnson–led Los Angeles Lakers and then in his second title, he used Weinke in a more drop-back style that was still explosive but less frenetic.

Despite his age and inflexible elements to his personality, when it came to football, Bowden was able to twist and bend both with different eras and personnel. Modern coaches like Tressel or Meyer are great in their own right, and Meyer is one of the few coaches who has the ability to win several more championships. Meyer has the smarts, the recruiting capabilities, and the resources to keep the Gators near the top of the college football world. He could eclipse Bowden as the greatest one day, many years down the road, if the NFL doesn't grab him first.

Coaches younger than Bowden, ironically, are not as capable at adapting and stick more stubbornly to their systems no matter the personnel. One of Bowden's greatest assets was that he didn't.

That did not mean Bowden wouldn't again experience heartache or even loss. After winning his second title, he knew it wasn't always going to be this smooth. Nothing in college football is. Nothing when it comes to family is either. This fact would be proven again when the Bowden coaching son most people know the least would cause some of the most uncomfortable headlines the family would ever experience.

The oldest of the four sons, Steve was a solid athlete like the other Bowden men. He was all-state in football and played on the West Virginia freshman team. His athletic career pretty much ended then. "Steve got a little tired of holding the dummies and the dirty uniforms," Ann says, "and he never wanted to coach." He did want to teach, however, and receive as much education as possible. He went to seminary and earned his master's and doctorate degrees in theology and ethics, respectively. As a teacher and counselor at Flagler College, Steve was a popular faculty member. As a teacher at Samford University in 1987, he was selected as the most outstanding professor. Steve later decided to go into the investment business as a way to mentally challenge himself.

With two others, he helped form a coach's retirement fund, Bowden, Bolton and Burgdorf. He received his Series 6 and 63 securities and insurance licenses and started to examine stock and investment options for Bobby and Ann. Steve was smart. He was a quick study, with a mind that could retain large amounts of information. He was an excellent money man. But he was not a good judge of character. And because of that, he soon became immersed in a shadowy universe full of criminal characters.

CHAPTER SIXTEEN

STEVE

Case number CR-03-BE-55-S: *The United States of America v. R. Stephen Bowden.*

People said Steve was a crook. People called him a two-bit con man. The truth, of course, is much more complicated. The case is less about a Bowden boy gone bad than it is a father and son trying to help each other. Or perhaps, most important, about a son trying to impress his famous father.

This part of Steve's life begins with an Alabama man named James Michael Hanks, who while working for others, recruited Brian Burgdorf, a former Alabama quarterback, and Steve, as sub-promoters of the Millennium Fund, billed as an investment chance for the privileged few, according to the government. A joint investigation by the FBI, the IRS Criminal Investigation Bureau, and the Alabama Securities Commission resulted in indictments alleging that the three men and three others conspired to offer and sell unregistered securities to fourteen residents of Alabama, Florida, and Tennessee, a document from the Alabama commission states. The investigation found that between June 1996 and July 1998, the investors were directed to transfer more than $10 million to Chateau Forte Consortium, the alleged manager of the fund; Trust Services, a Panamanian offshore trust firm; and/or Private Asset Management S.A., a Panamanian brokerage firm, in exchange for stock in the fund, the document states.

In effect, the government alleged, it was a Ponzi scheme. The fund guaranteed a 14 percent return, government lawyers said, from a fictitious source. "It was a scam, plain and simple," says Adolph Dean, an assistant U.S. attorney in Birmingham, Alabama, who handled the case.

Steve had recruited the Bowden men. At one point, Terry, Tommy, and Bobby flew with Steve to Panama, according to Dean, for what he says was a fancy presentation high on gloss but thin on facts. "Bobby was eventually supposed to be the hook to get other investors," Dean says. Throughout the process, Bobby continually emphasized to Steve that the fund needed to be proper. "Steve, be sure it's legal," he told his son. "I cannot afford to get my name into something. If there's any taint to it, it's going to be all over the country."

Bobby and daughter Ginger's husband, John Madden, invested in the fund. But not all the Bowdens were convinced it was legitimate. Terry, the more street-smart brother, also was a lawyer and much tougher to fool. Tommy had his doubts as well. "If you notice, Terry and Tommy did not put any money into it," prosecutor Dean says. "What does that tell you? My opinion is that they knew what was happening. But Bobby wanted to help his son."

Actually, it was a combination of the two men wanting to help each other. Bobby has long been concerned about whether he and Ann would have enough money in retirement. You never forget the sting of coming from the other side of the tracks, as Bobby likes to say. In the end, Bobby suspended disbelief so his son, as Dean says, "would have a place at the table with the big boys in the investment business." And Steve might have been trying to show people he could be as successful off the football field as his brothers were on it. When Steve later spoke to the court, records show he said: "It looked to me at that time as a wonderful opportunity to show my family and friends that, by golly, I can be successful financially and professionally in whatever I choose to set my hand to. Unfortunately, it turned out to be a hand as heavy as a lead balloon, and it caused a lot of grief and a lot of anguish and a lot of loss."

Several times after the 2003 indictment, Dean talked with the Bowdens and was so overwhelmed by their unity and sincerity, he began to enjoy speaking with them. He talked football with Bobby—favorite victories, Deion Sanders stories—and noticed something many people do when they come to know the Bowdens. "The women are incredibly strong," Dean says. "The men may be the coaches, but the women are the bosses."

"Bobby made me feel like a part of their family," he says. "It was genuine too. I liked them a lot, to be honest. I really can't say what the intent of Steve was. I do know what Bobby's intent in the whole thing was. It was to help his son. Intuitively, the deal probably sounded strange to Bobby. But he wanted to be a dad to his son. He wanted him to be successful. He wanted his boy at the table."

In the end, Bobby lost a total of $1.6 million, while all investors lost $10 million total, according to court records. Steve pleaded guilty and faced a maximum of forty-one months in prison and restitution totaling $4.3 million, but because he and the Bowden family were so cooperative, in October 2003 he was sentenced to six months of home detention and one year of probation, court records show. Steve also was ordered to pay $1.26 million in restitution.

Steve's sentencing leads to a question. Did he receive leniency because he was a Bowden? Prosecutors on the case vehemently denied this and say he would have gotten the same sentence if his name was John Smith and he was the son of a math teacher instead of the son of a coach.

At his sentencing, the Bowden family was there in full force, backing Steve. Sister Ginger, a prosecutor herself, stood up and made a passionate plea for his freedom. "I have tremendous respect, Your Honor, for the law," she told the court, "for the belief that the law applies to all men and that no man is above the law, not my brother, not myself, not anyone else. And with that said, I want this court to know that I know, and that my family knows, Steve to be an honest and honorable man, that he's been devastated by the ugly turn of events, that he's agonized over the fact that he may have somehow encouraged others to invest in what's now known to be a fraudulent fund."

Bobby also spoke at length. "As tight as our family is . . . I mean, there's no way any of my children would scam or swindle me," he said. "Steve still manages my money," Bowden told the court. "He and I are building a lot of condos down in the Destin area, and he manages it. . . . I guess the point I'm trying to bring out is that I have not lost one bit of confidence or trust or faith in him whatsoever during this."

When it was his turn, Steve took full responsibility for what he did in an eloquent speech to the court. Family members say Steve is the most gifted communicator of them all. "As difficult as it's been this past nine months to look at the charges against me and think that can't be me they're talking about," he told the court, "or to read the newspapers and know that the reputation I spent so many years building up has just dissipated like a vapor in the wind, and I can never grab it and claim it back again, because most of the people that will ever know my name will know me as the guy who stole $1.6 million from his father."

Says Dean: "All in all, I don't get upset about Steve getting probation. Did he know what was going on? Probably. Did he do it with malice? Probably not. Did he try to rip off his daddy? Probably not. He's no innocent, but he's no great criminal either."

No Bowden child is ever excommunicated. Steve had apologized profusely to Bobby and Ann, and they never believed he intentionally stole from anyone, let alone them. Perhaps the judge, Karon O. Bowdre, capsulated the family's posttrial reaction best during the sentencing of Steve: "You are indeed fortunate to have a strong family that supports you in this matter," she said, according to a court transcript, "and I know that with the support of your family and with the faith in God that you and your family have that you will weather this storm, and you will come through stronger as a result. It's hard at this point to see that, but I am confident that that will be the result."

So the family moved on, still close, still trusting. So much so that Steve still handles his parents' finances and investments. And the topic of Steve's legal troubles is never broached within the family. Ever.

BOBBY REMEMBERS A STORY. Shortly after the 2000 season, Bowden heard from Vince Dooley, the former coach at the University of Georgia. Dooley coached the Bulldogs from 1964 to 1988 and won over two hundred games. He and Bowden knew each other well, and he called Bowden not as the Georgia coach but as the school's athletic director. He had a question: Was offensive coordinator Richt tough enough to be a head coach? "I'm worried that he's too nice," Dooley told Bowden.

Bowden thought the question was fair. Richt was smart and he was also hardworking, but he was extremely nice. Sometimes in football that word—*nice*—is an expletive.

Richt had spent over ten years with Bowden and Bowden knew Richt well. He believed Richt's skin was sufficiently thick. "You're going to find that he's much tougher than he looks," Bowden said.

Richt departed Florida State for Georgia and led the Bulldogs on a rebirth that saw Richt become one of just nine head coaches in major college history to record 70 or more wins in his first seven years. Losing Richt would become arguably the greatest personnel loss of Bowden's long career. Some have traced the recent decline of Bowden's program to the exact date Richt left, which was December 26, 2000. "That was the day Georgia hired Florida State offensive coordinator Mark Richt as its head coach," wrote the *Sporting News*. "That's also the day the Seminoles' vaunted football program began to decay."

It seems like a simplistic thought. If a deep and rich program like Florida State's can't survive the loss of one coach, it deserves to lose. Yet the loss of Richt, without question, was a major factor for why Bowden has struggled recently. "Losing Richt hurt," says former running back Lorenzo Booker. "We may have been running the same plays, but the offense wasn't called the same. When and why you call a play matters." Richt was an uncanny and un-usual play caller in that not only was he excellent at picking the right play to call, he also called the play at the perfect moment in the game.

The fact Bowden lost Richt was only one reason why Bowden hasn't returned to a national title game. It was significant, but the biggest remains the fact that Bowden hasn't been able to recruit stars the way he once did. There simply are more good programs and fewer great players to go around. "We had guys like Charlie and Derrick," said Bowden, speaking of Charlie Ward and Derrick Brooks. "We need more players like that."

They need star power at quarterback perhaps more than any position, which was evident when the Seminoles played their rival Gators late in 2008. The Seminoles were beaten by Florida, 45–15. The game featured Tim Tebow, who won a Heisman Trophy in 2007 and was a finalist again in 2008. Tebow is the type of player Bowden used to recruit on a yearly basis, but the Seminoles haven't had a Heisman winner since Weinke. Keep in mind that one of the signature players at the position for Bowden was supposed to be Rix, but he never truly matured as a player (now Rix is a mature family man). He was followed by a number of other busts at the position.

Bowden believes he is close to getting those impact players again. Others disagree. In fact, some in the media continued to call for Bowden to step down, and by 2008 there was no pretense of civility. A headline in the *South Florida Sun-Sentinel* read, "It's alarmingly clear: Bobby Bowden must go." Wrote columnist Larry Williams of the *Post and Courier* newspaper several days before Bowden coached his 500th game in 2008: "No easy way to put this because picking on Bobby Bowden feels kind of like cutting in front of a senior citizen at the local dinner buffet . . . [but] everything we've seen lately tells us that Bowden needs to end this pursuit and hang up his headsets. And that's assuming he actually wears headsets anymore. You see, Bowden doesn't do much coaching these days. He just sort of hangs around and watches Florida State struggle to pull itself from a morass of stunning mediocrity."

Contrarily, in Bowden's mind, it's only a matter of time before the Seminoles make a resurgence. He believes people are underestimating him the way they did when he took over the program decades ago and have several times since.

"I know I'm older," he said. "But I'm not ready to go yet. I still got something left. This program still has a lot left. Don't count us out."

LAST MAN STANDING

*The Bear always said, "If I retire, I'll be dead a week later."
Well, he died a month later. Me? I'd just as soon die right out
there on the field.*

—BOBBY BOWDEN

*Who cares? When they bury me, are they going to put on my
gravestone "You're one win ahead of Bobby Bowden"? That's
good for you guys [media]. You need something to write about,
obviously. Bobby Bowden has been a great credit to our game,
everywhere he's coached. If he comes out with more wins than I
do when we're both out of it, I'm glad it's [him].*

—JOE PATERNO IN SEPTEMBER 2008
WHEN ASKED ABOUT THE ALL-TIME WIN RECORD

More scenes from the life of Bowden . . .

Sometimes Bowden's message of personal responsibility and accountability sticks, sometimes it doesn't, sometimes it takes years for that message to soak through the thickness of a young man's skull.

Clevan Thomas played four years at defensive back for Bowden beginning in 1997. During that time, he won four ACC titles and a national championship. When the 2001 NFL draft arrived, it looked like Thomas would be another standout in a long line of superb Seminole defensive backs to play professional football. There was just one problem. Thomas was an utter mess.

Just before the draft he tested positive for marijuana use. His personal life was in shambles. Thomas was losing his longtime girlfriend, and suddenly his phone stopped ringing. The NFL wasn't calling. His old Florida State buddies weren't either. For the first time since he was a kid, a six-year-old kid, organized football wasn't a part of his life. He traveled back to his old Miami neighborhood. There was nothing there for him. As with many athletes, when football is ripped from their lives, so is a great deal of their self-worth. And as has happened in the past with athletes who find themselves without football, thoughts of suicide crept into his head.

"I had too much pride," Thomas said. "And by having so much pride I was kind of blinded to what my reality really was. I thought about committing suicide, I really did. But what got me out of it was—each year Coach Bowden would make us go to church. I didn't grow up in a Christian home. I didn't have a church background. And Coach Bowden would always preach to us about getting married, about having a life outside of football. I used to take all that for granted."

Thomas started to remember specifically some of Bowden's teachings. By the end of 2001 he decided to become a born-again Christian. He joined the Arena Football League and became one of the best defensive players the league had ever seen. He got married and had two kids. The drugs were gone. The bad times were a memory.

This is the part where your doubt and cynicism reach DefCon status. And that's understandable. Thomas wouldn't be the first person to discuss his belief in God while bumping uglies with a mistress (or two) or playing the role of roughneck outside a club. Yet something about Thomas's story feels genuine. Thomas one day probably heard Bowden's voice in his head. "Look in the dadgum mirror," Thomas might have heard Bowden say, "and straighten out your life. It's not too late, son."

. . . .

THE MAT DRILLS. THEY are as ever present at Florida State as Bowden's drawl. They are so tough that Seminole players measure themselves by whether or not they vomited doing them. Those who don't are seen as lucky and possessors of gold-plated stomach linings.

There are two types of Florida State players. Those who have thrown up during mat drills and those who will. In April 2008, freshman Bert Reed threw up three times on the first day of mat drills in trash cans placed smartly around the gym.

The validity, if not the sanity of the drills, was publicly questioned when one of Bowden's Florida State players, linebacker Devaughn Darling, who was just eighteen years old, fell to the ground during the drills and died on February 26, 2001. A medical examination later determined that Darling had suffered from cardiac arrhythmia. A police investigation cleared the Seminoles of wrongdoing, and almost any Florida State player still lauds the benefits of the drills.

The death of Darling led to one of the most public awkward moments in Bowden's life. During the memorial service at Florida State's Ruby Diamond Auditorium, in front of a large audience, Bowden began that he hoped "this won't hit anyone the wrong way" but Darling was "the first player I've coached in forty-seven years who actually worked himself to death." It was a cold and inappropriate comment that caused a murmur among the audience. It was also shocking because it was so out of character for a coach who cares for his players as much as any other. Bowden says he was simply speaking about Darling's exemplary work ethic.

(Bowden would also receive criticism for adopting "Let's Roll" as the 2002 team's mantra, putting the words on the team's practice shirts. The phrase was used on September 11, 2001, by United Airlines Flight 93 passenger Todd Beamer just before the passengers stormed the cockpit of the plane; the plane crashed in a field in Pennsylvania. Some thought use of the phrase was insensitive.)

This wouldn't be the first time Bowden would get news that one of his players had died. In 1986, Pablo Lopez, a starting lineman for the Seminoles, was shot and killed after breaking up an argument at party. Lopez, who was married and had one young child, went to a dance on campus with his wife. After Lopez ended the dispute between a belligerent partygoer and teammate, the man went home, retrieved a shotgun, and came back to the party where Lopez and teammates were hanging out before heading home. The man shot Lopez in the chest, practically killing him instantly.

After getting the news of Lopez's death, Bowden raced to the hospital, and upon proceeding through the double doors, he saw that dozens of members of the football team were waiting for news. The players knew Lopez had been shot, but they didn't know how dire the situation was. Bowden gathered the team in the hospital's chapel, which was located in a corner of the building and wasn't much bigger than Bowden's Florida State office. The scene not only taught Bowden more about grief, he learned a lesson about how differently sometimes the races express the emotion. He writes in *Tales from the Seminoles Sideline* that after telling the players, who were mostly black, "They were just screaming, and laying on the floor, and kicking the floor. I didn't know people responded like this over a death. That must have gone on for ten minutes. It was my first experience around a minority race when somebody dies. This group's custom is to do this, and this group's custom is to do that. I didn't know this would be the reaction the kids would have. Since that time I've been to a funeral at a black church, and people cried out. They are more animated while we're more silent. It's their way of doing it."

In Darling's case, the family later sued Florida State, claiming Darling was deprived of water and other fluids during the drills. In 2004, a judge approved a $2 million settlement. Bowden also changed the mat drill program by adding longer water breaks and a full-time EMT on site who carefully watches the players as they drill.

The drills continue to this day and remain a vital staple of the Seminole program. Beginning in February, players are there, during the 5 A.M. hour, three days a week for four weeks. For an hour and a half they assemble on several large mats and run through various drills that push their minds and bodies further than they ever thought possible. "For the first time in your life, you reach a point where you really don't think you are physically capable of going any farther," quarterback Drew Weatherford said. "It's a lot more mental than it is physical. It definitely pushes your body to the limit, but it teaches you that your body can go a lot further than your mind really thinks."

"If you turned on a film from the first day to the last day, you would be shocked from the difference you see in players," said former Florida State defensive lineman Todd Stroud, who played for Bowden in the 1980s. ". . . I think in the past here at Florida State, the mat drills have kind of been a rallying point for the team to where they feel like they can't be beaten, and they've done something that no one else has done. They have walked through the fire of hell and back again together."

IN NOVEMBER 2008, FLORIDA State safety Myron Rolle missed a pivotal game against the University of Maryland. He had a good reason. Rolle temporarily left the team to find out if he was a winner of a Rhodes scholarship. The Seminoles played the Terrapins while Rolle hopped on a private plane to Birmingham for a final interview regarding the scholarship he'd indeed win.

"In my fifty-five years of coaching," Bowden told the author, "I've never had one quite like him."

WHAT BOWDEN *HAS* HAD in his five decades of coaching are questions about his disciplinary skills. Those questions have haunted him repeatedly and would again in 2008. Bowden suspended five Florida State players after they were involved in a campus brawl against members of the Phi Beta Sigma fraternity. The suspensions not only caused the Seminoles to lose the game, but the trouble further injured the image of a program still hurting from the academic scandal. In the 2008 season, nineteen players were held out of games for disciplinary reasons, mostly for academic issues. When those five players were suspended for the Boston College game, it was the seventh time that season Florida State suspended players for a game.

The fight also again demonstrated the duality of Bowden, one of the most decent men in the sport's history. He could reach and recruit players like Rolle, but he continued—all these years later—to fail to consistently discipline his players. "If I'm sitting up there [at NCAA headquarters] in Indianapolis looking at this," said Jim Smith, a former Florida attorney general who chairs the school's board of trustees, "I'd say, 'Those guys down there aren't taking this [disciplinary] thing very serious.'"

Bowden explained that he constantly warns his players about avoiding problematic situations. "I've done this every year," he said. "'Man, you have to back away from trouble. You might look like a coward but you must back away. My phone number is listed. Call me.'"

The problem is Bowden—and perhaps no coach—reaches all of his players. Of the five players suspended for the fight, three had been suspended previously for other reasons.

FOLLOWING A 2001 GAME against Maryland, the two head coaches, Bowden and Ralph Friedgen, approached each other to shake hands. The game was a wild one. The score was tied at 31 heading into the fourth quarter when Maryland turned the football over three times. It was Friedgen's first game against Bowden, and Bowden offered Friedgen a little postgame advice.

"Son, you can't turn the ball over," Bowden told Friedgen.

"I felt like saying, 'Thanks for the news flash,'" Friedgen said.

THE 2008 ACC MEDIA day had a distinct Bowden flavor. Tommy, the Clemson coach, sat at one table while his father Bobby sat several feet away at an adjacent one. It was natural for reporters to ask Bobby about his legacy. It was strange when one asked Tommy about his. "I'd like to talk about my legacy when I'm dead or re-tired," Tommy joked.

A smile came onto his face and there was a pause. He glanced at Bobby. "Now I sound like my father," Tommy remarked.

In the summer of 2008, Bowden arrived at Florida State's annual kickoff luncheon and was in typical Bobby form. He started his talk with a joke about his age. He spoke and pointed to music professor Tommy Wright, who more than five decades earlier had created the whimsical Florida State fight song. "I was reading a statistic the other day—I think you'll like this," Bowden told Wright and the crowd. "The average age of Amer-ican people is 35, in other words, 350 million Americans and the average age is 35. Now me and you are waaaaaay above average."

Then Bowden moved on to Ann. "Hard to believe Ann and I have been married fifty-nine years, which leads up to a story. Ann always says, 'Now don't you dare say nothing about me, don't you dare say nothing about me. . . .'" Ann was present and as Bowden paused for effect, he located his wife in the audience. "Ann ain't stood yet," Bowden said. "Or are you standing now?"

Then Bowden spoke about when he first met Ann. "I was speaking to the women's Extra Point Club last week and I told 'em the story that I met Ann when she was fourteen years of age back in 1946," Bowden said. "She had moved to Birmingham and was attending the same high school. Well, I was much older than Ann, but the first time I saw her, I liked her looks, you know. I went over there, I said, 'Where . . . have . . . you . . . been . . . all my life?' She said, 'Well, the first half of it, I wasn't born.'"

The *Tampa Tribune* wrote in 2008: "When linebacker Scot Brantley came out of Ocala Forest High in 1976, he chose Florida over Ala-bama. FSU wasn't even a consideration. 'They weren't on anybody's radar,' said Brantley, the former Buc who cohosts a sports-talk radio show in Tampa. 'How far they've come, to me, is a testament to one man. I think they should name the place Bobby Bowden University.'"

. . . .

One of Bowden's finer traits is his treatment of others. "Bobby is one of the few people I've ever known who when he meets you," says George Henshaw, a former FSU assistant, who has known Bowden for decades, "he focuses entirely on you. He's not looking to better deal you or thinking, 'How the hell do I get out of this conversation?' He treats the guy who donated $100,000 the same as the guy who donated $100."

Bowden's hospitable nature has always extended to the media. Bowden isn't just liked by many mainstream media members, he's venerated, mainly because unlike other coaches such as Alabama's Nick Saban or even the great Joe Paterno, Bowden has always respected most college beat writers. He has rarely lied about injuries. There have been few public outbursts aimed at reporters and even fewer attempts at manipulation or general deceit. Although Bowden has tightened access to his players in recent years, he has mainly treated the press with respect and cooperation. He also forgives. Bianchi, the *Sentinel* columnist, once shredded Bowden in a column after Bowden wrote a letter to a judge pleading for leniency on behalf of Michael Gibson, a serial rapist who played briefly for Florida State. It was a highly questionable decision by Bowden, and Bianchi rightly skewered the coach. Florida State administration officials and fans were infuriated with Bianchi. Bowden was so angry he wanted to telephone Bianchi at home and scream at him.

Bowden saw Bianchi a short time later. How did Bowden react when he saw Bianchi? "Hey, buddy, how ya doin'?" he told Bianchi. Was Bowden being phony? Not really. Bowden's way is to be angry for a limited period and then move on. It's one of his more defining characteristics.

In July 2008, *Birmingham News* reporter Ian Rapoport was phoning people who had worked with Dave Hart, the former Florida State athletic director who had just joined the University of Alabama. Rapoport decided to phone Bowden at home around 7:45 on a Wednesday night. The phone rang and Ann answered. Rapoport asked for Bobby. Ann responded that he was asleep; Bobby rises at 4 A.M. each morning and has done so for most of his life.

"Are you a telemarketer?" she asked. "What is your call in reference to?"

"I'm a reporter from the *Birmingham News*," Rapoport said, "but there is no need to wake him. I'm just calling about Dave Hart. He was just hired at Alabama."

"Oh, we love Dave," Ann said. "I'll wake my husband. Hold on."

Bowden awoke and gave the interview from the comfort of his bed.

Rob Wilson, the longtime sports information guru for Florida State, has been with the school for decades, and by Bowden's side equally as long. Wilson witnessed perhaps the most audacious example of Bowden's sense of media gentility. Following a game against Michigan, the entire Florida State team was on the bus ready to depart. Wilson began to get curious stares. Where was Bowden? He wasn't on the bus.

Wilson headed back inside the visitors' locker room to search for him. There, under the shower's spray, was Bowden, doing what people do in the shower. He was soaping up. A few feet away was a fully clothed sportswriter, dripping wet, interviewing a totally naked Bowden and furiously taking notes.

Bowden was giving an interview . . . in the shower. You don't get more cooperative with the media than that.

Bowden's office deep inside the stadium named after him is its normally aggressively uncluttered self. History books on World War II and one of his heroes, Bear Bryant, sit neatly on shelves (most of the books in Bowden's collection fall into three groupings: religion, military stories, and coaching). Papers are not strewn about (Bowden likes to begin each week with a clean desk). A small pink note with phone numbers to call sits in the center of his desk. The office is spacious but unpretentious, and many of the pictures on and around Bowden's desk are of family and coaching buddies.

Bowden chews on a massive unlit cigar; the end Bowden is

munching on looks like the head of a sliver of cauliflower. Bowden used to smoke them but he stopped after his sinuses became painfully irritated. His true addiction isn't cigars but chocolate. In the 1950s, when recruiting for South Georgia and driving through Tennessee and Alabama, Bowden would be on the prowl for milk and chocolate brownies almost as much as he was for good recruits.

He's now smiling, friendly as always, and talkative. If there are any worries, none is apparent now. Ann once said recently that Bowden has worried about their financial situation once he steps down. "He worries about when we retire, about [what if] we don't have enough money?" she said. "What if we get sick? What if we have to have 'round-the-clock nurses? I say, 'Look, I'm not worried about that because we're not going to need anything. We'll have each other.'" She then laughs: "You don't eat much when you're old." Bowden's worry is likely unfounded. He's guaranteed a $1 million bonus when he steps down as Florida State coach.

"We've been amazed at how we can still lay in bed next to each other and enjoy each other," Ann says. "The kids laugh at me when I say that. But it's the truth."

In April 2009, the Bowden family hosted a party for Bobby and Ann; attending the party were the couple's six children, twenty-one grandkids, and five great-grandchildren.

Bowden is asked about his legacy. Many times, over the past few years, Bowden has been hesitant to discuss the "L" word. In Bowden's mind, talking about legacy means the end of his professional coaching life is near. Again, to Bowden, after retiring from your job, there is just one last thing to do: die. He saw this happen to his father and Bryant, and he has always feared postretirement death would be his fate as well.

Bowden apparently isn't alone in that fear. Brent Musburger went on the *Dan Patrick Show* in October 2008 and spoke about Paterno. "This is a tough one for me because I have to say up front that JoePa is a dear friend of mine . . . I'll tell your listeners the truth as to why he still [coaches]," Musburger told the show. "He is fearful—and he looks back at Bear Bryant as the example—he is fearful that he would not be with us if he stepped away. He is a man that doesn't fish, doesn't play golf . . . he has no other interest other than his family and football. And he's just afraid what would happen with the rest of his life if he walks away from it."

Wrote SI.com's Frank Deford: "Yes, old is in. In college football, 80 is the new 60. If Penn State keeps winning, Old Joe Paterno—in the vernacular, JoePa (with the emphasis on the latter)—will be coach of the national champions at the age of—wow—82. But then, Pa can't stop coaching, or Old Bobby Bowden, who is merely 78 and has his Florida State team ranked No. 15, will pass him for most lifetime wins. Bowden has had two middle-aged sons fired as big-time coaches, while he keeps on rolling toward octogenarian land."

Bowden knows that coaching won't make him immortal, and he is keenly aware of his advanced age. After all, he started coaching on September 9, 1959, when Dwight Eisenhower was president and a fiery leader named Fidel Castro took control of Cuba. Bowden coached in his 500th game in 2008. Five . . . freaking . . . hundred. As Colorado coach Dan Hawkins said: "I think if you added up every basketball, baseball, softball, rec league, every game I've ever been in, I think it would probably add up to about 300. It's an amazing feat. I'm one of those guys who never says never, but I think as the years go on you're going to see that become very hard to do anymore."

On this day, however, Bowden is extremely contemplative. His words are passionate and emotional. During moments like these, it's understandable why Bowden has been such a sincerely effective coach, husband, and father. In these moments, you cannot take your eyes off him, and you believe every word that comes out of his mouth. The latter is something highly unusual for a big-time college coach.

"All my life, on Saturdays, I had a place to go," he said. "I got up in the morning, went through my routine, I left the house and coached. That's what I did. There's going to come a time when Saturday comes and I'll have no place to go. That'll be strange, you know? I won't be able to get up and go anywhere.

"I know people call me a figurehead. The problem is a lot of coaches are figureheads. A lot of coaches delegate. They do exactly what I do, but I catch heat for it. That's just the way it is. I know there are people who want me out, but I still have the fire. I still want to win. I do think there is something to the fact that I helped to build this program and deserve to leave when I want to leave. I hope that doesn't sound arrogant or anything but that's how I feel."

Bowden's legacy?

There were mistakes made. Over the years, he allowed some slick players to take advantage of his trusting disposition. Or maybe his normally keen senses about people were sometimes obstructed and overwhelmed by his strong desire to win.

Mostly, though, his legacy was one of almost unparalleled success on the field. He won. A lot. Just about more than anyone.

Former Florida State president Dr. Stanley Marshall was asked to reflect on the decision he made with the athletic director, John Bridges, to bring Bowden to the school. Marshall once said: "We hoped we were hiring a good, if not outstanding, coach. But we had no notion he would become what he has. The essence of the man to me is that he is fundamentally sound. He knows the game and hires excellent coaches. Plus, his personality helps in many important ways to sell the program. I can't think of any program that has achieved this amount of success in the same time. And it's all due to Bobby. It's a case of the right man, under the right conditions, at the right time."

"Sometimes, I hear certain people who are currently involved [with the university] feel like they understand and know Florida State," said Joe Camps, former Seminole player. He added: "They don't know Florida State. They don't know where Florida State was. When you go back to that era and watch it today, had it not been for people who didn't quit back then, Florida State may not be where it is today. Certainly Coach Bowden, with his tenure here, has proven that."

There has never been a sense of entitlement. Never. Not once. If he ever came close to arrogance, he always had Ann or the earthy reality of a large family to quickly snap him back. Or someone else. When Bowden once spoke at a church in West Virginia, he found himself in a small predicament. He repeatedly circled the lot, unable to find a parking spot. He finally gave up and double-parked in a spot that was far from legal. Bowden left a note on his windshield: "Dear officer, I am Bobby Bowden, football coach at West Virginia University. I have a very important engagement here at the church. I couldn't find a place to park, so I double-parked here. Please don't tow my car. Forgive us our trespasses."

When Bowden was done with his speech, he returned to the scene of the crime and indeed found that his car was still there, along with a fresh parking ticket and a note responding to his. "Dear Coach Bowden," the note read, "I have been patrolling this block for three years. I have a very important engagement too. It's my job. If I don't do it, I will lose it. Lead us not into temptation."

Bowden mostly won the right way. To be specific, while Florida State had its share of players who got into trouble off the field, it never reached the gutter depths of probation-plagued factories like Alabama and Auburn or other SEC horror shows. The SEC is to cheating what Superman is to comic book characters—simply the biggest and the baddest. Bowden's program never sunk to the levels of massive cash handouts or numerous times spent in the NCAA's principal's office. Again, Bowden's Seminoles weren't perfect, but Bowden mostly kept his head out of the NCAA muck.

More than anything, the pressure to win never changed Bowden. He was and remains one of the sport's greatest characters and quote machines. Bowden is as pleasant a person leaving Florida State as when he arrived more than three decades ago. With the help of Ann, he raised educated, grounded children despite them growing up in the maddening high-profile world of college sports, which, as Bill Walton mentioned, is one of the more challenging things any parent can do.

His legacy? The best coach in college football history, a dedicated husband, and a doting father. Not a bad legacy to have. Not a bad legacy to have at all.

"A lot of people in the past have asked me what about my legacy?" he added. "I've said this and that and I don't like talking about it all that much, but I answer the question the best I can. I want people to say, 'He was one of the best.' Not *the* best. Just one of the best. I want people to say I didn't cheat. We made some mistakes here, but I never had a win-at-all-costs mentality. We had that dadgum Free Shoes University thing, but we didn't know what the players were doing and anyone who says we did isn't telling the truth. I would've rather lost than be seen as a guy who won and cheated. I guess I want my legacy to be we won and we mostly won the right way, and along the way, people had fun, and I treated people with respect and decency. I was something Florida State could be proud of. They'd say, 'That dadgum Bowden was a good guy.' That's how I hope I'll be remembered."

ACKNOWLEDGMENTS

After a Tampa Bay Buccaneers game in December 2008, Derrick Brooks, wearing a dark suit and striped tie, walked slowly from the visitors' locker room in Atlanta's Georgia Dome to the team bus. He injured his ribs in what was a particularly violent game against Atlanta, and it showed on his face as he made the walk. He was in pain and was understandably not very happy. They'd lost the game, and to make matters worse he was in danger of missing the following week's game. He had not missed a game in his fourteen-year career.

Still, when I told him I was writing a book about Bowden, Brooks smiled. "I can talk about him forever," said Brooks.

In twenty years of practicing journalism, I have never seen such a large group of players stay so devoted to a coach so long after they played for him. Whether it's the players he coached at South Georgia College or Florida State. There has rarely, if ever, been anything like it with Bowden. Perhaps the closest comparison might be Bear Bryant or Paterno, but the loyalty Bowden engenders tops even those coaches.

The loyalty within the Bowden family, understandably, betters even that of the former players. One of the main objectives of this book was to have Bowden talking about his family and his family talking about him. I wanted those exchanges to be the star of the book.

Of course I cannot thank the Bowden family enough, particularly Bobby. A special thanks goes to Ginger, who spoke to me about such a painful topic and is one of the strongest people I've ever met.

Also, Bobby's trusted assistant, Sue Hall, was a great help, as was the Florida State public relations department. Both are remarkably classy.

As usual, my cherished childhood friend and great talent, Susan Thornton Hobby, did her usual excellent editing job. Jennifer O'Neill, the best researcher in the business, was a prolific help. Thank you also to the *Florida Times-Union*, a newspaper I'll always cherish, and also thank you to the *Times-Union*'s Maryann Sterzel for quickly arranging the photos that appear in this book.

Also thank you to CBSSports.com, particularly Mark Swanson, for giving me the occasional breather to work on this book.

My agent, John Monteleone, is the best I'll ever know, and my editor at HarperCollins, Mauro DiPreta, is brilliant and loyal. His assistant, Jennifer Schulkind, was incredibly helpful.

NOTES

INTRODUCTION

13   The Tigers looked elsewhere for a coach: NTSB identification number: IAD80AA018, January 11, 1980.

15   Terry would need to be ready for that battle: Joe Lapointe, "Bowden Has Still Got the Charm at Florida State," *New York Times*, October 13, 2001.

16   On the drive back, their car overheated: Sammy Batten, "Checking in on the Top Prospects from 1998," *Fayetteville Observer*, January 27, 2008.

16   Tommy Bowden also had his recruiting battles: Bobby Bowden, Steve Ellis, and Bill Vilona, *Pure Gold*, p. 98.

17   Instead, Terry eventually kicked Houston off: "Houston Gets the Boot," autigers.com, March 1998.

19   Bryant's reputation is mixed: David Climer, "Bear Bryant Stays a Symbol for Football," *Tennessean*, January 26, 2008.

19   Yet in 2006, *Sports Illustrated* wrote of Bryant: Frank Deford, "The Gridiron King & The Pursuit of the Record," *Sports Illustrated Presents*, August 30, 2006.

20   When Bowden and Ford first met: John Antonik, "A True Trailblazer," MSNsportsnet.com, July 29, 2006.

20   When Bowden became West Virginia's head coach: Ibid.

20   That was February 1970: Ibid.

21   Bowden refused: Cal Fussman, "What I've Learned: Bobby Bowden," *Esquire*, September 1, 2001.

21   SportingNews.com ranked its top coaches: Tom Dienhart,
      "Ranking the ACC Coaches," SportingNews.com, April 13,
      2007.

22   In his first fifteen years at Florida: Ben Brown, *Saint Bobby
      and the Barbarians*, p. 3.

23   Stagg pioneered the lateral pass: University of Chicago His-
      tory webpage, http://athletics.uchicago.edu/history/history-
      stagg.htm.

24   "Times have changed": Rick Rousos and Mike Cobb, "Papa
      'Nole: The Life and Times of Bobby Bowden," *Lakeland
      Ledger*, 2000.

24   Alphonso Carreker played on Florida State's: Mark Schla-
      bach, *What It Means to Be a Seminole*.

26   Ivan Maisel: "The Players and Coaches That Transcend the
      Game," ESPN.com, June 20, 2008.

CHAPTER ONE: TRAGEDY

29   "Ann was sixteen when I married her": "What I've Learned:
      Bobby Bowden," *Esquire*, September 1, 2001.

31   It had been a turbulent few days for Bobby: "Bowdens
      Mourn Together," *Atlanta Journal-Constitution*, September
      10, 2004.

33   Bobby was upstairs sleeping and raced downstairs: Bowden,
      Ellis, and Vilona, *Pure Gold*, p. 155.

34   In dealing with the tragedy, the family: Ibid., p. 10.

34   "It's just how they dealt with it": Ibid., p. 10.

34   Months after: www.fcapodcasting.com/oneonone, May 9,
      2009.

35   When she applied to law school: Ben Brown, *Winning's Only
      Part of the Game*, p. 65.

CHAPTER TWO: SON UNDER FIRE

45   Booker says he was so miserable: Mike Sielski, "Eagles'
      Booker Glad to Be Free of FSU Issues," Phillyburbs.com,
      June 5, 2008.

CHAPTER THREE: THE FEVER

53 Woodlawn was annexed by Birmingham: http://www.uab.edu/woodlawn/woodlawn_history.html.

54 Bobby was well behaved: Kyle Hightower, "Central Florida Sports Stars Share Their Favorite Christmas Memories," *Orlando Sentinel*, December 25, 2008.

55 In the year 1950 alone: http://www.thefreelibrary.com/Is+rheumatic+fever+making+a+comeback%3F-a053460614.

56 Bobby was born on November 8, 1929: Rick Rousos and Mike Cobb, "From the Sick Bed to the End Zone," *Lakeland Ledger*, 2000.

57 The church was organized: http://library.samford.edu/about/sc/treasure/ruhama.html.

62 "Some boys play football": Rousos and Cobb, "From the Sick Bed to the End Zone."

CHAPTER FOUR: APRIL FOOL'S IN LOVE

63 Ann Bowden stood smiling: Bobby Bowden and Mike Bynum, *Bound for Glory*, p. 56.

CHAPTER FIVE: THE COACHING LIFE

72 "Today's players are a lot bigger and faster": Jim Bowen, *Bobby Bowden: Memory of a Legend and His Boys from South Georgia College*, p. 36.

73 Ann would steer the subject: Ibid., p. 72.

77 9–1 and posted six shutouts: Rick Rousos and Mike Cobb, "Bobby's 'Brutal' Boot Camp," *Lakeland Ledger*, 2000.

CHAPTER SIX: MOUNTAINEER

80 He once told the team: *St. Petersburg Times*, http://pqasb.pqarchiver.com/sptimes/access/51730682.html?dids=51730682:51730682&FMT=FT&FMTS=ABS:FT&date=Aug+6%2C+1993&author=HUBERT+MIZELL&pub=St.+Petersburg+Times&edition=&startpage=1.C&desc=Peterson+legacy%3A+coaches.

81   Ann saw the rifle and didn't care: Bobby Bowden and Bill Smith, *More Than Just a Game*, p. 71.

89   McCartney met with Bowden: Mike Strange, "Big Hits Beget Big Honor for McCartney," Knoxnews.com, June 28, 2008.

92   "The biggest challenge": Antonik, "Hung in Effigy," MSNsportsnet.com, December 15, 2004.

96   "It was ugly": Ibid.

97   He cut out the editorial: Bowden and Smith, *More Than Just a Game*, p. 182.

CHAPTER SEVEN: PAPA 'NOLE

99   "When y'all started talking": Bobby Bowden, Jim Bettinger, and Julie S. Bettinger, *The Book of Bowden*, p. 60.

102   Economists believed then the nation: "Monthly Labor Review," http://www.bls.gov/opub/mlr/1985/03/art3full.pdf, March 1985.

102   "We were kind of running wild": Andrew Carter, "Bobby Bowden's Arrival at FSU Launched a College Football Powerhouse," *Orlando Sentinel*, December 26, 2008.

105   Bowden "fits": Brown, *Saint Bobby*, p. 4.

CHAPTER EIGHT: MATRIARCH

116   "The biggest thing that swayed me": Brett Malone, "Catching Up with Paul Piurowski," Noledigest.com.

117   Four years after being blasted: Floridastate.rivals.

123   In 1977, wide receiver Phil Williams: Schlabach, *What It Means to Be a Seminole*, p. 200.

125   "We could have gone": Ibid.

CHAPTER NINE: TERRY

136   "I was trying to decide": "Jeff Bowden Joins Terry Bowden's Coaching Staff," TimesDaily.com, January 31, 2009.

CHAPTER TEN: "TAKE FIVE MINUTES A DAY TO HATE FSU"

142   He shifted slightly from his pass-happy machinations: *Sports Illustrated*.

CHAPTER ELEVEN: TOMMY

155   "Out of all my kids": Bowden, Bettinger, and Bettinger, *Book of Bowden*, p. 59.

155   The note started: Bowden and Smith, *More Than Just a Game*, p. 181.

156   Bobby wrote to Terry: Ibid., p. 57.

157   Jeff called him back: Ibid., p. 59.

160   "Life right now is *Judge Judy*": Thomasville Times-Enterprise, http://www.timesenterprise.com/sports/local_story_104225904.html?keyword=topstory.

CHAPTER TWELVE: BOBBY'S SONG

163   "The Ballad of Bobby Bowden": Rod Kilbourn, the song title was later changed to "Sing a Song for Bobby" from the *Totally Nole* album.

167   "It's a long time ago": Tommy Deas, "What Might Have Been," *Tuscaloosa News*, September 29, 2007.

169   "I would assume": Ibid.

171   "Wayne wanted more control": Bobby Bowden and Steve Ellis, *Bobby Bowden's Tales from the Seminoles Sideline*, p. 141.

171   Brad Scott, the tight ends coach: Ibid., p. 141.

171   But Richt didn't want to do that: Ibid., p. 149.

172   "Art, why don't we throw to the tight end?": Ibid., p. 160.

174   "There is not a player that I played with": Brent Kallestad, "Talent-Filled 1987 Miami-Florida State Game Now Distant Past," Associated Press, October 19, 2007.

175–6   "I'm not going to wake him up": Bowden, Ellis, and Vilona, *Pure Gold*, p. 191.

CHAPTER THIRTEEN: LAW AND ORDER

177   Bobby Bowden's recruitment of LeRoy Butler: Gene Frenette, "Butler Made Difference On, Off Field," *Florida Times-Union*, July 20, 2002.

178   Butler was one of five players: Wilt Browning, "Legend Smiles at the Memory of His Part in a Famed Play," ACC.com, November 8, 2007.

179   in high school had a 4.0: Brown, *Saint Bobby*, p. 126.

184   In an alleged highly despicable act: "Defensive Tackle 'A Problem,'" *Palm Beach Post*, August 20, 2008.

185   Meyer's program isn't alone: "Coaches Step Up to Ensure Miami-FIU Brawl Won't Occur Again," *South Florida Sun-Sentinel*, September 11, 2007.

187   "It is now widely accepted": Michael A. Messner and Raewyn Connell, *Out of Play*, p. 48.

190   "In a lot of cases": "FSU Coach Bowden Still Reaching," timesfreepress.com, February 9, 2009.

CHAPTER FOURTEEN: WIDE RIGHT

195   "There were times when I was very small": Browning, "Legend Smiles," TheACC.com.

196   He began asking then sports information assistant Rob Wilson: http://www.youtube.com/watch?v=bUAlFzKTn38& feature=related, 1988.

198   The question about Bowden's age: Rick Rousos and Mike Cobb, "Just Call Him 'King of the Road,'" *Lakeland Ledger*, 2000.

199   The school's board of regents: Brown, *Saint Bobby*, p. 126.

202   "I sacrificed my own happiness": Greg Garber, ESPN, December 2000.

204   "You need to be helping players": Schlabach, *What It Means to Be a Seminole*, p. 299.

208   In the 1987–88 season: Rick Telander, SI.com, September 1998.

209   Churchill's quote: Brown, *Saint Bobby*, p. 278.

210   Many of the sixty-four thousand people: Ibid., p. 295.

212   Eventually Bowden sat him down: Austin Murphy, SI.com, December 1994.

CHAPTER FIFTEEN: CHAMPION

218   "Who would turn a sprinkler system on": Schlabach, *What It Means to Be a Seminole*, p. 286.

235   "We told the guys": Tim Layden, "Perfect Ending," *Sports Illustrated*, January 10, 2000.

235   "We should have beaten Tennessee": Ibid.

236   "Oh, yeah, my legacy is terrible": Ibid.

237   "Dear Chris": Bowden and Ellis, *Bobby Bowden's Tales*, p. 116.

AFTERWORD: LAST MAN STANDING

255   "If you turned on a film": Scott Carter, "Mat Drills Push FSU Players to the Limit," *Tampa Tribune*, March 7, 2008.

258   He also forgives: Mike Bianchi, "Dear Coach Bowden: Shut Up," *Orlando Sentinel*, March 5, 2004.

258   Bowden saw Bianchi a short time later: Mike Bianchi, "I Am Not Talking!" *Orlando Sentinel*, July 23, 2008.

262   "Sometimes, I hear certain people": Schlabach, *What It Means to Be a Seminole*, p. 145.

BIBLIOGRAPHY

Bowden, Bobby; Bettinger, Jim; and Bettinger, Julie. *The Book of Bowden*. Nashville, TN: TowleHouse Publishing, 2001.

Bowden, Bobby, and Bowden, Steve. *The Bowden Way*. Atlanta: Longstreeet Press, Inc., 2001.

Bowden, Bobby, and Brown, Ben. *Winning's Only Part of the Game*. New York: Warner Books, 1996.

Bowden, Bobby, and Bynum, Mike. *Bound for Glory*. College Station, TX: The We Believe Trust Fund, 1980.

Bowden, Bobby, and Ellis, Steve. *Bobby Bowden's Tales from the Seminoles Sidelines*. Champaign, IL: Sports Publishing, LLC, 2004.

Bowden, Bobby; Ellis, Steve; and Vilona, Bill. *Pure Gold*. Champaign, IL: Sports Publishing, LLC, 2006.

Bowden, Bobby, and Smith, Bill. *More Than Just a Game*. Nashville, TN: Thomas Nelson Publishers, 1994.

Bowen, Jim. *Bobby Bowden: Memories of a Legend and His Boys from South Georgia College*. Nashville, TN: Cold Tree Press, 2008.

Brown, Ben. *Saint Bobby and the Barbarians*. New York: Doubleday, 1992.

Jones, James. *F.S.U. One Time! A History of Seminole Football*. Tallahassee, FL: Sentry Press, 1973.

Maisel, Ivan. *The Maisel Report*. Chicago: Triumph Books, 2008.

Messner, Michael, and Connell, Raewyn. *Out of Play: Critical Essays on Gender and Sport.* New York: SUNY Press, 2007.

Schlabach, Mark. *What It Means to Be a Seminole.* Chicago: Triumph Books, 2007.

INDEX

ABC Sports, 127, 136
academic cheating scandal at
    Florida State (2007–2008),
    21, 44, 255–56
academics, and African
    American athletes, 182–84,
    186–89
Accorsi, Ernie, 27, 205
"acting white," 188
Adams, Lee, 146
"African American," use of
    term, 18
African American families
  disintegration of, 181, 186,
    187–88
  emphasis on sports, 186–87
African American players,
    177–78, 180–89
age questions about Bobby
    Bowden, 197–98, 206, 257,
    261
Alabama Crimson Tide,
    167–70
  Bowden as player at, 66

Bowden's flirtation with
    coaching job, 164–70
Bowden's love of, 69, 78
Bryant as coach at, 24–25, 78,
    117
Clemson Tigers game (2008),
    159
recruitment, 16–17, 116–17
troubled players at, 185
All-American Bowl (1986), 165
All-Americans, 84–85, 116
all-time career victories of
    Bobby Bowden, 26–27
American Football Quarterly, 129
Andrews, Mickey, 31
Angola State Prison, 202
Antonik, John, 93
Arena Football League, 252
Arkansas Razorbacks, 159
Associated Press (AP), 25, 124,
    133, 141
Associated Press Sports Edi-
    tors, 5
Astroturf cleats, 223–24

Atlanta Falcons, 165
Atlanta Journal-Constitution,
    134
Auburn Tigers
  Florida State fumblerooskie
    against (1990), 206–8
  Terry Bowden as coach of,
    14–15, 128–36, 152, 157

Baker, Art, 172
Baker, Robbie (Florida State
    center), 207
Baker, Robert (Auburn wide
    receiver), 131
"Ballad of Bobby Bowden
    (Goes to Alabama)" (song),
    163–64, 165–66
barnyard plays, 73–74
BB gun, 54–55
Beamer, Frank, 21
Beamer, Todd, 253
"Beat Anybody" (bumper
    sticker), 26
Becton, Lee, 218
Beitia, Xavier, 212–13
Belichick, Bill, 224
Bell, Trumane, 221
Beltz, Larry D., 42
Bentley, Scott, 211–12, 221
Berry Field, 54, 58–59
Bey, Raul, 228–29
Bianchi, Michael, 180, 258
Biletnikoff, Fred, 80
Bill Hurley Day, 138
Birmingham News, 69, 258–59
birth of Bobby Bowden, 56–57

Black, Jimmy, 119, 121, 122
"black," use of term, 18
Black America's PAC, 32
Blaine, David, 196
Blake, Harry, 194
blocking, 60–61
Blodgett Homes, 195
blue-collar values, 57
Boise State Broncos, 48
Bonasorte, Francis Joseph
    "Monk," 41, 143
Bonds, Barry, 118
Booker, Lorenzo, 44, 45–46,
    247–48
Boston Celtics, 4, 73
Boston College Eagles, 120,
    219, 256
Boulware, Peter, 178–79
Bound for Glory (Bowden), 106–7
Bowden, Bob Pierce (father),
    53–60, 64–66, 74, 84
Bowden, Bolton and Burgdorf,
    242
Bowden, Ginger (daughter). *See*
    Madden, Ginger
Bowden, Jeff (son)
  car accident and, 31, 34
  at Florida State, 157
  as Florida State offensive
    coordinator, 36–47, 50
  at North Alabama, 136
  at Southern Mississippi, 37
Bowden, Julia Ann Estock
    (wife), 110–13, 257
  Alabama job interview and,
    166, 167

car accident and, 33–35
dating Bobby, 63–64
daughter Ginger and, 33–35
daughter Robyn and, 38, 39
family life, 29, 31, 66, 73,
   80–82, 110–12, 206
as football wife, 9, 20, 59, 66,
   70–71, 110–13
as key part of Bowden's success, 5
LSU job offer and, 13–14
marriage to Bobby, 64–66
Marshall job offer and, 12
morning routine of, 113
player Rix and, 231
player Ward and, 214
political beliefs of, 32
relationship with Bobby,
   110–11, 112–13
son Jeff and, 36–37, 50
son Steve and, 241
son Terry and, 128–29, 134
son Tommy and, 154
at South Georgia, 70–71
at West Virginia, 81–82, 91,
   95, 98
Bowden, Linda White
   (daughter-in-law), 155–56
Bowden, Marion (sister), 53, 56
Bowden, Robyn (daughter). See
   Hines, Robyn
Bowden, Shryl (Terry's wife),
   127
Bowden, Steve (son)
   financial career of, 31, 242
   legal troubles of, 243–47

political beliefs of, 32
at West Virginia, 81
Bowden, Sunset Cleckler
   (mother), 53, 55–57, 59–60,
   64–66
Bowden, Terry (son), 126–36
   at ABC Sports, 127, 136
   at Auburn University, 14–15,
      128–36, 157
   brother Jeff and, 39
   brother Tommy compared
      with, 151–52, 156–57
   car accident and, 34
   father Bobby compared with,
      131, 134
   at North Alabama, 31, 136
   panic attacks of, 127–28
   racial prejudice and, 20
   at Salem College, 37, 126–27
   at Samford University, 37, 129,
      156, 166
   South Georgia players and,
      70–71
   at West Virginia University,
      15, 90, 128
   at Yahoo! Sports, 32
Bowden, Tommy (son), 151–62
   at Alabama, 16–17, 167
   at Auburn University, 152,
      159
   brother Steve and, 244
   brother Terry compared with,
      151–52, 156–57
   car accident and, 34
   at Clemson, 31–32, 153–54,
      156, 158–62, 256–57

Bowden, Tommy (*continued*)
  father Bobby compared with,
    154
  political beliefs of, 154
  at Tulane, 152–53
  at West Virginia, 90, 96,
    97–98, 151, 154–55
Bowden Process, 153, 155–56
Bowden Sportswear, 131
Bowdre, Karon O., 246
"boy," use of term, 20
Bradshaw, Terry, 99–100
Brantley, Scot, 257
Bridges, John, 262
Bright, Leon, 119
Brooks, Derrick, 178
Brown, Everette, 49
Brown, Jim, 2, 6
Brown, Kevin, 2
Brown, Mack, 48
Brown, Paul, 224
Brumfield, Kevan, 202–3
Bryant, Paul W. "Bear"
  Bowden compared with, 19,
    24–25
  funeral of, 128
  as hero of Bowden, 78, 259
  legacy of, 24–25, 169–70
  Piurowski recruitment and,
    116–17
  racial segregation and, 18, 19
  training camp, 76
Buckley, Douglas Terrell, 179,
    199, 200
Buffalo Bills, 217
Burgdorf, Brian, 243–44

Burress, Plaxico, 181
Busby, Thad, 223
Bush, George W., 32
Butkus, Dick, 115
Butler, Bobby, 118, 143
Butler, LeRoy, 42–43, 205
  Florida State 1987 season, 174,
    175
  Florida State 1988 season,
    193–97
  Florida State 1991 season, 210
  recruitment to Florida State,
    177–78

Calipari, John, 186
Camps, Joe, 119, 262
Capece, Bill, 141
Cappelen, Dave, 124
C.A.R.E. (Center for Academic
    Retention and Enhance-
    ment), 189
Carlen, Jim, 83–86, 93
Carr, Lloyd, 159–60
Carreker, Alphonso, 24
Carroll, Pete, 25, 48
Carter, Andrew, 5
Carter, Anthony, 145
Carter, Pat, 173, 174
Castro, Fidel, 261
Cebrun, Nate, 228–29
Census, U.S., 53, 57
Champs Sports Bowl, 162
Chateau Forte Consortium,
    243–44
cheating, 9–10, 129, 180,
    183–84

Chicago Bears, 115
Chicago Bulls, 224
Chicago Maroons, 27
Chief Osceola, 137
childhood of Bobby Bowden,
    53–62
Chronicle for Higher Education,
    48
Churchill, Winston, 209
Cincinnati Bearcats, 223
Cincinnati Bengals, 228
civil rights, 17–21
Claiborne, Jerry, 104
Clayton, Bertram Tracy, 56–57
Cleckler, Robert, 58
Clemson Tigers, 121
    Florida State puntrooskie
        against (1988), 172, 193–97
    Tommy Bowden at, 31–32,
        153–54, 156, 158–62,
        256–57
Cleveland Browns, 224
Clinton, Bill, 224–25
coaching relationships, father-
    and-son, 2–3
coaching style and philosophy
    of Bobby Bowden, 22, 25,
    77–78, 122–23, 174, 216–17
cocaine, 102, 131, 185
Coker, Larry, 115, 205
Coles, Laveranues, 179, 229,
    233
Collinsworth, Cris, 138
Colonial BancGroup, Inc., 132
Columbia State (newspaper), 44
Columbia University, 68

Connor, Theophilus Eugene
    "Bull," 20
Cook, Carroll Hoff "Beano,"
    194
Cook Springs Camp, 75–76
Cooper, Bert, 103
Corlew, Tim, 195–96
Corso, Leland "Lee," 42
Crist, Charlie, 179
critics (criticism) of Bobby
    Bowden, 21, 23, 36, 38–44,
    51, 91–92, 95–98
Croom, Sylvester, 19
Croom, Sylvester, Sr., 19
Crumbley, Paul, 64
Cuba, 261
Cunningham, Sam, 19
Curry, Bill, 167–68

D'Alemberte, Talbot, 38
Dallas Cowboys, 224
Daly, John, 2
Dan Patrick Show, 260–61
Darling, Devaughn, 253, 254
Davis, Chris, 47–48
Davis, John, 197, 208
Dawson, Rhett, 101
Dean, Adolph, 244–46
Decatur (Ala.) Daily, 132
Deford, Frank, 261
dehydration, 71
Deion Sanders Rule, 199–200
DelNagro, Mike, 138
DePasqua, Carl, 93–94
Detroit Lions, 86
devotionals, 225–26

Dinich, Heather, 52
disagreements between Bowden
    family members, 157–58
discipline
  at Florida State, 48–49, 102,
    105–8, 180–81, 232–33,
    255–56
  at South Georgia, 71, 74
Doak Campbell Stadium, 137
Dockett, Darnell, 184
Dodd, Dennis, 52
Dodge, Dedrick, 175
Dooley, Vince, 207, 247
Dorn, Greg, 223
DuBose, Mike, 169
Duke University Blue Devils,
    85
Dunn, Warrick
  on Bobby Bowden, 4, 43, 201
  Florida State 1987 season, 175
  Florida State 1993 season,
    214–15, 219
  Florida State 1999 season, 240
  murder of mother, 201–3
  name gap by Bobby Bowden
    and, 223
  "wildcat" offense and, 217
Durham, Bill, 137
Dye, Pat, 51, 130, 132, 135, 152

early life of Bobby Bowden,
    53–62
education (academics), and
    African American athletes,
    182–84, 186–89
Edwards, Harry, 182–83

Edwards, John, 32
Eisenhower, Dwight, 261
elopement of Bobby and Ann
    Bowden, 65
Emerald Bowl (2006), 45–46
Erickson, Dennis, 220–21
ESPN, 24, 41, 42, 52, 135, 158,
    162, 185, 226
Evict Richt Club, 41

faith, 14, 30, 34, 56, 58, 112,
    154, 190, 225–28, 252
Faith in the Game (Osborne),
    226
fast-break offense, 22, 25,
    216–17
father-and-son coaching rela-
    tionships, 2–3
father figure, Bobby Bowden as,
    190–91, 201–2
Faulkner, Chris, 144
Favre, Brett, 197
Feagles, Jeff, 175
Federation of Alabama Wom-
    en's Clubs, 56
Fellowship of Christian Ath-
    letes, 132
Ferguson, Chip, 198
Ferrell, Marvin, 204
Fielder, Cecil, 2
Fielder, Prince, 2
Fiesta Bowl (1987), 215
First National Bank of Bir-
    mingham, 57–58
Fisher, Jimbo, 11, 50
Flagler College, 241

Flamingo Studios, 192
"Float On" (song), 88
Florida Bar, 35
Florida Gators
  Florida State rivalry with,
    100–101, 205–6
  recruitment, 47
  troubled players at, 184–85
  winning percentage, 49
  1973 Florida State game, 101
  1976 Florida State game,
    120–21
  1978 Florida State game, 138
  1980 Florida State game, 143,
    144–45
  1983 Florida State game, 101
  1987 Florida State game, 176
  1993 Florida State game,
    214–15
  2008 Florida State game, 248
Florida Highway Patrol, 33
Florida International Univer-
    sity, 185
Florida Republican Party, 32,
    178–79
Florida State Seminoles (FSU),
    99–109
  academic cheating scandal, 21,
    44, 255–56
  All-Americans, 115–16
  Bradshaw and, 99–100
  Buckley and, 199, 200
  coaching drama at, 170–73
  discipline and, 48–49, 102,
    105–6, 107–8, 180–81,
    232–33, 255–56

Dunn and, 201–3
fiscal crisis of 1975, 102, 103
Florida Gators rivalry with,
    100–101, 205–6
fund-raising, 118–19
Henshaw and, 86–87
hiring as assistant coach,
    79–80, 81, 101, 104
hiring as head coach, 104–6
Jeff Bowden as offensive coor-
    dinator, 36–44, 50
loss of Richt, 247–48
McCorvey and, 200–201, 218
off-field issues, 168–69
overall record, 41
racial integration at, 18, 101
rankings, 124, 140, 141, 142,
    147–48
recruitment, 14–17, 47–48,
    111–12, 115–18, 177–78, 190,
    248
Sanders and, 174–75, 199–200
"The Seminole Rap," 192–92
speed of players, 204–5, 218
troubled players at, 179–84,
    190–91, 211–12, 226–33
Wadsworth and, 202–3
Weldon and, 198–99
winning percentage, 22, 25
1963 season, 79–80
1973 season, 101
1974 season, 101–2, 104
1975 season, 101–2, 103, 106
1976 season, 103–9, 119–23
1977 season, 123–25, 124–25
1978 season, 137–39, 143

Florida State Seminoles
(continued)
1979 season, 12–13, 139–41
1980 season, 141–46, 173
1981 season, 26–27, 37, 146–50
1983 season, 176
1984 season, 172
1986 season, 165, 254
1987 season, 172–76, 208–9,
215
1988 season, 192–97
1989 season, 175–76, 197, 200
1990 season, 96, 198–99,
206–8
1991 season, 95, 198–99,
209–11
1993 season, 214–25
1997 season, 239
1998 season, 239
1999 season, 48, 158, 234–35,
236–37, 239–49
2000 season, 48
2001 season, 40–41, 48
2002 season, 47–48, 212–13
2003 season, 158
2004 season, 42
2005 season, 49
2006 season, 25, 44–46, 50
2007 season, 50, 51
2008 season, 25, 41, 50–52,
161–62, 248, 257
Florida Times-Union, 5, 46
Foot Locker scandal (1999),
179, 228–29
Ford, Danny, 196
Ford, Garrett, 5, 19–21, 96

forward pass, 140–41
foul language, 57
Franchione, Dennis, 169
Franklin, Bill "Stumpy," 71
Frazier, Tommy, 221
Freedom Marchers, 20
Friedgen, Ralph, 256
FSU One Time! The Bowden
Years (Jones), 5
FSU Seminoles. See Florida
State Seminoles
fumblerooskie, 206–8
fund-raising by Bobby Bowden,
70, 118–19

Gator Bowl
1964, 79–80
1965, 22
1982, 37
Gators. See Florida Gators
Georgia Bulldogs, 16, 40, 142,
185, 247
Georgia Southern Eagles, 123
Georgia Tech Yellow Jackets,
167, 216
Gibbs, Joe, 80, 101
G.I. Bill, 71
Gibson, Michael, 258
Gillman, Sid, 83
Gladden, Jim, 171
Glynco Naval Air Station, 72
Goff, Ray, 232
Goin, Bob, 206
golf, 11
black caddie incident, 17–18
Gordon, Dan, 219

Gordon Military, 73
grandparent child-rearing, 187–88
grants-in-aid, 187
Great Depression, 57–58
Green Bay Packers, 77, 78, 107, 175, 178
Grobe, Jim, 21, 52
guns, 54–55, 67, 180–81

Haffner, George, 87
Hagan, Kay, 32
halfback pass, 73, 83
Hanks, James Michael, 243–44
Harlow, James, 98
Harris, Katherine, 32
Hart, Dave, 258–59
Hawkins, Dan, 26, 261
Hayes, Woody, 25
Heisman Trophy, 220–21, 229, 239, 248
Henning, Dan, 101–2
Henry, Jack, 86
Henshaw, George, 43–44, 85–89, 122, 145, 171, 194, 258
Henson, Drew, 238–39
Herring, Reggie, 143, 230
Hines, Jack, 38
Hines, Robyn (daughter), 31, 37, 38–39, 67, 96–97
hitchhiking, 67
Holtz, Lou, 104, 232–33
hospitable nature of Bobby Bowden, 258–59
Housel, David, 133–34

Houston, Martavius, 14–15, 17
Houston Cougars, 101–2, 143
Houston option, 83–84
Howard, Desmond, 199
Howard College Bulldogs, 54, 56, 66–67. See also Samford University Bulldogs
  assistant coach at, 67–68
  golfing black caddie incident, 17–18
  head coach at, 74–78, 151–52
Hurley, Bill, 138
Hurricane Frances, 33–35
Hurricanes. See Miami Hurricanes

Indianapolis Colts, 83, 232
Indiana University Hoosiers, 165
Inman, Dick, 82, 83
Iona Prep Gaels, 28
Iowa Hawkeyes, 185
Irvin, Michael, 174, 175, 206

Janikowski, Sebastian, 229, 234, 235
Jeter, Derek, 25
Jim Crow laws, 17
Johnson, Brad, 175, 198
Johnson, Earvin "Magic," 3, 241
Johnson, Hardis, 145
Johnson, Jimmy, 174
Jones, Cedric, 149
Jones, Keith, 143
Jones, Larry, 119

Jones, Willie, 138
Jones County Junior College, 72
Jordan, Jimmy, 121, 138–40, 142, 223
Jordan, Michael, 224
Junior College Coach of the Year, 74

Kansas Jayhawks, 49, 186
Kansas State Wildcats, 120
Kelly, Jim, 149, 217
Kent State Golden Flashes, 86
"Kentucky Derby offense." *See* fast-break offense
Kentucky Wildcats, 168, 186
Key, Sean, 235
Kilbourn, Rod, 163–64
King, Shaun, 153
Kinghorn, Bill, 75
Korean War, 66, 71
Ku Klux Klan, 101

Lake Forest College, 187–88
Lakeland Ledger, 5, 167, 197, 223
Landry, Tom, 224
Ledbetter, Clint, 194
Lee Jordan Band, 59
legacy of Bobby Bowden, 21–28, 260–64
Leggett, Jeff, 119
Leon High School, 139
"Let's Roll" (team mantra), 253
Limbaugh, Rush, 10–11
limited admissions, 189

Lombardi, Vince, 77, 107
longevity of Bobby Bowden, 23, 28
Lopez, Pablo, 254
Los Angeles Lakers, 3–4, 241
Louisiana State University (LSU) Tigers, 13–14, 50, 89, 99, 141, 148–49, 157
Louisiana Tech Bulldogs, 99–100
Lowder, Bobby, 131–32
Lowrey, Kelly, 194

McCartney, Ron, 89
McCollum, Bill, 32
McCorvey, Kezarrick "Kez," 200–201, 218–19
McDuffie, Wayne, 170–71
McEwen, Tom, 148
McGrotha, Bill, 123
McManus, Danny, 173, 223
McPherson, Adrian, 184, 230
Madden, Bowden, 30, 33–35
Madden, Ginger (daughter)
  brother Steve and, 244, 245–46
  car accident and, 30, 33–35
  car trip and, 81
  legal career of, 31, 35
  sense of humor, 35
  West Virginia University and, 15
Madden, John Allen, 30, 33–35, 244
Maddox, Nick, 16
Maines, Larry, 33

Maines, Margaret, 33
Maisel, Ivan, 26–27
Maisel Report: College Football's Most Overrated & Underrated Players, Coaches, Teams, and Traditions, 215
Majors, Johnny, 103–4
Manning, Archie, 2
Manning, Eli, 2
Manning, Peyton, 2, 232
Mara, Frank, 28
Mara, Sean, 28
marijuana, 102, 180, 233, 252
Marine Corps Reserves, 66
Marino, Dan, 141, 148
Marshall, Stanley, 102, 262
Marshall Thundering Herd, 12
Martinez, Mel, 32
Maryland Terrapins, 255, 256
mat drills, 123, 254–55
Matuszak, John, 102
Mayhew, Martin, 175
media relations, 23, 38, 105–6, 129–30, 181, 219–20, 256–57, 258–59
Memphis Tigers, 119, 140, 142–43, 186
Messner, Michael, 186–87
Mettler, Peter, 42
Meyer, Urban, 25, 47, 51, 185, 241
Miami Airport Hilton, 30
Miami Herald, 47, 112
Miami Hurricanes, 208–13
  Florida State rivalry with, 193, 205–6

recruitment, 47
Richt at, 40
troubled players at, 185
winning percentage, 49
1976 Florida State game, 119
1980 Florida State game, 144
1981 Florida State game, 149
1987 Florida State game, 172, 173–76
1991 Florida State game, 209–11
1992 Florida State game, 209
2002 Florida State game, 212–13
2004 Florida State game, 30
2007 Florida State game, 51
Michigan State Spartans, 118
Michigan Wolverines, 145, 153, 159–60, 259
Millennium Fund, 243–44
Mississippi State Bulldogs, 19, 143
modern athletes, Bobby Bowden's ability to deal with, 23, 24
Moore, Coyle E., 105
More Than Just a Game (Bowden), 18–19
Morgan, Kenny, 60–62
Morris, Ron, 44
Moss, Randy, 232–33
Mountaineers. *See* West Virginia University Mountaineers
Mowrey, Dan, 209, 211–13
MSNsportsnet.com, 5

Mudra, Darrell, 101–2, 103–4, 106, 119
multiple formations, 44–45
Munyon, Matt, 212
Murrow, Edward R., 55
Musburger, Brent, 260–61
Muse, William V., 129, 132, 133

name gaps by Bobby Bowden, 222–23
Nash, Steve, 217–18
National Coalition Against Violent Athletes, 227
Navy Midshipmen, 49
NCAA, 183–84, 187
Nebraska Cornhuskers, 205, 225–28
    troubled players at, 185, 226–28
    winning percentage, 49
    1980 Florida State game, 141, 143
    1981 Florida State game, 146, 147
    1987 Florida State game (Fiesta Bowl), 215
    1993 Florida State game, 214
    1994 Florida State game (Orange Bowl), 219, 220, 221–22, 224–25
nepotism, 38–39, 89–90, 158
New England Patriots, 224
New York Giants, 27, 181
New York Jets, 103
New York Knicks, 215

New York Times, 131–32, 221, 232
New York Yankees, 200, 224, 238–39
NFL (National Football League), 13, 165
Noah, Joakim, 2
Noah, Yannick, 2
North Alabama Lions, 31, 136
North Carolina State Wolfpack, 13–14, 42, 239
North Texas Mean Green, 121–22
Notre Dame Fighting Irish, 49, 142, 148, 218–19

Obama, Barack, 32, 169, 178–79
O'Brien, Pat, 196
O'Brien, Tom, 21
Ogbu, John, 188
Ohio State Buckeyes, 147–48, 189
Okefenokee Swamp, 69
Oklahoma Sooners, 48, 79–80, 120, 137, 140–41, 146
Old Blue Goose (bus), 71
Opelika-Auburn News, 133
Orange Bowl
    1979, 140–41
    1980, 13
    1981, 142, 146
    1992, 211
    1994, 220, 221–22, 224–25
Oravetz, Randy, 175–76, 239
Orlando Sentinel, 180, 258

Osborne, Tom, 222, 225–27
Owens, Arthur "Artie," 87–88

Parcells, Bill, 80, 101
Parker, Preston, 180–81
passing offense, 22, 77–78, 79–80,
    101, 140–41, 216, 240–41
Paterno, Joe, 44, 184, 251,
    260–61
  Bowden compared with, 22,
    25, 26, 27–28
Patrick, Dan, 260–61
Paxil, 127–28
pay-for-play scheme, 133
Peabody College, 67
Peach Bowl
  1969, 83–84
  1983, 122
Pell, Charley, 144
Pendry, Joe, 86
Penn State Nittany Lions,
    90–91, 96, 149, 185, 261
Perkins, Ray, 164, 166
Peter, Christian, 226, 227
Peterson, Bill, 79–81, 101
Phi Beta Sigma, 255–56
Philadelphia Eagles, 2, 45, 83,
    219
Phillips, Lawrence, 226
Piatt, Sam, 142
Pittsburgh (Pitt) Panthers,
    92–96, 98, 141, 143, 144,
    146, 148
Pittsburgh Steelers, 101
Piurowski, Paul, 5, 116–18, 139,
    143

Platt, DiShon, 47–48
Platt, Sam, 223
play calling, 82, 171, 247–48
Polen, Dick, 93
political beliefs, 32–33, 154
Post and Courier, 248
precision blocking, 60–61
press relations, 23, 38, 105–6,
    129–30, 181, 219–20, 256–57,
    258–59
Price, Mike, 169
Private Asset Management
    S.A., 243–44
Prop 48 candidate, 178
puntrooskie, 193–97
Pure Gold (Bowden and Ellis), 5

racial prejudice, 17–21
racial quotas, 21
Rapoport, Ian, 258–59
Reagan, Ronald, 105
Redmond, Kathy, 226–28
Reed, Bert, 253
Reid, Andy, 2
Rein, Bo, 13–14
religious faith, 14, 30, 34, 56,
    58, 112, 154, 190, 225–28,
    252
Renegade (horse), 137
Republican National Commit-
    tee (RNC), 32
Republican Party, 32, 178–79
rheumatic fever, 55, 58–60
Rhoden, Bill, 183
Rhodes Scholarships, 255
Rice, Jerry, 199

Richardson, Louie, 118

Richt, Mark, 39–40, 41, 125, 171–72, 217, 238, 239, 247–48

Ripken, Cal, Jr., 2

Ripken, Cal, Sr., 2

Rising Fawn, Georgia, 65

Rivals.com, 5, 47

Rix, Chris, 46–47, 184, 230–31, 248

Roberts, Selena, 232

Rockne, Knute, 27

Rodriguez, Rich, 153–54

Rogers, Corky, 196–97

Rolle, Myron, 179, 255, 256

rooskie, 195

Rose, Pete, 2

Rose, Pete, Jr., 2

Royal, Darrell, 84

Ruhama Baptist Church, 57, 58

Russell, JaMarcus, 50

Rutgers Scarlet Knights, 49

Ruth, George Herman "Babe," 224

Saban, Nick, 86, 159–60, 169–70, 258

Saint Bobby and the Barbarians (Brown), 5

Salem College, 37, 126–27

salicylate, 58

Samford University Bulldogs, 17, 37, 129, 156, 166, 241–42

Sanders, Barry, 86

Sanders, Deion, 101, 174–75, 199–200

Sanderson, Allen R., 187

San Diego State Aztecs, 3

Sang (dog), 62

Sapp, Warren, 206, 209

Sawyer, Corey, 228–29

Schlabach, Mark, *What It Means to Be a Seminole*, 5, 24, 101

Schlichter, Art, 147

Schnellenberger, Howard, 47, 149

scholarships, 16, 69

Scott, Brad, 115, 171, 177–78, 216, 217

Scout.com, 5

segregation, 17–21

"Seminole Rap, The," 192–92

Seminoles. *See* Florida State Seminoles

Shannon, Randy, 47

Sherwood, Mike, 92

shotgun offense, 216–17

Shula, Don, 43–44

Shuler, Heath, 220

Shultz, Roger, 169

Shumann, Mike, 102, 119, 125

Simmons, Ronald, 88–89, 123–24, 138, 143

Sims, Billy, 140

Sliger, Bernard, 13, 123

Sloan, Steve, 103–4, 124–25

Smith, Bill (sportswriter), 90–91

Smith, Billy (Florida State head of security), 33, 175–76

Smith, Jim, 256

Smith, Ken, 176

Smith, Leeon "Bull," 71

Smith, Sammie, 174

Smith, William, 68

Smothers, Betty, 201, 202

South Carolina Gamecocks, 84, 96, 156

Southern Crackers, 105

Southern Mississippi Golden Eagles, 37, 121, 124, 149–50, 193–95, 197

South Florida Sun-Sentinel, 248

South Georgia College Bull-dogs, 68–74

special plays. *See* trick plays

"Speech, The," 126–27

speed of Florida State players, 204–5, 218

Spitz, Mark, 2

Spitz, Matt, 2

Sporting News, 21, 160, 247

Sports Illustrated, 1, 5, 19, 124, 138, 139, 141, 142, 143–44, 147, 182–83, 211–12, 228–29

Spurrier, Steve, 167, 179, 206, 232

Stagg, Amos Alonzo, 23, 25, 27

Stallings, Gene, 76, 78, 168–69

Starr, Bart, 77, 78

Stockstill, Rick, 142–43

Stoops, Bob, 2–3, 48

Stoops, Mike, 2–3

Street and Smith's, 147

strength and conditioning pro-gram, 82–83

Stroud, Todd, 255

Stroudsburg High School, 87

Sugar Bowl (2000), 234–35, 236–37, 239–49

Summerall, Pat, 28, 205

Surratt, Joe, 51

Swinney, William Christopher "Dabo," 161–62

Switzer, Barry, 120, 140

Swyers, Holly, 187–88

Syracuse Orange, 138, 200

Tales from the Seminoles Sideline (Bowden), 254

Tallahassee Community Col-lege, 216

Tallahassee Democrat, 5, 44, 103–6, 123, 138, 162

Tampa Bay Buccaneers, 175, 206, 217

Tampa Tribune, 148, 257

Tangerine Bowl (1977), 124–25

Tarrant, Jim, 56

Tate, Walter, 207–8

Tebow, Tim, 248

Tennessee Volunteers (Vols), 89, 131, 232, 235–36

Texas A&M Aggies, 87, 169

Texas Christian University (TCU) Horned Frogs, 124

Texas Tech Red Raider, 84–85, 86, 102, 124–25

TheBigLead.com, 49

Thomas, Clevan, 5, 251–52

Thomas, Eric, 239

Thomas, Gerry, 210–11

Thomas, Joab, 165–68

Thomas, J. T., 101, 200

Thomas, Rudy, 119

Tiger Talk, 134

Toronto Blue Jays, 237–38

Torretta, Gino, 209

training camps, 75–76

training program, 82–83

Tressel, Jim, 25, 48, 241

trick plays, 45, 73–74, 174, 194

　fumblerooskie, 206–8

　puntrooskie, 193–97

Trust Services, 243–44

Tulane Green Wave, 152–53

Tuscaloosa News, 169

UCLA Bruins, 1

Unglaub, Kurt, 201

United Airlines Flight 93, 253

United States of America v. R.
　Stephen Bowden, 243–46

University of Tampa Minaret,
　102, 103

USA Today, 238

USC (University of Southern
　California) Trojans, 19,
　165

U.S. News & World Report, 189

Vanderbilt Commodores, 52

Vick, Michael, 234–35

Vietnam War, 102

Virginia Cavaliers, 216

Virginia Tech Hokies, 48, 194

　Sugar Bowl (2000), 234–35,
　236–37, 239–49

Wadsworth, Andre, 203–4

Wake Forest Demon Deacons,
　28, 50, 52

Wallace, George, 19, 56, 131,
　165, 166

Walsh, Steve, 175

Walton, Adam, 3

Walton, Bill, 1–2, 3–4

Walton, Chris, 3

Walton, Luke, 3–4

Walton, Nathan, 3

Walton, Susie, 1, 3

Wangler, John, 145

Ward, Charlie, Jr., 16, 22, 25,
　197, 199, 214–21

Ward, Charlie, Sr., 16

Warrick, Peter, 179, 229

Washington, Booker, 47–48

Washington, Leon, 47–48

Washington Redskins, 83

water breaks, 71

Watts, J. C., 140

Weatherford, Drew, 48–49,
　255

Weinke, Chris, 236–40, 248

Weldon, Casey, 198–99, 209–10

West Virginia University
　Mountaineers, 81–98

　coaching staff, 85–87

　critics and fans at, 91–92,
　95–98

　as head coach, 15, 84–98

　as offensive coordinator, 12,
　81–84

　racial integration, 19–21

　recruitment, 83, 87–89

　Tommy Bowden at, 90, 96,
　97–98, 151, 154–55

　winning record, 95–96

1969 season, 83–85
1970 season, 92–96
1971 season, 98
1972 season, 87–88, 96, 194
1973 season, 90–91, 96
1974 season, 91, 96–98
1982 Gator Bowl, 37
Wetherell, T. K., 34, 42, 189
What It Means to Be a Seminole (Schlabach), 5, 24, 101
White, Bill "Cannonball," 68
White, Shorty, 64
White House, 224–25
Wide Left I, 212–13
wideouts, 194, 232
"wildcat" offense, 217
Wilkinson, Bud, 147
Williams, Chette, 132
Williams, Dayne, 195–96
Williams, Larry, 248

Williams, Phil, 123, 148
Williams, Willie, 112
Willis, Peter Tom, 43, 198
Wilson, Rob, 196, 259
Wilson, Ronnie, 185
Wisconsin Badgers, 25, 162
wishbone, 83–84
womanizing, 85, 108
Woodham, Wally, 138–40
Woodlawn, 53–54
Woodlawn High School, 54, 59–62, 161, 191
Woodlawn High School *Tattler*, 62
work ethic of Bobby Bowden, 57, 118–19, 152, 156, 253
Wright, Tommy, 257

Yahoo! Sports, 32
Young, George, 27–28

Bobby Bowden gets a hug from his wife, Ann, after the field at
Doak Campbell Stadium was renamed Bobby Bowden Field in 2004.

Bobby Bowden speaks to fans and boosters at the Cypress Club and Ballroom in Orange Park, Florida. Bowden has been known to electrify Florida State followers at these gatherings.

The Bowden family on the Panama City, Florida, beach in July 2005.
The family has vacationed there for decades.

Bowden and Florida's Urban Meyer after a 2005 game. Bowden has had
some classic battles against in-state rivals Florida and Miami.

*Bowden watches
his players
hold up the
inaugural ACC
championship
trophy. Bowden's
Seminoles would
dominate the
conference for
years before parity
in the sport caught
up to the program.*

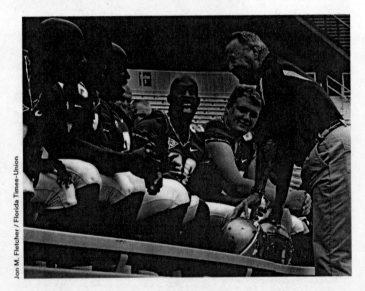

*Bowden speaks to his players in 2006. Perhaps no coach
in the history of college football has connected better with
his players than Bowden.*

Bobby and his son Tommy, pictured here while coaching Clemson University against his father, have fought on the field, but their battles haven't affected their relationship off of it. They remain extremely close, as do all the Bowden children.

Rick Wilson / Florida Times-Union

Don Burk / Florida Times-Union

Bowden with his son Jeff in 1999. Jeff would later become Bowden's offensive coordinator as well as a lightning rod with Seminole fans. Bowden would later accept Jeff's resignation after pressure from fans and boosters.

(right) *Bowden posing with his championship ring in 1994. He would eventually win two national championships.*

Bowden on the eve of his sixty-fifth birthday in November 1994.

Bobby and Ann relax in their Tallahassee home in 1993. Ann has been the most vital factor in Bowden's coaching career, allowing him to focus solely on football while she raised the family.

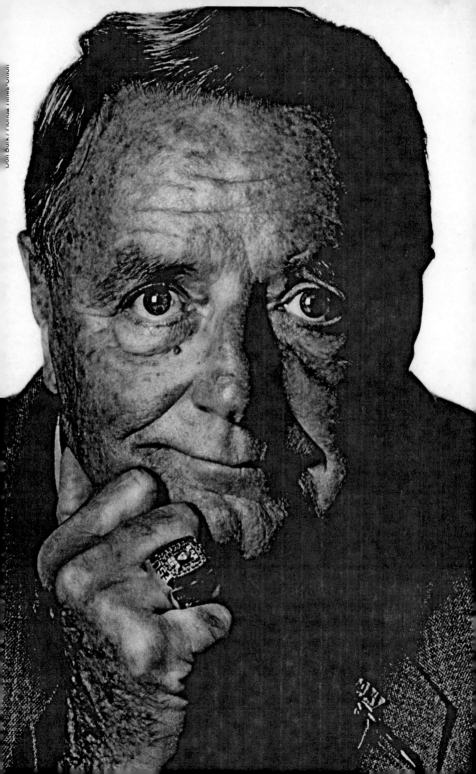

*Bowden became so popular soon after taking over the
Florida State football program that he probably could have
run for high office.*